HERMENEUTICS

Updated Third Edition

BY
PROF. D. R. DUNGAN
Author of '*Chang Foo*,' '*On The Rock*,' '*Rum, Ruin, And The Remedy*,'
'*Modern Phases Of Skepticism*,' Etc.

Edited and Updated by
BRADLEY S. COBB
Author of '*The Holy Spirit in the Book of Acts*,' '*Justified by Works*,'
'*Things Which Came to Pass*,' Etc.

Charleston, AR:

COBB PUBLISHING

2018

Published in the United States of America by:

Cobb Publishing
704 E. Main Street
Charleston, AR 72933
(479) 747-8372
www.CobbPublishing.com

ISBN-13: 978-1-947622-08-1

Foreword to the
Updated Third Edition

The book you now hold in your hands (or read on your screen) is a classic work on interpreting the Bible. Since it first appeared in the late 1800s, it has been valued for its logical treatment and presentation of language, figures of speech, prophecy, and the correct method by which God wants His word interpreted (that is, in short, taking the whole of what the Bible says on a subject, and then basing our conclusions on that information).

However, since the book's original release (and it's second edition in 1888), the English language has changed, both in vocabulary and phrasing. That truth is what inspired us to create this updated edition of Dungan's most famous volume.

In addition to correcting any typographical errors we found, we have also updated the verse numbering system (Dungan used xliv. 23, we have updated it to modern usage, 44:23), modernized spelling, replaced archaic words with their modern counterpart, removed excessive wordiness, and occasionally added an explanatory note where necessary.

We hope you will agree that this new edition is both useful and better suited for the understanding of modern readers.

Bradley Cobb
February 2018.

TABLE OF CONTENTS

CHAPTER I:
INTRODUCTION

Section 1.
OUR SUBJECT DEFINED.

Hermeneutics is the science of interpretation. It is derived from the Greek *Hermes,* the messenger of the gods and the interpreter of *Jupiter.* Every *Hermeneus* was, therefore, an interpreter, as he was supposed to inherit some of the mystic qualities of this god of philology, this patron of eloquence. Sacred hermeneutics is the science of interpreting the Scriptures. Exegesis (from *ex,* out, and *egeisthas,* to guide or lead), means to lead out. It is the application of the principles of hermeneutics in bringing out the meaning of any writing which might otherwise be difficult to understand.

Section 2.

GOD EXPECTS US TO USE HIS BOOK IN BECOMING ACQUAINTED WITH HIS CHARACTER, AND IN GAINING KNOWLEDGE OF HIS WILL.

(1). *The Bible is to be used like other books.*—Having an interpreter implies a misunderstanding between two parties, or at least a possibility of such a misunderstanding. And it is at once objected that if the Bible is from God, it should be so plain that no one could misunderstand it; that, if God *could* give us such a book, but would not, He was certainly to blame. But if He would give us such a book, but could not, He is not perfect in wisdom or ability to execute. This logic is not good. We might as well say that if God is the Author of Nature, its meaning should be so apparent that all would perfectly understand it, and therefore, understand it alike. And yet we know that our scientists are quite disagreed about many things in nature, and that the great masses of men are in ignorance, almost from first to last, respecting the whole question. God has, therefore, made it necessary to study nature in order to get its lessons. Geology, astronomy, physiology, etc., are known only to those who study them. It is reasonable, therefore, that He should make it necessary to study His word.

(2). *The weakness is with man.*—Man is fallible, and his judgment is very imperfect. Nothing has ever been written which has been understood by all alike. (*a*) *Our laws are made by our wisest and most careful men;* they are made with special reference to the people for whom they are intended, so that no man may be misguided respecting his duty, and no criminal go unpunished. And yet our shrewdest lawyers and ablest jurists are in doubt as to the meaning of much of our law. (*b*) Not only so, but the *creeds* that have been *wrought out by the ablest and purest of men,* are variously interpreted. Churches wrangle and divide over them. Leading divines differ widely as to the meaning of many of the articles, while the common people don't have even the slightest idea of their original intent. We can't say that they weren't plainly written in the first place. And, perhaps for the first quarter century after any one of these was published, all parties were agreed as to the meaning of its articles. But age has come, custom has changed, religious sentiment has veered, words and forms have become obsolete, or have changed their meaning: hence the many interpretations. Man misunderstands his fellow man, and even himself, and is competent to misinterpret the Lord also.

(3). *God does not inspire the interpretation.*—It is sometimes supposed still that the Holy Spirit directs men in their inquiries after truth, so that no hurtful mistake can be made. But we know that the very best of men differ very widely in their views of the word of the Lord. We know, too, that these men make their investigations a matter of daily prayer. And knowing that truth is never contradictory, that error is dangerous and injurious, that very pious men are permitted to blunder in reference to the meaning of the Scripture, we feel assured that, whatever helps the Lord may see proper to give His servants in their efforts to understand the Bible, He does not guide them by inspiration, otherwise the mistakes which are now made would not occur.

(4). *Divine wisdom has adopted the word-method of revelation.*—This being true, it is implied that all the weaknesses which belong to such a method of communication were adopted at the same time. There would be no reason in giving a revelation which would need inspiration to interpret. If the inspiration has to be given, there is no need of the word itself. The inspiration would make known all the truth as well without the word as with it. Indeed, it would be better to have the inspiration alone than to have a faulty word revelation, which might mislead those who do not have the needed inspiration. While the word would be of no practical value whatsoever, it might do a great deal of harm. Better that God had never given it, since its only power is to deceive. But when He made His choice between a direct revelation to everyone, and the selection of a few who should be the teachers of the many, He chose the latter. Hence we must look to those whom He has chosen as His revelators for a knowledge of the divine will.

It does not change the question to claim that a few men are now chosen to interpret that word. We must have some means of knowing that they are favored above the common people in thus being 'divinely endowed.' And since those who have equal claims to a special call to this work differ widely respecting very important matters, we are incredulous respecting these exalted assumptions. The truth is, their claims are not sustained. Besides, there is no reason that God should give special inspiration to interpreters now. He has no other truth now to reveal, nor can He make it any plainer than He did when He gave us the Bible. The words of the men whom He now inspires, if there are any, are as difficult to understand as the words of the men He inspired eighteen hundred years ago. If we cannot understand those, how shall we understand these?

The ancients supposed that they must look to the law and the testimony for a knowledge of the will of the Lord, and that the truth was to be had by the same methods of study that were applied to any other branches of knowledge.

> *For Ezra had set his heart to seek the law of the Lord and to do it, and to teach in Israel statutes and judgments. (Ezra 7:10)*

The secret things belong to the Lord our God; but the things that are revealed belong to us and to our children forever, that we may do all the words of this law. (Deuteronomy 29:29)

Nehemiah 8:1-8 shows how they had to learn the law, Ezra reads the law from morning till noon, and is assisted by chosen men who go among the people and explain to them the meaning of any words which they did not understand.

From Psalms 1:1-2; 19:7; 119:39-105, we shall get David's idea of coming to the knowledge of the will of the Lord. They must read that word, study it day and night, get all its precepts in the mind in this way, and then may they assure themselves that they have more knowledge than the ancients—than all their teachers.

Jesus makes Abraham say to the rich man, respecting his five brothers:

They have Moses and the prophets; . . . if they hear not Moses and the prophets, neither will they be persuaded if one rises from the dead. (Luke 16:29-31)

Paul holds this view of the question. He says to Timothy, that although he has known the Holy Scriptures from his childhood, which were able to make him wise to salvation, he must study to show himself approved to God, a workman that needed not to be ashamed, rightly setting forth the word of truth. Hence he must give attention to *reading*, to *exhortation*, to *teaching*.

Section 3.
CORRECT HERMENEUTICS WOULD GO FAR TOWARD HEALING THE DIVISIONS OF THE CHURCH.

(1). *A wrong interpretation is not the only cause of divisions.*— That the followers of Christ should be one, cannot be argued against. Jesus prayed for the unity of all those who should believe on him through the word of the apostles. The apostles condemned divisions on all occasions; even in an incipient form, they were regarded as being carnal, and proceeding from hearts not in unison with the will of Christ. Men who were division-makers were regarded as unworthy of a place in the church, and after the first and second admonitions were to be avoided. They were spoken of as not serving the Lord Jesus, but their own passions. But while we regard carnality, in the form of unsanctified ambition, as the great cause of the divisions that now serve to mar the beauty of Zion and destroy the peace and power of the kingdom of Christ, it is not the only cause.

(2). *Selfish ambition cannot be removed by rules of interpretation.*—Even in the days of the apostles, in the presence of divine inspiration, in the presence of the divine authority which had been committed to the chosen twelve, ambitious men rose up to draw away disciples after themselves, ready to make merchandise of them. Even then the mystery of iniquity was secretly at work. The desire for place and power led men then to adopt the claim of sanctity, so that they might gain a leadership which could come to them in no other way. It would be idle to undertake to prevent men from being hypocrites, from loving this present world, or from seeking their own, and not the things of Jesus Christ, by rules of interpretation. Sound exegesis can have but little effect on such conditions of the heart. But when we are *not able to change the goods, we may do something in changing the market.* A correct hermeneutic may do something toward rendering it impossible for these men to continue their work of deception. If we could bring all the followers of Christ to a common interpretation of the word of God, the power to create divisions would certainly be gone.

(3). *All divisions, however, are not the result of ambition, carnality, or a sectarian spirit.*—Among the purest and best of earth, there are many differences of faith and practice. They cannot be accounted for upon the basis of dishonesty, nor upon the ground of general ignorance, for these divisions in the church contain men of equal learning. Of course, many of these learned men were born in their particular views, and all their study in the Scriptures has been to sustain these tenets, and in their maintenance there may be the spice of dishonesty. Still, the unfairness that comes from the prejudice of early training will not account for the many conflicting faiths among the followers of Christ.

(4). *The Bible is not at fault.*—Skepticism today feeds and fattens on the divided state of the Christian world. It declares that the book which we regard as God-given is to blame for all this misunderstanding. Skeptics charge that the Bible either teaches doctrines which are contradictory, or that they are so obscure that a man is about as liable to make one thing of them as another. This we cannot admit. If the Bible is of God, it does not contradict itself, nor is it so obscure in its teaching that those who are seeking the way of life cannot understand it. We reason that God gave man such a book as he needed, and that man needed a book which, with honest effort, he could understand; hence, if the Bible is God's book, it can be understood by all those who wish to know the way of eternal life.

(5). *The method of interpretation is to blame for much of the inharmony which now exists.*—It is evident to every student of the times that the great body of Protestant Christians want unity; that they deplore the divisions which now disfigure the church and retard the progress of the truth; that divisions are not sufficiently accounted for upon the basis of dishonesty; and we cannot admit that the Bible is at fault in the matter: hence there is nothing else that we can say but that our manner of interpreting the word of God is wrong. These facts compel the thought that he who can bring before the world a correct system of interpretation, will do more to heal the divisions than any other man of this century.

Section 4.
SOUND HERMENEUTICS WOULD BE THE BEST POSSIBLE ANSWER TO INFIDEL OBJECTIONS TO THE BIBLE.

(1). *A wrong interpretation is not the only cause of unbelief.*—Much of the infidelity of the age is the result of impure hearts and bad lives. Many men have made themselves opposite to the purity of the gospel of Christ, and have gone beyond the limits of the faith-condition of the mind. Men may cultivate distrust in their fellowmen until it is impossible for them to trust themselves to the virtue and honesty of anyone. Skepticism is a plant that may be grown, nay, that is grown. It is suited well to a barren soil, and thrives in a foul heart. Many things are believed because men wish them to be true, while others are disbelieved for a like reason. In such cases, it would matter but little what the evidence might be, they would not accept the gospel.

(2). *But false interpretation is a strong support of unbelief.*— Someone has well said that "the Bible is its own best defense." But in order that it may be any defense at all, its teachings must be understood; and this can never be without a correct knowledge of the principles of interpretation. Before we assume that Geology and Genesis are at variance, we ought to be absolutely certain that we have accurately interpreted both. Because of the lack of correct hermeneutics, men have imagined that they have found discrepancies, and even palpable contradictions, in the Bible. They would find any other book equally contradictory if they should treat it in the same way. But men know that the laws of language must be observed in reading any other book. If they would use the same care and common sense when reading the Bible, infidelity would find no place to set the sole of its foot. Hence it becomes evident that a correct exegesis will greatly weaken the power of infidelity, if not utterly destroy it.

Section 5.
THE LAST GREAT NEED OF A SOUND EXEGESIS, OF WHICH WE NOW SPEAK, IS THAT WE MAY FIND OUR WAY TO HEAVEN.

(1). *Inquirers discouraged by the different answers given.*—The question, "What shall I do to be saved?" receives so many different and conflicting answers, that the seekers after eternal life are confused and disheartened, and they don't know what to do. They are told that there is nothing they can do, that they must wait for the Lord to come and save them; and that they cannot do anything that will contribute to their salvation. Others tell them that they can and must give themselves to Christ so that they may be saved; and that unless they do, they will certainly be lost. Still they do not tell them how to give themselves to Christ. If they are sent to the word of God to learn the way of life, they are not told how to read it or where to look for directions on the subject. They would be as apt to go to the book of Job as to the Gospels or the Acts of the Apostles, to find the way of salvation in Christ. If men were inquiring into any question of law or history, they would be told where they could get the desired information—what book treated on that subject. They would not only be pointed to the book containing the desired intelligence, but to the chapter and section where the information might be found. If the Scriptures were studied in this way, there would be but little difficulty on this most important of all questions.

(2). *Not only is the question of salvation involved, but the assurance of pardon also.*—Persons who have had the same religious experience, differ widely as to the import of what they have heard, and desired, and felt. One believes he is a child of God, and no doubt lingers to chill the ardor of his soul. Another, who has had the same experience, *hopes that he has a hope,* but is *only certain that he is not certain of anything* respecting his standing with God. It is vain to say that this must be the direct teaching of the Holy Spirit, or that a Christian knows by his feelings just what his relations are with God. For if God taught one of these servants in this direct way, He certainly would not have left the other to grope his way in darkness, doubt, and uncertainty on the same subject. The truth is, one has had the same joys and sorrows that are known to the other, and the reason that the one regards himself a favorite of heaven and the other is in doubt as to his standing with God, is in the creeds of the two men. They are equally good, equally pure, and have passed through the same repentance, and have the same trust in Christ as the only Savior of men; in fact, there is no perceptible difference between them, except that through their creeds they have interpreted these sorrows and joys differently. And this difference of creed has arisen from the difference in their modes of interpretation. To one, these things have had one meaning; to the other, they have had quite a different meaning. Now, if it is God's will that one Christian should know his sins are forgiven, it is certain that it is His will that all His servants should rejoice because of like intelligence. Right methods of the interpretation of the Scriptures will certainly remove the trouble, and enable our joyous and doubtful brethren to see themselves in the same condition before the "one God and Father of us all."

CHAPTER II:
THE THINGS WHICH HELP US TO UNDERSTAND THE
WORD OF GOD.

Section 6.
THE NEED OF UNDERSTANDING THESE THINGS.

If we do not know the things that will help us, we are not likely to invoke their aid. No man searches for that which he has no knowledge of. If there are helps, let us know what they are, and how they may be obtained; and then we will strive for that ability which will enable us to know what the will of the Lord is.

Section 7.
GOOD COMMON SENSE IS THE FIRST REQUISITE.

This is so self-evident that to present it further would be to waste time.

(1). *This is a natural qualification, but it may be greatly increased.*—Someone has said that if a man lacks knowledge he can get it from his fellow-man; that if he lacks religion, he can have it by going to God and asking for it; but if he lacks common sense, he has nowhere to go. But this remark has in it more of wit than of truth. We are not all equally endowed, but almost everyone has a talent, and if it is not hid in a napkin and buried in the earth, but properly employed, it will increase; if it shall only be put on interest, it will gain something. Common sense has its root idea in the ability to discover harmony in the things which agree; and, conversely, to perceive unlikeness in opposites. To a man devoid of common sense, there would be no difference between Islam and the religion of Christ; between the Law of Moses and the Gospel of Christ; between Catholicism and any form of Protestantism. Equally hidden from him would be the truths in all these systems, for he would not be able to distinguish truth from error.

It does not seem to be known that a man may be ostensibly learned in the abstract, and know but little of anything in the concrete. And yet it is true that he may give himself so entirely to the study of attenuated philosophy that he will almost cease to have any proper understanding of the events of life, and be quite incompetent to decide between one thing and another.

If it be true that one may injure his mind by employing it only on subjects that are abstruse, it is just as true that the mind may be strengthened and benefited by proper use upon themes and duties that concern everyday life.

(2). *The use of this gift in the interpretation of the Scriptures.*—If we were speaking of the interpretation of law or the study of medicine, no one would call into question our position for a moment. To understand the propositions of any branch of science, all are agreed as to the absolute necessity of common sense. But there lurks in the popular heart the suspicion that, the less of real knowledge, and the more of the dreamy speculative qualities of mind are possessed, the more likely will the interpreter arrive at the meaning of the Bible. They forget that God gave this book to the common people, that He has filled it with the experiences of men, and that its writers have spoken to us not only of the things that constantly surround us, but in the language which a plain people can the most easily understand. It is a book to accompany us through all the walks of life—to constantly show us the dangers on the one hand, and the way of safety on the other. In this book we are constantly dealing with those things that are in antithesis; in which are the deceptive tricks of the enemy of the race, put over against the truth of God; in which the way of truth is made plain by its contrast with the works of darkness. Hence the more the student will study plain questions, and the more he may know men as they are, the more likely he will be able to understand the word of God.

Section 8.

FAITH IN THE INSPIRATION OF THE SCRIPTURES WILL HELP THE STUDENT TO UNDERSTAND THEM.

(1). It is not meant to say that unbelievers cannot know anything of the claims of the word of God. They may know many things respecting the Bible. The Jews who did not believe in the divinity of Christ understood many things respecting the claims which he made. Indeed, if an infidel could not know such things, he would not be responsible. The ability which unbelievers possess to investigate these subjects is the measure of their responsibility before God.

(2). *And yet the condition of their mind is unfavorable to any thorough investigation,* or any proper estimate of the claims which are made. To receive a letter from Jay Gould, and yet believe it to be from someone else, who had sent it out of mere sport, would not likely benefit the receiver. If he should read it, curiosity would have to incite to the effort; and as soon as the reader would be sufficiently amused, he would lay the epistle aside, with little, if any, further thought. The communication might be one of very great importance, and yet in a few hours he would know little, if anything, of its contents. So it is with the Bible. The unbeliever reads it out of mere curiosity, or so that he may find some fault with it, and the probability is that all he will be able to find in the volume will be a few things that, to him, are curious, or unreasonable. He remembers here and there a text from which he can make an adverse criticism, but as to making any thorough investigation into the teaching of that book, such an idea does not enter his mind. He is not in sympathy with it; and in no way is he prepared to understand it.

(3). *Faith in the inspiration of the book will prompt the most patient and thorough investigation.*—Not only so, but the thought that it contains a divine message for him will help to bring about a clearer view of its contents than could otherwise be had.

Section 9.

MENTAL INDUSTRY IS ESSENTIAL TO ANY PROPER INVESTIGATION.

Mary, who sat at the feet of the Master, and attended diligently to His teaching, may have been as industrious as her sister, but her industry was of a different kind. She employed the head and heart more in the acquisition of truth. The disciples, who did not always understand the parables of the Savior, went to him afterwards and inquired about the meaning. It was their investigating spirit that made it possible for them to learn the deep things which the Master came to give them. Without this it would have been impossible for them to have graduated in His school. The Bereans are praised for this disposition of mind.

> *Now these were more noble than those in Thessalonica, in that they received the word with all readiness of mind, examining the Scriptures daily, whether these things were so. Many of them therefore believed; also of the Greek women of honorable estate, and of men, not a few. (Acts 17:11-12)*

There is no essential difference between the study of the Scriptures and the study of any other subject, respecting the mental expense necessary to success. An occasional hour or lesson may accomplish something toward learning, but not much. With all the advantages given Timothy through the early instruction received from his mother and grandmother, and the assistance of the apostle Paul, still it was necessary for him to *"study to show himself approved to God, a workman that does not need to be ashamed: rightly setting forth the word of truth."* So we find in the efforts essential to a knowledge of the word of God, that, like obtaining knowledge of other things, the mind must be employed intently and continuously. There can be no substitute for mental industry. We must apply the mind and heart, or not know the things of God.

Section 10.

A DESIRE TO KNOW AND DO THE TRUTH, IS NECESSARY.

It cannot be denied that the most careless and indifferent person may learn something about the word of God. But they are not likely to learn much, nor to learn anything very well. Being without interest respecting its claims, or, it may be, set opposite to them, wishing not to find the truth, as almost anything else would comport better with their lives, the truth will not be found by them. It would be as difficult for such persons to see the truth, as it was for the priest and the Levite to see the man who had fallen among thieves. Or, if they should see, they would immediately look on the other side, and so pass on. For a moment they may behold their face in the divine mirror, but they go away immediately, and forget what manner of men they were. The soil must be in keeping with the seed, or there will be but little accomplished by the sowing. There are men for whom the gospel of Christ has no more charms than pearls have for swine. There must be good ground; "such as have an honest and good heart, having heard the word, hold it fast, and bring forth fruit with patience" (Luke 8:15). The test given by the Savior is just to the point: "If any man desires to do his will, he shall know of the teaching, whether it be of God, or whether I speak from myself." It is this willingness to do the will of God that prepares the mind for that effort which is necessary to understand the law of the Lord. In the Acts of the Apostles (13:48), we have a picture. The Gentiles who glorified the word of the Lord, and were ordained to (*determined* for) eternal life, believed; and those who were opposed, remained in unbelief. Men can find what they look for, but what they do not want to see, it is difficult to make them understand. Hence if there is not a good and honest heart, there will be but little fruit from the sowing.

Section 11.

SPIRITUAL PURITY IS A LARGE FACTOR IN BIB-LICAL INTERPRETATION.

(1). As just seen in the previous section, *the mind must have a strong rapport with the teaching to be received.* But we now go further, and show that indisposition does not simply prevent the examination that is necessary to any thorough knowledge, but it is a condition that fences against the pure word of God. There are those who are competent to see in every remark that is made something that is unchaste. They can find double meanings to anything that is said. And they interpret actions in the same way. To them every word and act seen or heard is prompted by motives that are sinister. The world is a mirror in which they see themselves, as they attribute their own motives to the acts of others. To the evil, all things are evil. Nothing is pure to the eye of lust. "Blessed are the pure in heart, for they shall see God," does not have to wait till the day of judgment for its fulfillment. In all the bounties and splendors of earth, they can see the traces of the hand of a loving Father. But such views are never had by the impure. They do not like to retain God in their minds, and when they are compelled to recognize the Almighty, they make Him into the likeness of men, and of four-footed beasts, and creeping things. Any other thought is too high for them.

(2). *We do not mean to say that such men cannot learn anything about the word of God, for this is God's way of making men better.*— There is truth put within their reach, and which, if they will lay hold of it, will lift them up to that better condition, in which they can know more of God and of the beauties of his word. They may learn much of sacred history; they may understand the teachings of prophecy and the claims of the Messiah; they are competent to examine the claims made respecting New Testament miracles, but there are great spiritual truths that will not be recognized by them.

(3). It is possible for men to become so gross as to be removed even from the probabilities, if not from the very possibilities, of faith. I cannot do better here than to quote a few passages of Scripture containing this thought:

For the time will come when they will not endure the sound doctrine; but, having itching ears, will heap to themselves teachers after their own lusts; and will turn away their ears from the truth, and turn aside to fables. (2 Tim. 4:3-4)

You stiff-necked and uncircumcised in heart and ears, you do always resist the Holy Spirit: as your fathers did, so do you. Which of the prophets did your fathers not persecute? and they killed them which showed of the coming of the Righteous One; of whom you have now become betrayers and murderers; you who received the law as it was ordained by angels, and kept it not. (Acts 7:51-53)

Here is both the teaching and the living picture of the ability to harden the heart against truth, until the soil of the soul is utterly destroyed.

And to them is fulfilled the prophecy of Isaiah, which says,
By hearing you shall hear, and shall in no way understand;
And seeing you shall see, and shall in no way perceive:
For this people's heart is waxed gross,
And their ears are dull of hearing,
And their eyes they have closed;
Lest haply they should perceive with their eyes,
And hear with their ears,
And understand with their heart,
And should turn again,
And I should heal them. (Matt. 13:14-15)

The meaning of this language cannot be mistaken. The reason they were not saved was they had not turned to God, and the reason they had not turned was that they did not understand with the heart; the reason they did not understand with the heart was that their grossness prevented them from considering the claims of Christ in any proper way.

> *How can you believe, which receive glory one of anoth-er, and the glory that comes from the only God, you seek not? (John 5:44)*

Here, even, the desire for the praise of men is presented as a bar-rier sufficient to prevent faith.

> *"You are of your father the devil, and it is your will to do the lusts of your father. He was a murderer from the beginning, and did not stand in the truth, because there is no truth in him. When he speaks a lie, he speaks of his own: for he is a liar, and the father of it. But because I say the truth, you do not believe me. (John 8:44-45)*

It is plain that this was not the original condition of this people. Once they might have accepted the truth and been made free by it, but they had turned their hearts over to the control of the wicked one till they had become like him.

With this evil heart in them, it would have been more agreeable for them to have heard a falsehood than a truth, and it would have been easier for them to receive the falsehood.

> *And then the lawless one shall be revealed, whom the Lord Jesus shall slay with the breath of his mouth and bring to naught by the manifestation of his coming; even he, whose coming is according to the working of Satan with all power and signs and lying wonders and with all deceit of unrighteousness for them that are perishing; because they did not receive the love of the truth, that they might be saved. And for this cause God sends them a working of error, that they should believe a lie; that they all might be judged who did not believe the truth, but had pleasure in unrighteousness. (2 Thess. 2:8-12)*

These persons were perishing because they believed a lie, and not the truth. This they did because they did not receive the love of the truth, but had pleasure in unrighteousness. And because they would not have the truth, God turned them over to the falsehoods which they preferred.

> *But and if our gospel is veiled, it is veiled in them that are perishing: in whom the god of this world has blinded the minds of the unbelieving, that the light of the gospel of the glory of Christ, who is the image of God, should not dawn upon them. (2 Cor. 4:3-4).*

The god of this world, in this text, was the riches, honors, and pleasures of this life. These things become a god to man through the devotion which he chooses to render. And in return for all this service, the worshiper has his mind blinded to all that is good and pure.

In this way the Gentile world fell away from all that was pure and holy. Once they knew God, but they neglected his worship, and so went astray, step by step, till they reached the lowest possible spiritual condition (Rom. 1:18-32).

Paul thinks it possible for those who have once known the truth, and have been made partakers of the Holy Spirit, to fall so far away that they cannot be renewed again to repentance (Heb. 6:1-6).

(4). *Not only may men fall into evil thoughts and evil lives, and thereby destroy their disposition to receive the truth, and even go so far that they cannot turn back again, but every degree in depravity renders it that much more difficult to accept the pure thoughts of the word of God.*—There are carnal-minded church members, who are too gross in their hearts to know the height and breadth, and length and depth, of the riches and beauty and glory of the revelation which God has made to us.

This proposition might be regarded as having been established already. Still it is proper to refer to a text or two—first to make the point still clearer; and second, to get the meaning of these passages clearly before the mind of the reader:

> *"Now the natural man does not receive the things of the Spirit of God: for they are foolishness to him, and he cannot know them, because they are spiritually judged (1 Cor. 2:14)*

This text has been a battle-ground, and as we enter it we announce our utter lack of sympathy for either party. The first and most common view of the passage is that until a man is converted and enlightened by the Holy Spirit, he cannot understand the word of God; that this natural man is the unconverted man. The second view is much more reasonable: The natural man is the man in a state of nature, and, therefore, without the revelation which God has given. And the reason that he cannot understand the things of God is that he has not had a teacher; but with a teacher, he could know these things quite well enough. I do not accept the interpretation of either of these parties, for the following reasons:

(*a*) Paul was not speaking *to,* nor *of,* men in a state of nature having never received revelation, or to whom it had never been offered.

(*b*) He was not speaking *to,* nor *of* unconverted men, in antithesis to converted men.

(*c*) The spiritual judgment is the antithesis, and the carnal judgment is that which naturally opposes it. Hence the conclusion is that the word rendered "natural" would be better rendered *carnal.*

(*d*) The reason that this natural man did not receive them, was not because he had never heard of them, but because they were foolishness to him. They could not be foolishness to a man who never heard of them.

(*e*) The word *psuchikos,* here rendered natural, is better rendered carnal. It occurs five times in the New Testament: 1 Cor. 2:14; 15:44, 46; James 3:35; Jude 19. In the Corinthian letter, it is rendered in the Common Version by the word *natural,* but in the other occurrences, by the word *sensual.* The latter is its meaning in all of the occurrences, as will be seen by the opposing thought being that of spiritual purity.

(*f*) Paul was writing to church members, whom he denominated saints—those who had been set apart to the service of the Lord. Hence neither of the old interpretations can possibly be true.

(*g*) *He was condemning them for their carnality.* In the third chapter he tells them that their divisions proved that they were carnal and walked as men. In the fifth chapter they are condemned because they had an incestuous man among them, who was living with his father's wife, and they did not mourn on that account, but were rather puffed up. In chapters ten and eleven it appears that they had turned the Lord's Supper, on the first day of the week, into a kind of Sunday club dinner, and thus spoiled the occasion of all its sanctity. But they were not only impure in their practices; they were erroneous in doctrine. Some of them, as it will be seen in the fifteenth chapter, denied the resurrection of the dead. Their condition is well presented in the following passage:

> *And I, brethren, could not speak to you as to spiritual, but as to carnal, as to babes in Christ. I fed you with milk, and not with meat; for you were not yet able to bear it; nay, not even now are you able; for you are yet carnal; for whereas there is among you jealousy and strife, are you not carnal and walk after the manner of men? For when one says, I am of Paul; and another, I am of Apollos; are you not men? (3:1-4. [That is, are you not worldly men, or men of carnal minds?]*

The reason that Paul had not given them the higher spiritual instruction was because they were not in a condition to receive it. And even then, when writing this letter to them, they were too low and carnal to receive the rich truth which otherwise they might have received long before. But in their then present condition, such lessons would have been wasted on them.

I lay it down, then, as being true beyond any possible doubt, that even Christians may be of the earth, earthy, to the extent that they will be incompetent to get the grand and spiritual thoughts of the word of God. This will account, in part at least, for the fact that the apostle John saw more in Jesus of Nazareth than any of the other writers of that most wonderful life. John had become more like the Master than anyone else, and was, therefore, prepared to understand Him better.

There is many a learned criticism that does not come near the truth because of the icy distance of the writer's heart from the subject on which he treats. On the other hand, the true follower of Christ finds the truth almost by intuition. The glory of heaven's richest revelation has been withheld from the wise and the prudent, and has been revealed to babes. It is first a humble, willing heart, good and honest, that will be easily instructed in the way of life in Christ Jesus. Those eyes are best adjusted to the divine light, and therefore they better understand both the truth and Him who taught it.

Section 12.
A CORRECT TRANSLATION WOULD HELP PRODUCE RELIABLE EXEGESIS.

This is especially true with the ordinary reader. Indeed, it is true of ninety-nine out of a hundred of the whole number of the real students of the Bible, for they are almost wholly dependent on the received translation as a means of knowing what has been said to us by the Lord. There are many contradictions now found in the Bible, or the language which is tortured into contradictions, which a correct translation would entirely remove. There are many harsh and seemingly brutal things in the Bible that would be modified by a clear and just translation. There are statements, forms, and phrases that occur to the refined ear as vulgar, that would be shorn of all offensiveness by judicious rendition. There are many things which are exceedingly dark, which an accurate version would illuminate, and, in their place, give us the clear and beautiful truth of God.

We do not mean to cast any reflections on the translators of the King James Version. They did well: for the times and circumstances, they did very well. It should be remembered, however, that they labored under many difficulties that have been removed since that time.

(1). There are words anglicized and transferred into our version which ought to have been translated. And the failure in that respect has contributed very much to the misinterpretation that would long ago have given place to better views.

(2). Incorrect translations were retained for fear of injury to the long-standing customs and traditions of the church. There is no reason for the word bishop, the meaning of which never occurs to anyone, when the word *episcopos* meant an overseer, and should have been so translated. It was wrong to give us Easter, in Acts 12:4, when it should have been Passover. The Accepted Version thus maintains an error that would have died out, but for the assistance rendered by a wrong translation.

(3). Many words have become obsolete since the translation of King James was made. *Wist,* and *wot,* and "*we do you to wit,*" are expressions without meaning to us.

(4). Many other words have changed their meaning entirely. The word *let,* then meant to prevent, to hold back, to restrain; now it has the opposite thought. Paul had desired many times to see the brethren at Rome, but had been *let.* He informed the brethren of Thessalonica that there would come a great falling away, and that man of sin would finally be revealed, but that which then *let* would continue to *let* till taken out of the way. Such language is unintelligible to us. *Prevent* (from *pre,* before, and *venio,* to come) meant to come before, to precede, to anticipate. So David said: "My prayer shall prevent the Lord;" "my prayer shall prevent the dawning of the morning." And Paul gravely tells the brethren that those who shall be alive and remain to the coming of the Lord, "shall not prevent those who are asleep." The word *conversation* once related to action and its results, rather than the use of words by one person to another. Hence Paul says, "our conversation is in heaven." The meaning of the passage is easy, when we have it correctly rendered *citizenship.*

We are in great need of a *translation,* not simply a *revision.* But while the world would not likely be willing to receive such a work, it would be better that all students should provide themselves with a copy of the Revision of the Old and New Testaments. Not that this work is faultless—that would be too much to expect of any human production—but because it is much better than the Common Version. The translators are equally learned with those of King James, and they have had many advantages which the former never possessed. While they have been too conservative in retaining many things that ought to have been removed, and while the Revision is marred by much of the bad grammar of the Common Version, still there are many valuable changes. And I think it is not too much to say, that in many respects the Revision is the best work of the kind ever furnished to the reading world.[1]

Section 13.

A GENERAL AND THOROUGH EDUCATION IS OF GREAT VALUE IN THE INTERPRETATION OF THE WORD OF GOD.

(1). No one is at liberty to suppose, from my advocacy of learning, that it can always be trusted. It cannot take the place of good common sense, and certainly not of a true heart and that spiritual purity which is so greatly needed in order to understand the things that are freely given to us of God.

(2). There is an idea that learning is destructive of piety. But I know of no evidence of the correctness of that view. Of course, there are many men so engaged in their investigations of science, and even in their literary pursuits, that little or no time is left for the cultivation of their hearts by the soul-stirring truths of heaven. Anything that will take up the mind entirely will do that. Farming, merchandise, politics, anything, if it is sufficiently absorbing. Learning will do this no more than any calling which will elicit the mind and direct the energy of the man. But instead of learning standing in the way of faith and piety, it can greatly aide it. The man of knowledge may lose his respect for many of the traditions of the fathers, but his faith in God and His word will not be injured thereby, but greatly aided.

(3). There is a mental drill in the attainment of knowledge that will greatly assist you in preparing for that effort necessary for a full and complete investigation of the Scriptures.

(4). I would begin my recommendations respecting the necessary features of education, with the knowledge of one's own vernacular. With us the English language is the great medium of knowledge. If our knowledge of that medium is defective, the benefits derived from its use will be greatly lessened. Most readers of the Bible, as before

[1] The author here speaks of the English Revised Version, which was later modified and became the American Standard Version in 1901. *Editor.*

stated, are entirely dependent upon the English Bible, and *all* are more or less dependent upon it: Not only so, but the commentaries, lesson helps, and all the valuable suggestions by way of essays, sermons, etc., come to us through the English language. Hence it is of great importance that we should have an accurate knowledge of our own language.

(5). A knowledge of the original languages, in which the Scriptures were written, would be of great assistance in getting an accurate and intimate acquaintance with the Bible.

There are many thoughts in the Greek and Hebrew Scriptures that cannot be so clearly presented in any other language than that in which they were written. In translating any book from one language into another, much of the beauty and strength is lost. The translator may be learned and faithful, but there are not the words to express those peculiar shades of meaning that belonged to the original. The peoples using these tongues have differed both in their thoughts and in their modes of expression, and it is therefore almost impossible to translate a book from one of these into the other, and retain the beauty and vigor of the composition. Other things being equal, the scholar in Hebrew and Greek is the better interpreter.

(6). A thorough immersion in logic would greatly aid investigation in the Scriptures. This is true in reading any work of merit. But it is especially true of the Bible. I once heard a man of prominence say that the Bible is not a book of logic, but of assertion. This, however, was a short-sighted observation. Even if the Bible were a book only of direct revelation, still the propositions made to men are to be understood by the rules of logic. There is no more direct assertion found in the Scriptures anywhere than in the teaching of the Master. He ever spoke as one having authority. And yet the strictest and closest logic is constantly observed. This was especially true in His many encounters with the Pharisees and Sadducees. When He stood in a synagogue on the Sabbath day, and a man was there who needed healing, He said to them: "Is it lawful to do good on the Sabbath day, or to do evil?" They might have said it is lawful to do neither one. But they could not consistently do so. Help was needed, and it must be rendered or refused; hence a choice had to be made. Inactivity in the matter was an impossibility. When Peter had committed himself and the Master by saying that the Master paid tribute, Jesus said to him, "Do kings collect revenue from their sons, or of strangers?" Peter said, "of strangers." "Very well, then," said the Savior, "the son goes free." Nevertheless he sent Peter to take the fish. The blunder of this apostle was thus pointed out by the use of logic. Take all the conversations at Jerusalem; during the last feast that the Master attended, his parables—full of logical acumen. He taught the Sadducees the resurrection from the account of the burning bush. He went to the very root of the question, and showed them that they were fundamentally wrong. Men did not lose their identity by death, as they supposed, and therefore there would be a resurrection from the dead. But especially the apostolic speeches and writings are full of logic. Peter, on the day of Pentecost, argued from what they then saw and heard, from the language of the prophet Joel, and from the Psalms, and, having finished his quotations, he drew logical conclusions so strong and so just that the whole crowd was carried with him. And wherever the apostles went, they argued before the people, opening the Scriptures and alleging out of it that Jesus was the Christ, and that he must needs have died and risen from the dead; and their logic was faultless. Open to any of the epistles, and you will find them replete with the finest argument, and presented in the most logical form. Perhaps no more logical writing can be found anywhere than Paul's letter to the brethren at Rome. And if one is in need of the knowledge of logic in order to comprehend the great speeches of Webster, Clay, and Garfield, he will equally need that skill before undertaking to analyze the epistle to the Romans.

(7). A good knowledge of contemporaneous history will greatly aid in the study of the Scriptures.—For several hundred years before Christ we have history, more or less reliable. And with all the imperfections that gather about these productions, they greatly assist us in knowing just what was done, and hence just what was referred to by the divinely directed writer. Old Testament history is by no means well studied, without comparing the statements of the Bible with the best thoughts on Egyptology, and the most reliable records of the Medes, Persians, Assyrians, Babylonians, Syrians, Phoenicians, Grecians, etc. And there are many things in the New Testament that will never be clear to the mind unacquainted with the history of the times. Matthew, Mark, Luke, and John wrote for those who were well acquainted with the facts, and therefore they did not stop to explain many things which cannot be understood by us, except as we study history and come into possession of the facts before *their* minds at the time they wrote these accounts. For the most part they speak of Herod as if there had been but one. Of course, to those for whom these records were first intended, there was no need of anything further being said. But without the knowledge of history, we will not know whether the writer is speaking of Herod the Great, Archelaus, Aristobulus, Antipas, Philip, Agrippa 1, or Agrippa II, and everything will be confused.

(8). *A good knowledge of the lands of the Bible will render many things plain which, without such knowledge, would be dark.*—The things that were said and done would have much more meaning and interest to us if we knew where they were and what they were looking at when these things were done and said. The allegories of the *true vine* and the *good shepherd;* the teaching of the Master on the great day of the feast; the directions to the blind man, *"Go wash in the pool of Siloam,"* crossing the sea to the land of the Gadarenes, or coming through the midst of Decapolis; the teaching of the Master in the borders of the city of Caesarea Philippi; the transfiguration that followed, are at least partially lost to us without a knowledge of the geography of the country. But while this is true in the study of the Gospels, it is especially true when we come to read the Acts and the letters of the apostles to the various churches. Every student of the Scriptures ought to become familiar with all the lands mentioned in the Bible. In the study of Old Testament history, this is especially true. The forty-two encampments of the children of Israel will never be understood without a good knowledge of the country through which they passed. Egypt, Sinai, the wildernesses of Paran and of Zin; the land of Edom; the mountain ranges; the land of the Amorites, of the Moabites, of the

Midianites east of the Jordan, should all be known. The student will be well paid for all the time and energy expended in the study of Biblical geography.

(9). *One should become as thoroughly acquainted as possible with the customs of the people during the times of the Bible.*—Many things are perfectly inexplicable unless we are in possession of this key of knowledge. Words and ways are full of meaning to us when we know the customs of the people; whereas, without such knowledge, we would not be able to divine their intent.

Section 14.
WE SHOULD EXPECT TO UNDERSTAND THE BIBLE.

The Bible is regarded by many as a sealed book, and not to be understood, unless by some gift from God which shall make it possible, either because of some office, or on account of conversion. The ability to read it as any other book, and understand it by reading it, is not supposed to belong to unaided mortals. In another place we will examine the cause of this hurtful superstition, but for the present we are content to say that we must expect to understand the word of God or our investigations will amount to a total waste of our time. If we should read any other book in this way, no one would expect us to know anything about it when we had finished reading. The words might be pronounced or heard, but no impression would be made on the mind. We would not be looking for anything, and, as a consequence, we would not find anything.

There are those now who regard the Scriptures as a mystery, and therefore not to be understood by the common mind. Indeed, they suppose that the Scriptures themselves teach that they are a mystery. On this account it is necessary to quote a few passages, so that we may realize our privileges.

> But you abide in the things which you have learned and
> have been assured of, knowing from whom you have
> learned them; and that from a babe you have known the
> sacred writings which are able to make you wise to sal-

vation through faith which is in Christ Jesus. Every scripture inspired of God is profitable for teaching, for reproof, for correction, for instruction which is in right-eousness: so that the man of God may be complete, fur-nished completely to every good work. (2 Tim. 3:14-16)

The Scriptures which Timothy had known in his childhood were those of the Old Testament, which are much more difficult than the communications found in the New Testament. And these, too, as they were fulfilled in Christ, were sufficient to perfect the man of God, filling him with all needed truth.

How that by revelation was made known to me the mys-tery, as I wrote before in few words, whereby, when you read, you can perceive my understanding in the mystery of Christ; which in other generations was not made known to the sons of men. (Eph. 3:3-4)

Then again in the eighth and ninth verses:

To me, who am less than the least of all saints, was this grace given, to preach to the Gentiles the unsearchable riches of Christ; and to make all men see what is the dispensation of the mystery, which from all ages has been hidden in God, who created all things.

Here it is evident that the most difficult things that had to be pre-sented to the world—those which were more mysterious than any former revelation—were to be read and understood by the whole church. Not only so, but Paul was commissioned to make all men see this mystery as he did.

And when this epistle has been read among you, cause that it be read also in the church of the Laodiceans; and that you also read the epistle from Laodicea. (Col. 4:16)

This letter to the brethren of Laodicea has been lost, but it was probably much like that which was sent to the church at Colossae. We cannot say that it is unusually difficult, and yet he who can read that letter and understand it, is able to read any of the letters of the apostle

Paul. He supposed the whole church at Colossae could hear and understand it, and that the church at Laodicea could do the same.

> *I adjure you by the Lord that this epistle be read to all the brethren. (1 Thess. 5:27)*

Here again, though the first written of the apostolic letters, it is one of the most difficult. And yet Paul had no such thought that the members of the church could not understand it. Indeed, the evident purpose of all the epistles was that they should be read to the whole church, and that the whole church, in this way, should be instructed in divine things. And yet there is as much skill needed in the interpretation of the epistolary communications as any other portion of the Scriptures, unless it be Revelation, or Ezekiel.

Then let us remove the fog of superstition that has prevented so many from any proper investigation of the Scriptures, that all may know their rights to search this volume for themselves, and that they may understand it. Indeed, they should be made to realize that they are responsible for their ignorance. God has made a revelation of His will to us, and if we do not avail ourselves of the privilege of reading it and of knowing its contents, it is our own fault. All should be made to feel that, under such circumstances, ignorance is a sin against God and ourselves.

Section 15.
THE BLESSING OF GOD IS NEEDED, AND MAY BE HAD FOR THE ASKING.

This does not mean that knowledge is to be had by asking alone, when there are other conditions of receiving it. But it does mean that God has promised to bless us in this respect as well as in others.

> *But if any of you lacks wisdom, let him ask of God, who gives to all liberally, and does not chastise; and it shall be given him. (James 1:5)*

While the preacher *then* had to study to show himself approved to God, that he might be a workman that does not need to be ashamed, rightly setting forth the word of truth, still this blessing is promised.

And all we are authorized to say about it is, that while we use the means which God has provided for our education in divine things, it is our privilege and duty to ask that God will bless the effort. And we have God's promise, through an apostle, that he will do so. We may not know just how God will choose to assist us in learning his will, but his promise will certainly be kept. We may, in part, answer our own prayers, for the very hungering and thirsting for this divine knowledge will prepare us for a ready reception of the truth.

CHAPTER III:
THINGS WHICH HINDER A RIGHT INTER- PRETATION OF THE SCRIPTURES.

It is about as necessary to understand the things that prevent us from the investigation that would acquaint us with the word of God, as to know the things that will help. Because even while we may be availing ourselves of assistance, we may be injured by many things that so modify the favorable forces, that we shall get but little benefit from them. We wish to know, therefore, the things that will hinder, as well as the things that will assist us in understanding the word of the Lord.

Section 16.
A DESIRE TO PLEASE THE WORLD.

(1). It is not meant to say that all desire to please the world is wrong; indeed, we are required to please our neighbor for his good. No real man of God can have any interest in offending. For when we have offended the world, we have lost our power with them to do good, at least to a degree.

(2). But it is the *inordinate desire to please the world* that hinders a right interpretation. Many men have been decoyed from the truth by popular applause. They have said something that sounded like heresy, and it received the approval of persons of means and standing, and, desiring more approval, they ventured on more and graver utterances of the same kind. If they did not absolutely run away into heterodox woods, they at least climbed up to the top of the orthodox gate-post, and gave a longing look in that direction. And for that look they received a benefit. And then with vanity on the one hand and flattery on the other, all sorts of doctrines have been preached, to tickle itching ears, and bring the rounds of applause for which a vain heart palpitates. To such men the word of God may never have been very precious, but the honor that comes from men continually lessens their feeling of loyalty to divine authority, until they are willing to preach anything, true or false, if it will only give them favor with the people. They become willing to sell their pulpit—and themselves also—to the highest bidder. And the bid from the ungodly becomes a bribe to blind them to the truth.

Section 17.
THE BIBLE MADE THE PROPERTY OF THE PRIESTHOOD.

(1). This has been one of the great faults of the Catholic Church. In the decision of their councils, that the laity of the church should not read that book, lest they should reach wrong views, they have left it entirely to the control of those whose special business it has been to furnish the people with a knowledge of heaven's will. This enables them to establish a monopoly of interpretation. So that, to the people, the Bible is not the book itself; but the meaning of the book, as interpreted by the priesthood, *is to them the Bible.* All the restraints are thus removed from these men, and they are at liberty to interpret the Bible in that way that will best suit their purposes. This kind of power is always dangerous, as much in this respect as in any other.

If, in answer to this, it shall be said that only the more ignorant of the membership of that church are thus prohibited, and that many of them are at liberty to read the Bible, and that they are encouraged to do so, I am willing to grant that such is the case in some places, and especially of late. But this does not remove the correctness of our position, nor the justness of our charge. Much has been done in opposition to the thought that the common people can understand the word of God; and in this way it has been kept from their hands.

(2). Protestantism is an improvement, perhaps, but not such an improvement as will give us any particular cause of boasting. The creeds that are in use have been made a long time, at a time when knowledge was lower and prejudices were higher than at present. And yet in the light of these catechisms we have been compelled to conduct our investigations. So it has not been, even to Protestants, so much, *"What does the Bible say on the subject?"* as, *"What does the creed or catechism say?"*

(3). There has descended to us a kind of reverence for *authority found in great names,* that is very hurtful. These authorities have been canonized by us, and are not to be disturbed. This is partly because of superstition from which we are not yet free, and partly from laziness that makes us willing to accept statements, rather than look for the truth ourselves. In this way errors are handed down from one generation to another, for centuries, without having been suspected of being untrue. Some great man has made a hasty statement, which, at the time, he intended only to be understood as a kind of guess, and then it has been copied by one after another, till a dozen or twenty scholars can be quoted as holding that view; and this will be evidence enough for the faith of all the rest, for centuries to come.

(4). It is not intended to encourage disrespect for candor and learning. *Authors may be used as aids in study of the Scriptures,* as well as in the study of anything else, but it should be remembered that nothing but the word of God will do as a guide for the faith and practice of His people. We should accept the assistance of these great men in getting that knowledge, but nothing more. Reformations have been checked, and really prevented, by too much reverence for the reformers. They have had but a single truth which they have urged before the world, which they saw with great clearness. On many other points they have been weak, like other men. But their admirers have stereotyped them as the sum of all intelligence, and refused to have any view of theirs called in question. This has resulted in making these men the standard of doctrine, and preventing the world from learning anything else than what *they* learned under the most difficult circumstances.

Section 18.
USING THE BIBLE TO PROVE DOCTRINES IS A GREAT SOURCE OF MISUNDERSTANDING.

The Bible is not a book with which to prove doctrines; it is the doctrine itself. Almost anything can be proven to the man who wants to find the proof. It leads to a wrong use of the Scriptures, so that instead of searching them for whatever they may contain, the doctrines have been first assumed, and then the Bible is compelled into some sort of recognition of the position. (See Section 34).

Section 19.
MYSTICISM.

Spiritualizing the word of the Lord.—Instead of regarding it as a sensible communication from the God of heaven, it is turned into a kind of Samson's riddle, and made to say almost anything except that which it meant to say. (See Section 28).

Section 20.
MAKING THE BIBLE MERELY A BOOK OF WONDERS.

The disposition manifested in this does not differ greatly from that which guides the Mystic Method. And yet it is treated this way by many persons who do not have the slightest idea that they are influenced by like motives and feelings. It is treated as a kind of mental and spiritual *museum*—a box of curiosities. Men who search for quaint texts, and Sunday-school teachers who have their scholars searching for some strange question, are constantly contributing to that kind of disregard for the word of the Lord, though they do not intend it. The school is asked to tell how many times the word girl occurs in the Bible, or what was the name of David's mother, or what man had twelve toes; and the energies and time of the scholars are taken up with such incidentals, to no profit.

Section 21.
READING WITHOUT INTENDING OR EXPECTING TO UNDERSTAND IT.

(1). *Reading from a sense of duty,* or simply to be able to say that they have read it through. I have known persons who regarded it a duty to read the Bible through once a year, and having done this for a number of years in succession, they seemed quite fond of telling about it. This exercise will be something better than a pilgrimage to Mecca, but as a means of becoming acquainted with the Scriptures, it is very poor. If we should read any other book in this way, we would not be expected to know much of its contents. The mind must be fixed upon the thought and purpose of the work, with the intent of knowing what they are; and no more should be read than is understood, or at least partially digested.

(2). *The Bible is read irregularly and without any system.*—This is quite common in family worship. One time it is a Psalm; at another, it is a chapter from the Gospels, or one from the Prophets. Something, of course, may be learned in this way, but not very much. Like the reading mentioned before, it leaves nothing except that which sticks to the mind of its own accord. It comes from the lack of method, which will be more fully discussed in another place. (See Chapter 4).

(3). *Reading only favorite Scriptures.*—This is pardonable, to a degree, in a hobbyist. A man who has a particular hobby to ride may be expected to know but little of the Scriptures outside of the round of texts that can be made to harmonize with his doctrine. These he has thoroughly committed—at least, he has the places well marked, and quite well worn. Now and then I find a Bible owned by one of these men, and it is worn out at his favorite texts, and perfectly new everywhere else. But there are many others who treat their Bibles much in the same way. They have their favorite chapters, which they read again and again to the neglect of other and equally weighty Scriptures. If any other study should be pursued in this way, no one would expect anything to be gained by the effort. If a student should come into school and study only the chapters and sections in his book which he preferred, he would know little more at the conclusion than at the beginning of his studies.

There are a great many hindrances, which we will not now name, of the same kind. But let this suffice. Anything that will prevent thorough and continued study will prevent knowledge, to the full extent of its influence. Whether we read hurriedly or slowly is a small matter, for each one has some advantages; but the reading that is not pondered, is nearly worthless.

Section 22.

INTERPRETING FROM SINISTER MOTIVES.

(1). *This is frequently done to save property.*—Being found in the possession of goods that it is not right for us to have, we begin to excuse ourselves by some peculiar theory on that subject. Then the mind is drawn out in the defense, not simply of the theory, but of the property which the theory protects. We did not first advocate slavery in this country, and then seek the slaves. The property came into our possession, we could scarcely say how. And rather than to let the servants go, the Bible was brought into the defense of the institution. Legislators make laws to shield themselves in the possession of property, and many interpret law for personal gain, or for protection in the business which they know to be ruinous to the people. Of course they will quote and apply the Scriptures in the same way. Many, perhaps, do no intentional wrong in the matter. They have simply permitted themselves to become blinded by their own interests. This desire for security in their business and property colors all their interpretations and makes ineffective all their exegesis.

(2). *A wish to do as we please; to continue our customs, or begin new ones which we prefer.*—Many men today are in the condition of the prophet Balaam; they are very anxious to do and say whatever the Lord may direct, provided the Lord will direct them to do and say the things they prefer. When Judah heard that his daughter-in-law had played the harlot, he was so indignant that he wished her to be burned; but when she showed the cane and the bracelets, which he had left with her, there was a wonderful modulation in the tone. In the days of Christ, the Pharisees and lawyers were ready to lay grievous burdens on the shoulders of others, but they were not willing to touch one of them with even a little finger. The rules they would make for others were strict, but those they would make for themselves would be quite different. So it has ever been with the world. I knew a man who had a hobby on marriage. He was of the opinion that no man could marry twice without being a polygamist—in heaven, if not on the earth. His wife might die, but that had nothing to do with it; if he married again he would be guilty of polygamy. You could not talk with him five minutes without having his hobby brought out and made to canter in your presence. But his wife died, and in less than a year from that time his theology changed on that point. Almost anything that men want to do, they can find some text of Scripture that will sound like it is giving it support. And it is exceedingly difficult to make any man see that he has been preaching that which is not true. He has posed before the people on that subject, and is not willing to incur the humiliation of saying, "I was wrong, and my opponents were right." The question, "How religiously dishonest can an honest man be?" is hard to answer. Whether this is the right way to state it or not may be doubted; but one thing is certain—a man's wishes will blind his mind to the truth, if they happen to be on the contrary side. During the last war, good men would read the same dispatches, and reach opposite conclusions from them. During a political campaign they will do the same. We should be as far above such prejudice as possible.

(3). *Sectarianism is responsible for much of the wrong interpretation that prevents the world from knowing the truth.*—The desire to be with the successful party furnishes a strong temptation to use the Scriptures so that the party shall be approved. Indeed, the love of party will develop genius in its maintenance. In political matters, it is not strange that men will bend the truth for party purposes, and interpret all facts according to the interests involved. But that good people will do this in matters of salvation, seems out of place. If we were listening to such a statement for the first time, we would not be willing to accept the charge without a wide margin on which to write exceptions. But facts are stubborn things; the world does very frequently subordinate the truth to the interests of sectarian preferences. It is possible for well-meaning people to be blinded by these things. They get into an argument, and are put to the worse; and, being sure that their position is correct, and yet not being able to make it appear, they are ready to seize any passage that can be made to do even temporary service. In their sober moments they would say that the interpretation of the passage in hand was not the correct one; but not seeing what else to do at the time, they give that exegesis to push back the opponent till they can have time to cast about for something better to say. But for the sectarian prompting, nothing of the kind would have occurred. Prompted by their love for their party, or, perhaps, what is worse, their hatred for the opposite one, they become willing that the word of God shall be misrepresented for the time. They find themselves in the heat of battle, and anything then to win—at least, to prevent defeat. This interpreting the Bible for party ends is one of the greatest hindrances of today to a correct knowledge of the revelation of God to men. How to avoid this, and yet retain the parties, is difficult to say. About all that we are now warranted in saying is that it is needful to put everything out of the mind but the desire to know the truth of God when we open His book. Let go, as far as possible, everything of self and sect, and free the mind and heart from every wish or interest that may, in any way, prevent the knowledge of the word and will of the Lord.

(4). *Moral or practical atheism.*—This is the disposition to do as we please about divine things. There is a feeling of indifference as to what God may have said on the subject. Men are ready to conclude that it matters little whether they do God's way or not. In their opinion, it will do well enough to obey the Lord in His commands, but it is not essential. If they do not prefer to do the Lord's way, He will accept them while they do *their* way. These persons may believe that there is a God; they may believe that He is the author of the Bible; but it has not entered their minds that it makes any particular difference whether they do His will or not. This is practical atheism. Like the Samaritans of old, they fear the Lord and serve other gods. With such views of the authority of Jehovah, it is not possible to have any correct understanding of the Scriptures. Everything is vitiated by such heedlessness:

Section 23.
THIRST FOR DISTINCTION: DESIRE TO BE KNOWN AS PERSONS OF LEADING THOUGHT.

Whatever desire there may be to do good, by bringing out the meaning of the word of God, is certainly laudable. Or if there be a wish to excel in this effort to benefit the world, it is to be allowed and encouraged; but when the ambitious mind has only in view *the exaltation of self,* the exegete comes to stand in the way of every other effort than that which he is making, and his thirst for distinction even prevents the acceptance of the plain and simple truth of the gospel. Scientists do this, sometimes, and stop all investigation respecting everything on which they have pronounced. Lest they should not be regarded as the end of all wisdom, they go to work to destroy every hypothesis that, in any way, seems to call in question any position which they have taken. So do these, for the purpose of maintaining a reputation for independence of thought, adopt anything and everything that promises to bring them to public view. One man was capable of finding all the ordinances of the church in the book of Job. And all the quaint or curious things from first to last, have come from this desire for leadership. Hence they must find in the Scriptures what no one else has been able to find, or their claim to acuteness will not be well maintained.

Section 24.
EFFORTS TO HARMONIZE SCIENCE WITH THE BIBLE ARE DOING MUCH HARM.

We have no objections to any investigation into the subject of science and revelation. But what we do object to is the demand that Scripture interpretation must keep pace with the *guesses* of scientific speculators. Every new theory that is advanced demands a new hermeneutic. Words must be bent and shaded till they will fit the wards and cells of the new science.

The old theologians took advantage of science, and declared that everything that did not accord with their interpretation of the Bible could not be true, and, therefore, should not be tolerated. This, of course, was very discouraging to scientific research. No man was at liberty to push his investigations beyond the creed of the church. All can now see the injustice and injury of such unrighteous jurisdiction.

But in latter times it has been changed, so that the scientist comes and sets himself up in a kind of espionage over the interpreter of the word of God. These are both wrong, and both to be condemned. Before any man is ready to say that the Bible and science are not agreed, he should know two things: first, he should everything all about the Bible; and second, he should know everything about science. In the meantime, the best thing he can do is to learn everything he can of either one, or both.

It is not to be denied that we may know some things, at least approximately, and that so far as facts have been really introduced and tested, we may be governed by them, just to the extent of our absolute knowledge. But no interpreter should trouble himself to make exegesis keep up with scientific hypotheses. Science has no more right to lord it over religion, than religion has to lord it over science. He who made the universe made the Bible, and when we come to understand them both, we will be delighted with their beautiful harmony. And it is, therefore, the privilege and duty of every man to push his investigations as far and as fast as he can.

CHAPTER IV:
CONCERNING METHODS.

Section 25.
THE VALUE OF METHOD.

(1). *Definition of method.*—According to Webster, Method is—

1. An orderly procedure or process; a rational way of investigating or exhibiting truth; regular mode or manner of doing anything; characteristic manner.

'Though this be madness, yet there is method in it.'—Shakespeare.

2. Orderly arrangement, elucidation, development, or classification; clear and lucid exhibition; systematic arrangement peculiar to an individual.

'However irregular and desultory his talk, there is method in the fragments.'—Coleridge.

'All method is rational progress, a progress toward an end.'—Sir W. Hamilton."

We use the word, in the present work, to indicate the arrangement or plan of investigation. It is the system by which facts are to be introduced and conclusions reached.

(2). *Method is superior to rule.*—Methods are general and rules are special, hence the method governs all rules, or directs their use. One of the weaknesses of hermeneutics is the lack of a system, or of any thought that a system is necessary in the study of the Scriptures. Rules have been furnished in abundance, but the great need has been that of method. Rules may explain how to cut stone and lay up the wall, but without method you would be as likely to have one form as another in the building. The material that went into the temple at Jerusalem could have all been put into a building ten feet high and ten feet wide, by extending it far enough. If rules were all that had been needed, the men of King Hiram would have known just how to erect the temple of Solomon without any directions from him. But rules were not enough; it took the divine plan to govern them, to render them of any particular value in erecting the temple. An army might have all the rules necessary to success—marching, camping, cooking, fighting—but, without method, they would not unite against any foe, or conduct a campaign with any profitable results.

Section 26.
WHY METHOD HAS NOT BEEN EMPLOYED.

Several superstitions seem to have combined to prevent the world from the exercise of common sense in dealing with the word of God.

(1). The idea that it is a supernatural book, and, therefore, must have a supernatural interpretation, has done much to weaken efforts at close and profitable study of the Bible.

(2). It has been regarded as the right of those who have been divinely appointed to bring out its meaning and that it would be presumption for others to meddle with their prerogatives.

(3). Men have looked upon the Bible as not having been given according to any plan. They have regarded it as a mass of truth irregularly thrown together, and that we are as apt to find its meaning without system in our investigation as with it. They suppose its truth to be gold pockets, and not to be mined after any plan; and if we accidentally happen to hit upon a deposit we are fortunate. Getting the meaning of the Scriptures, to them, is more a question of genius or accident, than of study or research.

(4). Others, as we will see, have looked upon the Bible as a blind parable, and if it mean anything, then it is as likely to mean one thing as another.

They would not think of treating any other book in this way. When they read books of law and medicine, they suppose that intelligence and a wish to communicate has made the author present his thoughts in a way in which he could be the most easily understood. And why they have imagined that God has acted less kindly and sensibly than men do in making their communications, I cannot understand. Against this injustice, thinking men have arrayed themselves for many centuries. But they have been too few in number, and have been overborne by the thoughtless masses.

Milton says:

> We count it no gentleness or fair dealing in a man of power to require strict and punctual obedience, and yet give out his commands ambiguously. We should think he had a plot upon us. Certainly such commands were no commands, but snares. The very essence of truth is plainness and brightness; the darkness and ignorance are our own. The wisdom of God created understanding, fit and proportionable to truth, the object and end of it, as the eye to the thing visible. If our understanding have a film of ignorance over it, or be blear with gazing on other false glisterings, what is that to truth? If we will but purge with sovereign eyesalve that intellectual ray which God has planted within us, then we would believe the Scriptures protesting their own plainness and perspicuity, calling to them to be instructed, not only the wise and the learned, but the simple, the poor, the babes; foretelling an extraordinary effusion of God's Spirit upon every age and sect, attributing to all men and requiring from them the ability of searching, trying, examining all things, and by the Spirit discerning that which is good.

This presents us no method of reading the Scriptures, but contains a valuable truth in respect to the divine purpose in giving the word of God to men. In the mind of Milton, there is no reason to suppose that God intended any other rules to be employed in the investigation of His book, than those which are needed in the examination of all other books.

Prof. Moses Stuart, of Andover, says:

> Nearly all treatises on hermeneutics, since the days of Ernesti, have laid it down as a maxim which cannot be controverted that the Bible is to be interpreted in the same manner, that is, by the same principles as all other

books. Writers are not wanting, previously to the period in which Ernesti lived, who have maintained the same thing; but we may also find some who have assailed the position before us, and labored to show that it is nothing less than a species of profaneness to treat the sacred books as we do the classic authors with respect to their interpretation. Is this allegation well grounded? Is there any good reason to object to the principle of interpretation now in question? In order to answer, let us direct our attention to the nature and source of what are now called principles or laws of interpretation: Whence did they originate? Are they the artificial production of high-wrought skill, of labored research, of profound and extensive learning? Did they spring from the subtleties of nice distinctions, from the philosophical and metaphysical efforts of the schools? Are they the product of exalted and dazzling genius, sparks of celestial fire, which none but a favored few can emit? No; nothing of all this. The principles of interpretation as to their substantial and essential elements, are no invention of man, no product of his effort and learned skill; nay, they can scarcely be said with truth to have been discovered by him. They are coeval with our nature. Ever since man was created and endowed with the powers of speech, and made a communicative and social being, he has had occasion to practice upon the principles of interpretation, and has actually done so. From the first moment that one human being addressed another by the use of language, down to the present hour, the essential laws of interpretation became, and have continued to be, a practical matter. The person addressed has always been an interpreter in every instance where he has heard and understood what was addressed to him. All the human race, therefore, are, and ever have been, interpreters. It is a law of their rational, intelligent, com-

municative nature. Just as truly as one human being was formed so as to address another in language, just so truly that other was formed to interpret and understand what is said.

(5). More than any other thought or feelings a *want of sound faith,* has contributed to a wrong system of hermeneutics, and even to the abolition of all system. At a very early date, philosophies were introduced as the equal of the teaching of the apostles. And even up to the time of the Reformation, the study of Christian philosophers was thought to be more desirable than the study of Paul. And it made such a lasting impression on the minds of the people that they have not entirely recovered from it yet. Men studied Augustine, and were regarded sound, or otherwise, as they agreed with that saint. The schools of theology were not so much to study the Bible as to become acquainted with the views of their great men.

Blackburne, in his "History of the Church," pp. 226, 227, gives us a good statement respecting the condition of things in the ninth century:

A subtle philosophy was brought into the controversies of the West by John Scotus Erigena (Irishman), the adviser and confidant of the French king, Charles the Bald, who had some of the tastes of his grandfather, Charlemagne. John was the teacher of the court school. He was the enigma and wonder of his time. He suddenly comes, and all at once disappears; so that we know not whence he came nor whither he went. He was undoubtedly the most learned man, and the deepest, boldest, and most independent thinker of his age, in which he was neither understood nor appreciated, and he was scarcely deemed even worthy of being declared a heretic. The churchmen of Paris rectified the omission in 1209, and burnt some of his books and pantheistic followers. Though he wished to retain some of the essential doctrines of Christianity, his system was one great heterodoxy, based upon Plato, Aristotle, Plotinus, and himself.

Theology and philosophy were, in his view, merely forms of the same truth. He said: 'Authority springs from reason, not reason from authority.' He was the Western writer who used logic as a means of discovering truths. His philosophy was rationalistic; his pantheism foreran that of Hegel. The French king directed him into a new field. It is a startling feature of the times that one whose theories were so divergent from the teaching of the Church, was called to speak as an authority on two of the most awful topics of the faith. These were the doctrines of predestination and the Eucharist, which, owing to the great activity of thought engendered in the Carlovingian schools, were now discussed with unwonted vehemence.

This is but the case of an individual philosopher, but the Christian world in general conducted no investigations in any religious matter for a thousand years, except as they did it by questions which were discussed. The opponent of Christianity appealed to philosophy as much as its friends, but to another class of philosophers. And heterodoxy consisted more in not agreeing with them respecting the philosophers who were to be guides for them in this wilderness of speculation than in anything else.

Guided by the thought that the apostles of Christ were only splendid philosophers, and that truth could be as easily and as safely gained from the others, it is not strange that there was no system of hermeneutics thought of; for there was but little attempt at investigation into the word of God.

And yet we may reserve our sympathies for ourselves, as we have nearly the same need of method in our attempts at investigation that they had. But we are coming to the light, and, it is sincerely hoped, in the near future we shall have the common sense and common honesty to treat the Bible as we do other books: let it speak for itself.

Now and then, we find a man in the dark ages contending for something like a correct method of interpretation. But his voice is soon hushed, and a century goes by before the world is favored with another reformer of sufficient force to be known and felt.

Section 27.
WRONG METHODS OF INTERPRETATION ARE RESPONSIBLE FOR MUCH OF THE MISUNDERSTANDING RESPECTING THE MEANING AND INSPIRATION OF THE SCRIPTURES.

(1). *By their use many things are sustained that we know to be false.*—The unbeliever says, "There, that is what your Christianity teaches;" and we do not dare to deny it, for by the use of false methods of interpretation the church has adopted it. And we are in the condition of the Egyptians when Cambyses came against them. In front of his own men he drove a large number of their calves, and dogs, and cats. The Egyptians did not dare to injure them. They were their gods. As they could not reach the Persian army save through their own divinities, all that was left for them to do was to flee before the approaching enemy. So when the enemies of our religion can defend themselves by our creeds, we are helpless. When the Bible is made to teach that there are no good impulses in our nature, and that we can no more believe than we can make a world, except by a power that must come to us from above, the logical mind concludes at once that if he fails to believe, the fault is not his. And hence, if he is to be damned, it will be for that unbelief which he could not help. We argue in vain against his atheistic fatalism, for he can show that our Christian fatalism is no better. When we make the Bible teach that a man cannot even think a good thought, of himself, the thinking world says your Bible teaches what every man knows to be false. Supposing that the Scriptures have been fairly dealt with, the thinking man turns away from them in utter disgust.

(2). *Not only is the Bible made to teach what we know to be untrue, but also to contradict itself.*—It is said that to come to God in any acceptable devotion, we must not only believe that God is, but that He is a rewarder of those who diligently seek Him. Then we are told that faith is a direct gift of God, and that the only thing that one can do in order to become a believer is to ask God for that faith by which he can be saved. The logical mind balks at the sight of such confusion. He says: I cannot be heard and have my prayer answered, unless I have faith when I go to Him. But I have not that faith, and am told that I must pray for it. That is, I must have the faith before the prayer can be heard, and I must pray before I can have faith. He says that such doctrine is nonsense. And, supposing that the exegetes have done their work all right, he declares the Bible to be self-contradictory, and, from that hour sneers at the claims of inspiration made in its favor.

(3). *False methods have turned over the Bible to the clergy, as a kind of convenient toy.*—We are amazed that Christianity has outlived the treatment it has received at the hands of its friends. From the beginning of the fifth century to the close of the fifteenth, real scriptural examination was almost entirely dispensed with. The most ingenious travesty on the word of God was accepted as evidence of the fitness for the ministry of the man who could arrange it. Theology related to the forms of church government, or some question about Transubstantiation, Trinity, Predestination, Indulgences, Penance, or whether *tonsure* should be made by shaving the head from the forehead, backward over the crown, or to begin at one ear and shave over the crown to the other ear. This was a grave question, on which the English Church and the Church of the Pope could not agree, until it was settled by King Oswy, before whom the question had been argued by the ablest theologians of the time.

There were reformers, here and there, who wished to give to the people the word of the living God, and to urge them to follow it as their guide to heaven; but, as said before, they were few in number, and their power for good was scarcely felt. Religious people were controlled by scientific theology, and not by the word of God. As the philosophical puzzles of the day had little or nothing to do with the Scriptures, everything was left to those who had the time and were paid to attend to such things.

We think that it was a great misfortune to have lived in that day, and yet how much have we improved? Orthodoxy and heterodoxy are determined now, more by the canonized authorities than by the word of God. If a missionary now be questioned as to the soundness of his faith, it is to be decided more by the custom of the *church,* than by the word of Scripture. The sensational sermons of today are excused on the ground of dullness of the people and the need of something to appetize them. But whatever the cause, it is lamentably true that the masses are getting little help in understanding the Bible from the pulpit at the present time. Upon the weaknesses of the pulpit, not of ancient, but of modern time, in matters of exegesis, I have nowhere seen a clearer or more manly statement than is to be found in a work of Homiletics, "The Theory of Preaching," by "Austin Phelps, D. D., late Professor of Theology in Andover. He says:

> *It should be further observed, that the past and present usages of the pulpit respecting truthfulness of interpretation is not entirely trustworthy. Explanations which exegesis has exploded are sometimes retained by the pulpit for their homiletic usefulness. Preachers often employ in the pulpit explanations of texts which they would not defend in an association of scholars. The pulpit suffers in its exegetical practice by retaining for polemic uses explanations which originated in an abuse of philosophy. I do not say in the use of philosophy. We have seen that there is a legitimate use of philosophy, within certain limits, in aiding the discoveries and application of sound philology. But philosophy has often tyrannized over philology. In the defense of the creeds of the Church, the exigencies of philosophy have overborne the philological instinct of the popular mind, as well as the philological learning of the schools. A modern exegete affirms that the interpretation of the seventh chapter of the Epistle to the Romans, which makes it a description of Christian experience, was never heard of in the Church till the time of Augustine. He originated it to support his theory of original sin. He held the opposite interpretation, as now held by many German exe-*

getes, till he was pressed in the argument with Pelagius. The authority of Augustine, and the force of his theology; have sent down to our own day the interpretation he then adopted.

Again the same author says:

Still further: the pulpit suffers, in its exegetical authority, from the habit of spiritualizing all parts of the Scripture indiscriminately. Ancient usage justified any use of a text, which, by any eccentric laws of association, could be made serviceable to any practical religious impression. Popular commentaries have largely contributed to this abuse. Some of them no preacher can read respectfully without insensibly surrendering somewhat of his integrity of exegetical taste.

Such are the more important reasons for the caution which I have advanced, that the past and present usage of the pulpit respecting truthfulness of interpretation is not entirely trustworthy. You cannot safely accept that usage as authority. It is improving, but it is no model for a youthful ministry. Do not be misled by it. Form your own model, and let it be one which scholarship and good taste and good sense can approve."—See pp. 160, 161, 162.

The foregoing are brave, true words, and voice the sentiment of the present time. The fact is, we are just entering upon more thoughtful and conscientious times. A new and more reliable hermeneutic will have to be accepted. The people are beginning to demand it. The time-servers among the clergy may as well get ready to faithfully interpret the word of God for the people, as that will soon be the means by which they shall be able to hold their places.

The time has come when men will demand that the meaning of the Scriptures shall be presented, instead of human vagaries. When that voice shall be heard from the pew, the pulpit will address itself to the task. Then the question will be, not, 'What can I make out of the text?' but, 'What has the text in it for me and the people?' not, 'How can I display my genius, in discovering some new way of filling the text with a meaning it never had?' but, 'What did the Lord mean when he directed its use?'

To present all that ought to be said on this subject in the most direct way possible, we shall consider the several methods that have been proposed. We shall not then have to charge the many failures in the interpretations of the word of the Lord to some unknown evil, but to definite mistakes.

Section 28.
THE MYSTICAL METHOD.

(1). *This originated in heathenism.*—Because of its origin it is called "*mythical.*" It was maintained that no man could interpret the communications from the deities unless he was *en rapport* with said divinities. This gave position and prominence to those men of holy calling. The church adopted as much of heathenism as was thought best to render Christianity popular with the people; hence the same, or similar claims had to be made for her priests. This was not done all at once but came, like other things which have no authority in the New Testament, little at a time, until the whole distance was overcome.

(2). The several *reformations* that have taken place have *removed somewhat* this veneration for the priesthood, but have not entirely removed the mistake; for while we have ceased to regard ourselves as the subjects of priest-craft, we continue a superstition quite akin to it. A common error remaining is that God's book is to be miraculously interpreted—that no one is competent to understand these things unless he has been called and divinely qualified for the task. This about as effectually removes the Bible from the masses, as the old theory of its interpretation belonging only to the priesthood. It leaves us dependent upon those highly fortunate ones who have been thus specially endowed for the work. They may be priests, or not. But in either case they must have been 'called by God' to this work. If this theory were true, the Bible would be of no value whatsoever. The inspiration in these interpreters would be sufficient, without any Bible. Hence the effect of this theory has been to prevent the people from looking to the Bible for instruction. Regarding themselves as dependent upon inspiration, they have waited for it to accomplish its work, and break to them the will of God.

(3). The *evil results* of this theory might be called *legion,* for they are *many.* All kinds of ambitious pretenders have found security under such claims. If we deny their rights to such espionage over the great family of God, they are able to beat us back by their assumptions that it had been given to them only to understand their prerogatives. *Sects* and parties *have grown from this seed* in great abundance. Men who have *wanted a following,* have been thus enabled to *lead away multitudes* of disciples after them. As these leaders have *differed* as to the things of God, many of their followers have been led into doubt and skepticism. *If these inspired men cannot agree* concerning the things which their God wishes them to do, the *common people* cannot be expected to *know anything* about it. They know, too, that where there is contradiction there is falsehood, for it is not possible that truth should disagree with itself.

(4). *If the Bible does not mean what it says,* there is no way by which we can know what it does mean. Indeed, if it is a revelation at all, then it must signify just what such words would mean if found in another book. If they have any other meaning than that in which they would be understood by the people to whom they were employed, then they were absolutely misleading. In that case the Bible is *not only not a revelation, but a false light,* doing a vast amount of injury by leading simple-hearted people into the wrong way.

Section 29.
THE ALLEGORICAL METHOD.

Definition.—This method treats the word of God as if it had only been intended to be a kind of combination of metaphors—a splendid riddle. Interpreting by this method is not *exegesis* but *eisegesis*—they do not obtain the meaning of the text, but thrust something into it. Its statements of history are mere figures of speech, and mean one thing or another, or nothing, as the interpreter may choose. What the Bible may mean to any man will depend upon what the man would like to have it mean. The genius that would be able to make one thing out of it would be able to make it have the opposite meaning if he preferred. Clement of Alexandria maintained that the Law of Moses had a four-fold significance—*natural, mystical, moral and prophetical.* Origen held that the Scriptures had a threefold meaning, answering to the body, soul, and spirit of man; hence that the meanings were *physical, moral, and spiritual.* Philo of Alexandria gives a fair specimen of al-legorizing in his remarks on Gen. 2:10-14:

> *In these words Moses intends to sketch out the particular virtues. And they, also, are four in number— prudence, temperance, courage, and justice. Now, the greatest river, from which the four branches flow off, is generic virtue, which we have already called goodness; and the four branches are the same number of virtues. Generic virtue, therefore, derives its beginning from Eden, which is the wisdom of God: which rejoices, and exults, and triumphs, being delighted and honored on account of nothing else except its Father, God. And the four particular virtues or branches from the generic virtue, which, like a river, waters all the good actions of each, with an abundant stream of benefit.*

Clement of Alexandria had definitions for the interpretation of the Scriptures not unlike the rules found in a dream-book. He said the *sow* is the emblem of voluptuous and unclean lust for food. The *eagle* meant robbery; the *hawk,* injustice; and the *raven,* greed.

Emanuel Swedenborg is a fair illustration of the workings of this theory. He is commonly written down as a mystic, but he is properly denominated an allegorical interpreter. Every statement of the Bible, according to his view, has a meaning such as no sane person would gather from the use of these words if they occurred anywhere else. He is able to find four distinct thoughts in almost everything that has been said, anywhere in the Scriptures. He is mystical in his claims to the means of knowledge. He is lifted above other mortals into the realm of clearer light, and therefore he is able to say that the Bible does not mean what it says, but means that which has been revealed to him. His position, as stated by himself, is:

> *The word in the letter is like a casket, where lie in order precious stones, pearls, and diadems; and when a man esteems the word holy, and reads it for the sake of the uses of life, the thoughts of his mind are, comparatively, like one who holds such a cabinet in his hand, and sends it heavenward; and it is opened in its ascent and the precious things therein come to the angels, are deeply delighted with seeing and examining them. This delight of the angels is communicated to the man, and makes consociation, and also a communication of perceptions (The True Christian Religion, 4:6).*

This, however, only accounts for the power of knowing the higher import of the Scriptures, through his science of correspondences. But his interpretations are allegorical, and should be classed as such.

Section 30.
SPIRITUAL INTERPRETATION.

This method differs only in liberality from the Mystical. Instead of supposing that a few persons are favored above the rest of mortals, it regards such power to be within the reach of every one. Piety and a possession of the light of God in the soul will enable everyone to understand the Scriptures in this spiritual way. Of course, many plain passages of the word of God will, to them, have the meaning of something very different from what has been said. For with them, it is not so much what the Lord has said, as what He revealed to them as the meaning of that language. The Friends have held this idea most firmly, though there are many in other churches now who hold similar views. It is strange that those who are thus enlightened of the Lord do not interpret the Bible in the same way. Even the Allegorists are better agreed. They follow some law of language, and hence, necessarily, reach conclusions a little similar. But the Spiritualizers are not bound by any law. Whatever may be the pious whim of the exegete, he will be able to find it in the Bible. Every one becomes a law of interpretation to himself. Of course like all other people, those who live together or read the same books will spiritualize the word of God in the same way, and reach nearly the same conclusions. The reason is that they have formed ideas and convictions just like other people, and then in their ecstasy, suppose they receive these impressions from above. The Bible is, of course, worth little to them, for the inward light in the soul of each one would be quite sufficient. When a man's practice is found to be contrary to some direct statement of the word of God, the easiest way to reconcile his conduct with Christian faith, is to say that such a passage is "*spiritual.*" By that he ordinarily means that the text agrees with his practice, whatever may be its statement to the contrary; at any rate, it is above and beyond the comprehension of the reprover. No one would think of dealing thus with any other book. Law, or medicine, science, history, mechanics, anything else except religion, must be submitted to the rules of common sense. Everywhere else words are supposed to have a meaning, to be interpreted by the laws of language, but this superstition relieves its disciples from any bondage to law respecting exegesis.

Jesus said, "The words that I speak to you, they are spirit and they are life." This metaphor is not difficult of interpretation. He is the bread from heaven, the vine, the door of the sheep; and the bread and wine of the supper were His body and His blood. Christians should be filled with wisdom and spiritual understanding; should speak of spiritual things by spiritual words, for they receive spiritual blessings, and are built up into a spiritual house, to offer up spiritual sacrifices to God. The city in which the witnesses lay for three days and a half was denominated *spiritually* Sodom and Egypt. In spirit it would be like these places. But this says nothing about spiritual interpretation, but uses the figures most common in the presentation of such thought.

Section 31.
THE HIERARCHICAL METHOD.

(1). *This method differs from the Mystical, or Mythical,* not so much in the manner of *receiving* the knowledge from heaven, as in the *assumption* of authority in presenting it. It affirms that the church is the true exponent of the Scriptures. As the church was built before the New Testament Scriptures were finished, and was appointed as their guardian, it has, therefore, the right to interpret them.

(2). *This interpretation is to be given by the priesthood.*—When we ask what is meant by interpretation being given by the *church,* we are told that the word *church* does not mean all the members of the body, but simply that portion of its membership appointed to speak for it. Hence *not* the members of the *church* are intended in any general way, but its *priests* only.

(3). *But when priests are not agreed,* then there must be provision for a *higher tribunal* than the parish priest. If his opinion shall be doubted, the bishop of that Holy See may settle the question. But even then there may be trouble. Bishops differ like other men, and then we will have to go to the archbishop, or the matter may be carried to the Pope, if it should merit the attention of the Holy Father. In the past there have been some who have even doubted his infallibility, and carried the question up to a Council. Of course that will end its consideration. However, the Pope *now commits no more mistakes!*

(4). *After all, their decisions have been reached something like those of other people.*—Some have maintained that whatever has always been believed must necessarily be right. This has been a conservatism to retain the opinions of the past, and prevent any further search for truth.

(5). *Pinning our faith to the sleeves of the fathers* is one of the features of this method that remains, to some extent, even among Protestants at the present time. Just now, however, the world is waking up to the fact that error may live and thrive for a thousand years, and never be disturbed during that time. While that which has been held to be true by good and competent men should not be hastily thrown aside, yet it may be utterly false. There are many traditions which have scarcely been doubted during the whole Christian era, that never had any foundation in truth. To begin with, they were only the unstudied guesses of popular men. Others suppose that they have duly considered them, and therefore adopt them without any further investigation. Still others, seeing *their* names to the theory, adopt it the more readily; and so on to the end. And yet when we come to look for evidence of truth in the matter, we find it wholly wanting. In this way we have had a traditional Mount Calvary, and have told and sung about the Savior's transfiguration on Mount Tabor. In the same way, many errors have lived long, simply for the want of any examination. But this method prevents any falsehood from being disturbed. As it has long been the faith of the church, *it must be correct!*

(6). This method is followed, *not so much to find what the Scriptures mean,* as to know what the Lord would have them believe and do as *revealed through the church.* Hence, in the use of this method, the Scriptures are not the guide of the faith and lives of the people, but rather the priest, the bishop, the archbishop, the Pope, the Council. The question is not, 'What saith the Scriptures?' but, 'What saith the church?' While, then, we would retain a proper respect for the opinions of good and great men, we cannot assent to this method of interpretation, as it sets the word of God at naught to make room for the traditions of men. In the seventh chapter of Mark and the twenty-third chapter of Matthew, we discover this to have been the trouble with the ancient Pharisees, and for it they received the condemnation of the Master.

(7). *In the plan of revelation according to this method,* God has chosen *strange ways* of causing His people to understand the good and the right way. The correctness of a doctrine has been ascertained by the *ordeal.* In confirmation of this truth, its advocate partook of the *Host,* and that publicly. And as the emblem of the Savior's body did not kill him, he was supposed to be right. Of course, this was looking to the supposed *miracle* for divine direction, and *not to the word of the Lord.* It is quite common for Protestants to smile at Catholics for superstitions so groundless, and yet to practice others just as unreasonable. Even now there lingers the suspicion that the Lord directs His people in the line of duty, and shows them that they are right while they do not follow the Scriptures. We ought not to speak of the superstition of Catholics when we are doing the same things. Now, if we are to learn the will of the Lord in this way, what use do we have for the Bible? It is better that we seek its meaning and follow its direction, or confess that God *could not or would not give us the kind of book we need.*

(8). *This method stands in the way of Christian liberty.* It prevents all investigation, and so hinders the people from knowing more of the word of God than they did during the dark ages. Luther began the Reformation in direct opposition to this idea. And yet we are ready to stop all search after truth, and bind the world to the opinions of the last reformer. This was the tyranny against which he rebelled, and yet we are trying to fasten upon the rest of the world this usurpation. If the right does not now exist to differ from the views of canonized authority and hoary tradition, then it did not exist in the days of Luther; and, if it did not then exist, we ought all to be in the bosom of Rome. Of all methods of interpretation yet considered, if we shall call this one, it is the most unreasonable, and attended with the greatest amount of evil.

Section 32.
THE RATIONALISTIC METHOD.

(1). *It is very nearly the rule of unbelief.* Though many of these exegetes have professed to strive only to know the exact meaning of Scripture, yet they have done more to compel the Bible to harmonize with the latest philosophies than anything else. They have differed only from the dogmatists in the standard by which all Scripture statements are to be compared. With them, *"Nature is the standard, and Reason the guide."* If the Bible can be made to harmonize with the notions of the reasoner, then it is to be understood as meaning what it says; but if not, it is to be regarded as mythical, or used by way of accommodation, or the writer has been mistaken respecting his inspiration, or we have been imposed upon by apocryphal books. After all has been said respecting the efforts at exegesis in the use of this method, we regard it not so much exegesis as *exit-Jesus!* The interpreters are the guide and rule of life, and the Bible is merely called upon to sanction their conclusions. Not that they feel themselves at all in need of its light and instruction, or that it would be any proof to a sensible world of the correctness of their positions, but to patronize believers a little, they quote their sacred books to show that, after all, they are not bad friends. I speak of the German critics especially, not because they are alone in the use of this method, but because they are leading. Some of these claim to believe in the inspiration of the Bible, and others do not. But no man holding their views of the right to compare the Bible with the thoughts and feelings of men, and to compel the sacred text to agree with erring men, can have any particular conviction respecting its inspiration. It would be better if they were all avowed infidels, for then the world would not be deceived by them.

(2). *The theory of Strauss.* In his *Life of Jesus,* he lays down the following rules to guide in the investigation:

> *A narrative is not historical (1) when its statements are irreconcilable with the known and universal laws which govern the course of events; (2) when it is inconsistent with itself or with other accounts of the same thing; (3) when the actors converse in poetry or elevated discourse unsuitable to their training or station; (4) when the essential substance and ground-work of a reported occurrence is either inconceivable in itself, or is in striking harmony with some Messianic idea of the Jews of that age.*

This theory has been exposed so many times, and this has been so well done, that no more is now necessary than to call attention to its unreasonable demands. (1). *That all miracles must be rejected.* That is, no man can pretend to be an interpreter of the Bible till he is prepared to deny its claims to inspiration and to its record of miracles. (2). If any accounts differ, they must both be false. (3). If the actors were inspired, and, therefore, spoke in a manner above those of their time and station, the account is to be regarded as untrue. (4). If the interpreter cannot conceive of the correctness of the statement, or if any affirmation is made that harmonizes with ideas common to the Jews respecting their coming Messiah, then it must be untrue. Now, for unreasonableness and dogmatic unfairness, this has no parallel. According to David Friedrich Strauss, no one can interpret the life of

Jesus, or any other portion of the sacred volume, till he is a confirmed infidel.

(3). *Other theories of the same kind.*—Those of Kant, Baur, Renan, Schenkel and Eichhorn, while they may differ from each other in many things, have the same general plan of investigation. Human reason is held to be superior to anything that can be revealed in the Bible. Hence they do not interpret the Scriptures, but simply interview the interpreter, and then demand that the Bible shall say the same things, or be set aside as a work of fiction; and, having been the child of a dark age, it must hold an inferior position. We shall not deny that good Christian men have held this view as the right method of investigation, that is, that everything must be made to harmonize with something they call reason; but we do say that the rule is of no value whatever, as it determines beforehand what must be found, and thereby limits all investigation.

(4). Further objections to the Rationalistic Method.

(*a*) *No new truth* or fact could be received; hence all investigation would be stopped. Every discovery is at variance with some preconceived idea, and therefore adverse to what some interpreter will regard as the eternal and universal law. This new truth being opposed to his previous ignorance, it would be rejected at sight. The king of Siam is said to have reasoned in this way; and when the missionary told him that in his country, in the winter, water would turn to ice, and on the lakes and rivers there would be a crust strong enough to bear up wagons and horses, the king decided that he was trying to practice upon his credulity, and told him plainly that he had no further interest in anything he might tell him. All his knowledge of nature's laws were set at naught by this daring man, and he felt outraged by him, and drove him from his presence. He was using this method consistently.

(*b*) *It is a wrong use of reason.*—The critical ability of every investigator should be employed (1) to determine whether the Bible is from God, or only from man; and (2) all the mental resources should be brought into requisition to ascertain what it teaches. If the Bible is not of God, then interpret it according to its contents; or if it is of

God, do the same. But no man who shall first decide that the message is from God, can retain any right to contradict its statements, or differ from its conclusions.

(*c*) *For a man to make his reason the guide* and standard of all truth, is to say that the *reason of others is worthless*—that he alone is the standard of appeal. This is indelicate.

(*d*) *A man's reason can decide nothing of itself.*—All that belongs to that faculty of the mind is to properly argue, and dispose of all facts reported by perception. Perception only gathers depositions from one or more of the five senses. Hence, when a man decides that nothing at variance with his reason can be admitted as true, he asserted that he has had all possible facts reported to his mind that can have any bearing on the subject, and that he has properly considered them, so that in their use no mistake could have occurred. This is too assumptive for any modest man, and, we might say, for any *man of common sense.*

Section 33.
THE APOLOGETIC METHOD.

(1). *It maintains the absolute perfection of all statements in the Bible.*—It was brought into being by the Rationalistic Method, as the mind swings from one extreme to another. As the former denied everything but what agreed with the views of the exegete, this view finds its adherents to everything, and anything that can be found in the Bible, and regards it all as from God. Whether the witch of Endor, Cain, Ahimelech, Laban, Esau, Judas Iscariot, or the devil himself, everything is filled with inspired truth, and made to serve as a perfect guide to the world. *This is unreasonable.* Very much of the Bible was spoken by the enemies of God's people, and for the correctness of what they say, the Bible is in no way responsible. It has reported them correctly, and that is all it had to do in the matter. Suppose, then, that Abraham and Isaac did equivocate respecting their relation to their wives, or that Rachel did deceive her father concerning his *teraphim,* the Bible is not to blame for her falsehood in the matter. David did many things that were wrong, and the Bible tells all about it. Suppose that David was a favored man—that does not demand that he should have been perfect in all that he did. If it could be shown that Jephthah did really offer up his own daughter, it does not make the word of God endorse the deed. When Paul speaks of him as an example of faith, he does not affirm that he was without fault, nor does he indicate that God did not hold him guilty for the act.

(2). *This method opposes one of the very first rules necessary to any fair and thorough investigation*—TO KNOW WHO SPEAKS.—The question of speaker is of first importance in all matters of investigation. Was it the language of Balak, or Moses; of one of the three comforters, or Job? Was the man inspired? Did he claim to be? Was he truthful, even? Was he competent to speak on such a subject? Job's wife offered very poor advice, and yet it is a part of the Bible. To regard it as authoritative is to do more than Job did, for he said she talked like a foolish woman.

(3). *This method takes it for granted that if a man was ever inspired, then he always was.*—But when we come to examine the Scriptures on the subject, this is not found to be true. A man might have been inspired for one message only, and all his life before and afterward may have been without such divine guidance. Caiaphas once spoke by inspiration, as well as Balaam; but it does not follow that they always did so. The beast on which Balaam rode had an inspiration, but it was for one occasion only.

Section 34.
THE DOGMATIC METHOD.

(1). This method is noteworthy for two things: first it assumes the doctrine to be true; and, second, it regards it as certainly true by being proven. It proceeds by assumption and proof. We have found more or less of this in all the methods yet considered. It has, indeed, been the rule that the thing which was desired to be found, was looked for, and the conclusions reached were those that were desired at the beginning. Men have been able to find what they have looked for.

(2). *It came into existence during the dark ages,* when speculators and Christian philosophers were the only guides of the people. These were soon found to differ from each other; hence there must be found some way to test the correctness of the positions taken. This correctness was *determined by argument, tradition, and Scripture.*

(3). *It has been kept alive by the same power that brought it into existence.*—The *desire to rule* in spiritual matters made it necessary for leaders and parties; and the desire now, on the part of men and sects, continues the use of a method which, without such potencies, would soon die out. But men and parties hold and teach doctrines nowhere found in the Bible, and they must do something to support their theories. To go to a plain reading of the word of the living God for support would be ruinous; hence, resort must be had to what is known as proof. The assertion is made, and then something is found that sounds like the position already announced. This is satisfactory to those who want the theory sustained.

(4). *This method was begun in Catholicism, and is continued in Protestantism.*—We are now in the same condition, largely, as those to whom this plan was a necessity. Many of the practices of Mother Church are continued today. For them, there never was any Scripture warrant. Once they might have been upheld by the direct voice of the church, as it spoke in its councils. But now having denied that these councils have had any right to change divine regulations, and finding no directions for our practices, we have to resort to methods of proof that would not be recognized in any other search for knowledge.

(5). *Truth has been found in this way,* and yet the manner of investigation has been a great hindrance. It should be said that men have found truth in *opposition* to the method, rather than *by* it. A very honest mind will sometimes see that the proposition, though made by himself, is not sustained by the facts, and turn to that which is true; but it is the exception, and not the rule. He who has taken a position and made it public, is in a poor condition to see that his affirmation is not correct. He may see it, but he *is not likely* to do so.

Wishes and previous conclusions change all objects like colored glasses, and convert all sounds into the assertions which the mind prefers to have made. The horse hears no sound in the morning that indicates it to be his duty to stop, but in the evening, when he has traveled all day, almost anything would convey to him that thought. In the morning there were many frightful objects that suggested the propriety of running away, but in the evening he is not troubled with any such evil apprehensions. The reason of this difference is very obvious: in the morning he wanted to run, and in the evening he wanted to stop, and he understands everything in the light of his desires. When Moses and Joshua went down the hill together, and heard the children of Israel in their frolic around the golden calf, Joshua thought he could recognize the sound of battle in it, for he was a warrior. Moses had a different thought about it. They reached different conclusions, not because they heard differently, but because their minds were on different topics. So it is with most of us. If we start out to find some particular doctrine or dogma in the Scriptures, we shall probably find it. It may not be there; there may not be anything on the subject; but we can find a hundred things that comport with that thought, and hence conclude that it must be true.

(6). *This does not indicate that the Scriptures speak in riddles, or that they are not clear.*—Such misuse may be made of any book. A man may not only prove anything he wishes by the Bible, but he may do so by any other book, if he will treat it in the same way.

(7). *It exalts traditions and speculations of men to an equality with the word of God.*—In the heat of argument, with a determination to find a theory in the Scriptures, anything is accepted as proof. If the desired proof cannot be found in the Bible, it will be found somewhere else. The fathers, the canonized authorities, the practice of the church—anything, to save the doctrine, from which we are determined not to part.

(8). *This method now very greatly hinders the unity of the people of the Lord.*—Much as we dislike to own it, we maintain our creeds by its use. It serves us, not as a means of ascertaining the meaning of the Bible, but as a means of supporting our theories. In our very best books of discipline, we say that "The Scriptures of the Old and New Testaments furnish the only and sufficient rule of faith and practice, so that whatsoever is not read therein, *nor may be proved thereby,* is not to be required of any one to be believed, or thought requisite or necessary to salvation." It may not be *"read therein"* but if it can be *"proved thereby,"* then it is to be continued in the church. Hence it *will be continued,* beyond any possible doubt. If proof is desired, proof will be found, and the doctrine will continue to be taught, and those who prepare themselves for the ministry will have to run the gauntlet of this doctrinal test. The Bible may know nothing about the doctrine, but it is kept alive by this method of assumption and proof.

(9). *The Bible is not a book of proof for doctrines, but is the doctrine of God itself to men.*—We are to go to God's book, not in search of our views, with the intent to find them in some way or other, but to go to it *for what it has in it for us.* Many of the interpreters of prophecy are prophets first, and then they go to the Bible to see if they can get the old prophets to agree with the new ones. Of course they always succeed. The man who fails to make out his interpretation should be regarded as wanting in common genius. I am hopeful of overcoming this method, notwithstanding its strong hold on the people. All works on Hermeneutics of recent date condemn it. I give a short quotation, by way of example. *Immer's Hermeneutics,* pp. 144, 145:

> *One of the most frightful causes of false explanations is dogmatic presupposition. See Matt. 7:16-20. This passage has been thus understood by Luther and by other old Protestant exegetes in an anti-Catholic interest: The tree must first be good before it can bring forth good fruit—i.e., man must, through faith, be regenerated, before he can perform good works. But this contradicts the connection and the clear intention of the passage. Immediately before, Jesus has warned his disciples against false prophets, who appear outwardly like innocent and pious sheep, but inwardly are ravening wolves. He now gives them the criterion by which they may distinguish the false and the good teachers from each other, viz.: their fruits—i.e., good works, conduct corresponding to the words of Jesus.*

The writer continues to show, at considerable length, the many blunders that have been maintained in this way. The doctrine is assumed, or presupposed, and then everything is bent, to give it support.

(10). *The manner in which it is done.*—Conclusions are reached without the facts necessary to warrant them. Sometimes it is by a mere jingle of words, something like the theory. The author may have no reference to anything relative to the subject that the interpreter is considering, but the application is made. The exegete supposes that the author has his subject under contemplation, for what else could he be thinking about? It is of such importance to him, that of course the writer or speaker must have been discoursing on that topic. Again, misinterpretation is very innocently reached by associating one of the premises of the speaker with one of his own, and then drawing a conclusion. In this way one man frequently misrepresents another—he hears a statement made, which, if associated with a position of his, a certain doctrine would be advocated. Then it is common to clothe that thought in one's own speech, and say that a certain man taught it. And yet he may never have thought of such a thing in his life. He did not hold the premise that we did, and therefore did not teach as we said he did. But the position was in our mind, and we assumed that it was in his without inquiring about it. When Jesus was dining at the house of a Pharisee, somewhere in Galilee, there came behind Him a woman whose character was not good. Simon said in himself: "If he were a prophet, he would know what sort of woman this is." Now, he assumed that if Jesus did know, He would send her away; and because He did not send her away, therefore He did not know what sort of woman she was. This was his mistake. Jesus did know what kind of woman she was, but He was not like the Pharisee in the disposition to order her away.

(11). Dogmatism first determines what it is willing shall be found in the Scriptures, and then goes to work at once to find nothing else there, and even *to refuse that anything else shall be found.* The infidel has this dogmatism as largely developed as any one. In all the reading that he may do, his determination never wavers for a single moment. From first to last he is determined to find that the Bible is only the work of man. Hence the evidences which he has no way of meeting, or turning to a bad account, he regards as unintelligible, or he deliberately shuts eyes and ears to all that has been said therein. It is just as difficult for a man to be made to believe what he does not want to believe, as it is to cause him to throw away long cherished opinions. And no investigation will ever be worthy of the name while conducted under this controlling power of prejudice.

(12). *Liberalism is just as dogmatic as the most orthodox creed.*— They who boast of their liberality are, many times, the most narrow and unreasonable bigots. They are liberal while they differ from the old church authorities, and are perfectly willing that you should join them in their new views of inspiration, or of obedience to Christ, but they are unwilling that you should differ from them. Hence it is plain that they have reached their views without the boring introduction of facts and the uncompromising use of logic, but have simply jumped to their conclusions without any such examination, and are determined that the rest of the world shall adopt their views of liberality. And those who are not able to do so are denominated by them *"legalists."* They may adopt as many forms as any others, and those, too, that are not known to the Scriptures, but when others fail to adopt their liberal ideas and still cling to the word of the Lord and the ordinances as they were first commanded, they are denominated bigots by those who are continually advertising their extreme 'liberality.' This is the way dogmatists deceive themselves quite commonly. With them, the world is perfectly illiberal, because it will not adopt their dogmatic opinions. Dogmatism here is just what it is everywhere else, only the points assumed at the beginning differ from those which have generally been regarded as orthodox; but the manner of maintaining them is just the same.

Section 35.
LITERAL INTERPRETATION.

(1). This is most commonly employed by dogmatists, in order to maintain a view that cannot be supported in any other way.

(2). *It makes all the language of the Bible literal.*—It treats the word of God as if it were an essay on chemistry or mechanics. Hence, almost anything can be proved by its use. Something can be found, by taking a jingle of words, that will establish any theory. They do not stop to consider that God spoke to men in their own language, and by such methods of speech as would render the thoughts of God most easily understood. If they would read Oriental writings on any other subject, they would be convinced that much of it is highly figurative. But, coming to the Bible, it must be made to bow down to a gross materialism, and take a yoke upon its neck that will make it the merest slave of the merciless task-master, who allots the talley of bricks, and will be satisfied with nothing less. These exegetes do not pretend that David's heart melted within him like wax, that all his bones were out of joint, and were staring at him in the face; that he was a worm, and not a man; for they have no theory dependent upon the literal use of these figures. But let their theory be involved for a moment, and then, if the literal meaning will avail them anything, they will use it, and deny that any other is possible. If the word in question has a low meaning, then it has been used only in that sense. Many of our spiritual conceptions are expressed in the Scriptures by the use of words once employed in material affairs; hence they are enabled to shut out everything but the grossest meaning the word had in its first use. The materialists of the present time insist on making the soul of man as material as his body, or at any rate, dependent upon it for its existence.

The disposition, however, manifested by materialists, does not differ much from the spirit of dogmatists generally. Everywhere the aim is to carry the point and maintain the doctrine, whatever may come of Scripture truth. Others, from the same determination respecting the doctrine to be proved, will compel a word into any peculiar meaning which is only possible to it under peculiar circumstances. But, the word having been used in that sense somewhere, it must have that unusual import in the passage under consideration, for two reasons: first, the word could be used in that sense; and, second, the doctrine in question is in need of that being regarded as the meaning in this place.

This trifling with the word of God does not come from that dishonesty to which we are ready to attribute it. This dogmatism has fostered the idea that whatever may be proved by the Bible, no matter in what way the proof may be found, or extorted, must be right, Hence there is a kind of undefined feeling of right to manufacture teaching in that way. And the work seems to be undertaken and accomplished without any compunctions whatsoever. Not one of these persons would think for a moment of interpreting the words of a friend in that way. A letter having been received from father or brother, they would feel insulted if anyone should insist on such a mode of interpretation. With such a communication before them, the question would be, 'What does the writer mean?' not, 'What can we *make him mean?*'

The latter forms of materialism go even farther, in one respect, than any former effort, to maintain the desired doctrine. It is not uncommon to assume a meaning for a word which it never has, and then make a play on the sound of the word, using it so repeatedly in that sense that many persons will come to the conclusion that such must be its meaning. In this way very much is being done at the present time to establish religious speculations nowhere mentioned in the Bible. We have before seen the evils resulting from the Allegoric method, and yet it is but little, if any, more likely to prevent the right interpretation than the Material or Literal. Either one is a foolish and hurtful extreme. Much of the Bible is written in language highly figurative. And not to recognize the fact, and treat the language according to the figures employed, is to fail entirely in the exegesis. This, of course, does not imply that God has said one thing while He means another, but simply that He has spoken in the language of men, and in the style of those to whom the revelations were made. No one reading the Prophecies or the Psalms without recognizing this fact, will be able to arrive at any reliable conclusions whatsoever as to their meaning.

78

Section 36.
THE INDUCTIVE METHOD.

(1). *What is it?* Leading or drawing off a general fact from a number of instances, or summing up the result of observations and experiments. Roger Bacon, to whom we are largely, if not wholly, indebted for this method of philosophy, was less clear in the definition of terms than in the use of the method itself. Still, we can arrive at his meaning fairly well. This is what he had to say of it:

> *In forming axioms, we must invent a different form of introduction from that hitherto in use; not only for the proof and discovery of principles (as they are called), but also of minor, intermediate, and, in short, every kind of axioms. The induction which proceeds by simple enumeration (*enumerationem simplicem*) is puerile, leads to uncertain conclusions, and is exposed to danger from one contradictory instance, deciding generally from too small a number of facts, and those only the most obvious. But a really useful induction for the discovery and demonstration of the arts and sciences, should separate nature by proper rejections and exclusions, and then conclude for the affirmative, after collecting a sufficient number of negatives.*

The thirteenth century was a little too early for such a philosopher to be well understood, and far too early for him to be appreciated. Still his views gained some support even then, and have been gaining ever since, and now they are quite extensively adopted.

In the uses of this method of interpretation, all the facts are reported, and from them the conclusion is to be reached. Of course during the time of the collection of these facts, there will be incertitude as to whether some of them are facts or not. Still, judgment is to be formed as best as it can, for the time. But when the whole number of facts is reported, it is probable that all the facts will stand approved as such, and the guesses that were incorrect will be found to be lacking the necessary evidences, and will be easily thrown aside. After the pyramid shall have been built, it can be put into line, and whatever material there gathered which will not harmonize with the whole amount will be readily refused as not being according to truth. Hence we may say that in the inductive method, we have necessarily the deductive. We will not only induce, or bring in all the facts, but we will reach conclusions as to truth from these.

(2). *The law of analogy.*—Everything must be found to agree. Harmony is one of the first demands of truth. Two truths are never contradictory. It is impossible for contradiction to be found where there is truth in all concerned. Hence, when any fact has come to be known, and about it there can be no longer any doubt, whatever may be reported after this, which is contradictory thereof, is rejected at once as being certainly untrue. And yet this rule must not be employed so as to prevent investigation, for it is possible that we may be perfectly satisfied with an error. We have long regarded it as truth, and may make it the reason for the rejection of facts that would be of great value. But if the new fact is admitted, then that which has been accepted must be displaced, for it is impossible for both to be correct. Hence no interpretation can be true which does not harmonize with all known facts.

(3). *This method demands that all facts shall be reported.*—It assures all concerned that if all facts are reported, and they are permitted to speak for themselves, error will not be possible. But it is not always possible to obtain all facts that have bearing on any given subject. Indeed, it is very probable that complete success in this respect has never yet been attained. All the mighty works of Jesus were not reported; but enough were presented for the faith of all who were willing to believe. John said that He did many other signs beside those which he recorded, but that the record he made was sufficient. This method demands that when all the facts cannot be had, as many shall be reported as possible. The falling of one apple would not be enough to prove the law of gravity, for there might have been something peculiar (1) in the then present condition of things; or (2) in the form of the falling body; or (3) in its contents; or (4) something present which had attraction for it and not for other bodies. On the other hand, it is not necessary that all bodies shall have been observed in their relation to each other; a large number will do, if they embrace the several kinds of material, and are tried in many circumstances—provided there is no opposing fact. One opposing fact will be enough to introduce an exception, at least, to the rule. Hence it would not be a universal law. Before reaching a conclusion, then, all facts attainable should be gathered.

(4). *To always heed this command is difficult.*—Men have ever been ready to deduce without having properly induced. Sometimes a number of exceptions are reported as the rule. One man is an enemy to the Christian religion, and therefore he proves that it is of no value to the race, by finding a number of cases in which it has done no good, or, at least, it has not made the right kind of persons out of those who have professed it. The argument is augmented by finding a large number of men who are out of the church who are better persons. Now, this examination is very imperfect. It should be known (1) what they were before conversion, so that the life afterward might compared with what it was before. It ought to be known (2) what they probably would have been without this religion. (3) On the other hand, too, it should be known if the men who have been presented from the outside of the church are fair representatives of those who have never made any profession of Christianity. (4) And again, it should be known what have been the effects of Christianity on them. It might be that although they had never been church members, the morality which made them so respectable was all obtained from that very religion. (5) Then again, on the other hand, it should be borne in mind that other influences than those of the religion under consideration may have controlled those church members, and that the religion is not so much to blame as the other forces that have controlled them. (6) Finally, it should be known whether the persons compared are fair representatives. If they have been the exceptionally bad on one side and the exceptionally good on the other, then there has not been an induction of facts, but an induction of falsehoods. Neither the inside nor the outside of the church has been properly reported. He who would pursue such a method would be about as truthful in his investigations as the man who undertook to prove that his neighbor's ground was not as good as his. To do this, he went into his neighbor's field and plucked ten ears of corn, of the smallest and smuttiest that he could find. He then went into his own field, and took the same number of the largest and best filled ears that he could find. Then he made a comparison.

The same unfairness is exhibited sometimes in the examination of the results of temperance laws. A large number of exceptions are reported as the rule; hence the conclusion is reached that such laws are accomplishing no good. In order that all facts shall be considered, we should ask, (1) Are the statements made correct? or are they only part of the truth? or are they wholly false? (2) Has the law itself been what it ought to have been? or has it been full of flaws and weaknesses? (3) Is it a new law, and therefore not understood, or loyally accepted; as it contravenes longstanding customs? (4) Is the party in power in favor of the law, or is it opposed to it, and therefore will not enforce it? or (5) while the party in power wishes well to the law, is there a large number of its members on the other side, so that the leaders of the party are afraid to do anything in the way of enforcement, for fear of dividing the party? (6) Are other laws, under similar circumstances, disobeyed as much as those? I refer to these things because they are within easy reach of everyone nowadays, and to show what I mean by the inductive method.

But men have been no more rash in these matters than in many other things. In medicine, a cure is reported by a certain remedy, but the condition of the patient is not known; indeed, it may not have been properly diagnosed, and hence the report may have contained falsehoods instead of facts. Or, if the Condition has been made known, it may be that other assistance may have been received from other sources to which the recovery was in part due, and may be wholly due.

Experiments in science are conducted hastily, sometimes, and *deductions* made before the facts have been *induced.* If a deformed creature is found in some part of the earth, forthwith someone is ready to reach the conclusion that it is the representative of a race, and hence that the connecting link has been found. We might find a large number of hunchbacks and unfortunate creatures in this country, and we are at liberty to suppose that abnormal conditions have existed in other places; and hence, from such a partial introduction of facts we have really no report at all.

(5). The inductive method has long been used in almost all departments of investigation except that of theology.

(*a*) I could quote many passages from the great *jurists* of the world, showing that in the interpretation *of law* they follow this method. One quotation, from *Blackstone's Commentaries*, Vol. 1 pp. 59-61, must suffice for the many we would like to give:

> *To interpret law, we must inquire after the will of the maker, which may be collected either from the words, the context, the subject-matter, the effects and consequences, or spirit and reason of the law. (1) Words are generally to be understood in their usual and most known significance; not so much regarding the propriety of grammar, as their general and popular use. . . . (2) If words happen still to be dubious, we may establish their meaning from the context, etc., of the same nature and use is the comparison of a law with laws that are made by the same legislator, that have some affinity with the subject, or that expressly relate to the same point.*

This shows that in the mind of this jurist the great aim of all research in legal investigation was to arrive at all the facts in the case. Whether constitution or code of legislative enactment was to be interpreted, the absolute intent of the maker was to be sought after, and any failure to get a right understanding of such purpose would result in a misapprehension of the enactment to be interpreted. And to know this aim of the law-making power, all facts that bear upon the subject should be employed. I know of no jurist or constitutional lawyer that differs from this opinion.

(*b*) When witnesses give testimony in our common courts, they are sworn to tell "the truth, the whole truth, and nothing but the truth."

This demand is made upon the presumption that the only way of meting out justice to all concerned, is to render a decision according to all the facts. And as these must be gained by the testimony of witnesses, they must make known to the court the whole of their knowledge relating to the question in hand. In the pleadings too, before the court, decision is to be according to the facts revealed in the trial. Indeed, the jurymen are sworn to render the decision according to the law and evidence. And all the arguments allowed in the case are to prevent the misunderstanding of either law or evidence. At least, such is the ostensible purpose of the pleading in the civil courts. Speculation as to the possible meaning of law is not tolerated, when the facts can be had by which the purpose of the law-makers can be known.

(*c*) The great teachers in the science of medicine have long held to this method of investigation. Medical associations have for their main object the increase of knowledge by the induction of facts. Hence, anyone in the regular practice who knows of any special remedy for any ailment of the human body, is duty bound to give others the benefit of his discovery. The thought of all this is that, in order to deal successfully with the enemies of human life and health, they are in great need of all the facts that can be had; that, when all these facts are revealed, the healing art will be perfected. It is not to be denied that there are theorizers in medicine as well as in theology, but it remains true that Medical Science presumes, at least, on the induction of facts, and by their light the men of healing are guided. Of course, every year they are discovering that some of the former decisions were not correct; but this is the method by which facts are finally reached.

(*d*) The things already said of law and medicine may be truly said of *political economy, history,* or any other science or study that engages the attention of man. *Facts alone* are supposed to guide men in forming their conclusions. Speculators there may be, but the science of investigation in any of these departments of thought is supposed to be conducted in the light of the inductive method. When our historians gathered up the accounts of the last war, they did it so that the whole truth might appear. In doing so, they found that many things

84

which had been reported and had been believed by very intelligent men were not true. During the war it would almost have been impossible for any historian to have written correctly of any battle. All the facts could not at that time be ascertained. Hence they had to wait patiently till they could be gathered and compiled, and a history, true to the facts, given to the people.

(*e*) *The Bible recognizes the correctness of this method.*—When Jesus appeared to the two disciples as they went into the country, he expounded to them all things found in the law and the prophets concerning himself (Luke 24). He thus introduced all the facts from that divine source that would bear upon their minds, that they might understand the truth. When the apostles met with the elders and the whole church at Jerusalem, to consider the question of admitting the Gentiles into the church without circumcision or keeping the law, they first heard the testimony of Peter respecting the work of the Lord by him among the Gentiles, at the house of Cornelius. Afterwards they gave attention to Paul and Barnabas, while they recounted the things which the Lord had done by their hands during the missionary journey which had just closed. After this, James makes a speech to them reminding them of another witness which they had overlooked—the testimony of one of their prophets (Amos 9:11-12). Now, when all these facts were introduced, there was but one conclusion possible for them, which was that the Gentiles were under no such obligations as those Judaizing teachers had affirmed. When Moses wished to prepare Israel to go over into the land of Canaan, and inherit it according to the promise of the Lord, he made them three speeches, which constitute nearly the whole book of Deuteronomy. In these speeches he brings before their minds nearly all their history, with all the obligations that rested upon them to keep the commandments of the Lord. He does this so that they may have all the facts in the case before them, that they may be guided thereby. When Philip would convince the Ethiopian nobleman that Jesus was the Christ, and the only way of salvation, he began at the same Scripture which the man was then reading, and preached to him Jesus. Now, what he did was to make him understand the testimony of the Lord respecting His Son.

Fact after fact was in that way presented to his mind till he became convinced, and asked for admission into the service of the Son of God. Nothing more respecting the Scripture method need be said, for it is everywhere apparent that when the Lord would conduct an investigation on any subject, He did it by the inductive method. When the devil wished to gain a point, he did it by quoting a text for its sound. When the Jewish rulers condemned the Savior, they affirmed well but proved nothing.

(6). *Inference may be used legitimately in the ascertainment of facts, and also in the conclusions reached from them.*—Many do not seem to know what an inference is; they speak of it as if it were a kind of guess, and therefore never to be used either in induction or deduction. The truth is, it is the logical effort to know the facts in the case, and to ascertain the facts from phenomena. 'Certain things seem to have been done; were they done or not?' may require the best effort of the mind to determine. This is done by associating the whole number of things which are known, and reaching conclusions, in a logical way, as to what else was done or said at the time, or in connection therewith. A few illustrations will help us to know the place of legitimate inference.

(*a*) Abraham went down from Canaan into Egypt; when he came out from that country Lot returned with him. Though it is not said that Lot went into Egypt with him, we infer it. They had journeyed from Haran together; the same wants were common to them both; they remained together for some time afterwards; hence, though we did not see them going together into that country, the mind naturally infers that they did. And we are about as certain of this fact as we are that Abraham went there.

(*b*) There were four kings who came from the east and fell upon the kings of the plain of the Jordan, and overcame them, and took away much goods. Abraham took his trained men, and, joining with his friends, followed the returning victors and overcame them, and returned, not only with the spoil, but with the family of Lot and the women. Here are persons said to be brought back, that have had no mention as being among the captured, but we infer that they were captured. And we are just as certain of that fact as we are of the facts that have been recorded.

(c) If we read in the book of Joshua that the conquering army of Israel did to certain kings just what they did to the king of Jericho, and we learn that they hanged those kings, though nothing be said about what they did to the king of Jericho at the time they took that city, yet we infer that they hanged him. We have the necessary premises, and cannot reach any other conclusion.

(7). *Things assumed in the Bible* are to be regarded the same as those which have been stated. In the first verse of the Bible it is said that "in the beginning God created the heaven and the earth." It is not stated in this verse that God existed; that he had the wisdom and power to accomplish this work; but it is assumed, and, being assumed, no interpreter has the right to call it in question. Of course great caution should be had in the use of this rule, that we may not at any time be mistaken as to what has been assumed. Anything that God takes for granted is true; hence, anything which He has assumed or taken for granted, we are bound to regard as true. Illustrations:

(a) *God has everywhere treated man as if he could repent.*—(1) He has nowhere said that man could not repent. (2) He has commanded all men everywhere to repent. Here our ideas of divine knowledge and justice come in to help us in the solution of the case in hand. We say that God knew whether man could repent or not; that He would not have required man to repent if it had not been possible for him to do so. With all this in the mind when we hear an apostle saying that He has commanded all men everywhere to repent, it is assumed that all men can repent, and that if they do not, the fault is their own; and if they are damned, they will have no one to blame but themselves.

(b) *An honest heart is necessary to the reception of the truth.*—It is never stated in so many words. And yet every attentive reader of the Scriptures recognizes the correctness of the statement at once. When the "sower went forth to sow," the seed must have found soil congenial, or there would have been no results whatsoever. And that which brought forth the thirty, sixty, and a hundredfold, referred to those who received the word in a good and honest heart. The result of this condition of mind is seen in the difference between the people of Thessalonica and those of Berea, who "received the word with all readiness of mind, and searched the Scriptures daily, to see if these things were so." Therefore, many of them believed. On the day of Pentecost, those who "heard the word gladly," obeyed the requirement of the Holy Spirit made known by the apostle Peter. The honest-hearted Cornelius was in the right condition to receive the pure gospel of the grace of God. His good and honest heart was the right kind of soil in which to sow the divine seed, and from which there was an immediate and very large yield.

(c) *Man's general wants are assumed.*—When God provides for man a teacher, sending the revelator before him to make known to him his duty, it is not thought to be necessary to announce that man is ignorant and needs an instructor. God's treatment of His creatures is sufficient for that. When a sacrifice was required it was not preannounced that man was a sinner, and that for the sin he had committed, his right to live had been forfeited, and that God would accept a substitute. His treatment of men carried that thought, and the lesson was taught in that way as effectively as it could have been done by the use of words. God does not stop to inform man that he is weak and wayward, that he is in need of a government to control and protect him. It would be a waste of time. He simply gives him that government and protection, and furnishes the necessary instruction respecting man's condition by the things He does for him.

And yet the wants of the world are known just as well in this way as if Jehovah had written a systematic theology on the subject. It does not seem to be known that God can teach in any other way than that which men have employed to get their theologies before the minds of their fellows. The truth which God *acts* is just as valuable as that which He has *revealed in any other way.*

(8). When a result is spoken of which is commonly attributed to several causes, though, in mentioning the result at a given time, no cause should be assigned: they are understood to be present.—It has first been determined that these causes are necessary to the result, hence if they had not been present the result would not have been reached. Since, then, their presence is necessary to the result, and the result has been reached, it follows beyond question that the causes were present. The same is true with a part of these causes. If we find the result, and yet one or two of the causes are not mentioned, it is taken for granted that they were present. They have been associated with the result as causes, and though not mentioned in a given case, we assume that these unmentioned causes were present.

(9). *Religious truth may be gathered from approved precedent.*— We learn from the authorized conduct of the children of God. If we can first be assured that what is done is approved, we can know certainly what we are at liberty to do under similar circumstances. Indeed, if the conduct has been directed by men under the guidance of the Holy Spirit, we learn from the example what we ought to do. If the Scriptures are to be our guide from earth to heaven, then to be religiously right we must be scripturally right. Or the statement may be made stronger in this way: no one can be religiously right and scripturally wrong at the same time. Or again: no one can be religiously wrong while he is scripturally right. Now, if the will of God has undergone no change since the New Covenant was completed, what was His will then is His will yet. And if those men did that will, and we do the same now, we will be accomplishing His pleasure.

But there is need of caution.—(1). Because a man has been inspired for a *given work or a single message,* it does *not* follow that he is *always* under the direction of such wisdom. When Elijah directed the contest on the top of Carmel, and when he saw the plentiful rain in the little cloud, hanging over the Mediterranean, he was inspired. But when he was frightened at the threat of Jezebel, and fled to the Mount of God in the wilderness of Sinai, he acted on his own motion, for God does not approve of his course. When *Peter* spoke on the day of Pentecost, he did so as he was moved upon by the Holy Spirit, and when he went to the house of Cornelius and gave to them the way of salvation, his way and his speech were directed by the Lord. But when he went down from Jerusalem to Antioch, and ate with Gentiles till "certain came from James," and then withdrew from Gentile associations, he was doing things Peter's way. Paul afterwards, writing by the inspiration of the Lord, says that he withstood Peter to the face, for he was to be blamed (Gal. 2:11-14). (2). We must also be careful not to confound mere incidents or accidents with the approved precedents. The disciples met together in an upper room in Jerusalem, and so did those at Troas, but that does not make it binding on the disciples of today to meet in upper rooms. These were nonessentials or conveniences. And to elevate them into divinely appointed rules for the service of the Lord would be to miss the purpose of the record altogether. The Master took all his journeys on foot, but it does not follow that we are only at liberty to travel in that way. (3). There are things which they did not do, yet which it would be perfectly right for us to do. But they belong to the same class. There are matters of propriety that would, under some circumstances, render some things improper, and, though there would be no harm in the act itself, yet, owing to the surroundings, it would not be wise to do them. Customs being entirely different in another place or at another time, these very things may be well enough. The apostles built no church-houses or colleges, but this is not proof that the existence of these things is offensive to God. These things, too, they could have done, but they did not choose to do them. They were busily engaged in other work, which, for the time, was of more importance.

But the question then arises, 'How shall we determine what is an approved precedent?' 'How shall we be able to separate the many things done in the times of the apostles which are merely incidental, from those that were meant for our benefit, that we may know what to do?' (1). Those actions performed by the apostles or other disciples in their day, which have a divine approval, or if done by an apostle, nothing has been said by inspiration in opposition to it. (2). Customs of the Church under the eye and sanction of *apostles*. For if, in an unguarded moment, an apostle should turn aside, he would not continue in that condition. And if it could be possible for one apostle to continue to err in his public character, it would not be so with all of them. A general custom is established in harmony with that which is allowed, taught, approved by the many. If we shall find the whole church engaged in a common custom in religious service, no matter how we may come to that intelligence, if we can certainly know that such was the custom everywhere among the disciples in the days of the apostles, such practice will show certainly what was the will of God.

(10). To know the meaning of any statement, we should *know what the author was trying to say.*—The purpose before his mind will be a safe guide before the mind of the investigator in gathering the facts to put to record. We know intuitively that no man should be made to say what he does not intend to say.

(11). *In searching for causes, that upon which all facts agree is the cause, or one of the causes.*—If any known fact denies that it was one of the causes, then it must be dismissed from such a responsible position. On the other hand, if any fact claims it as a cause, then it must be so enrolled. As there can be no opposing facts, we may experience a little difficulty in deciding between two supposed facts, one claiming it as a cause and the other denying it such an honorable place. In that case, we must continue to search till the mistake is discovered, then introduce the triumphant fact and listen to its decision. If it shall enroll any thing or act as a cause, it must be so regarded till there shall be some dispute, there being found some other fact, or supposed fact, which denies the conclusions already reached. When such questions arise, we are required to pass through the investigation again, and satisfy our minds as before.

(12). *We are not to reject a cause for the lack of philosophical probability, when a miracle is declared or assumed to be present.*— When Israel was called out of Egypt, many things were commanded which philosophy would never have suggested. No one could have seen why they should sprinkle the blood of the lamb on the lintel of the door and the two door posts. Philosophy would have said: The angel now knows whether the inmates are Hebrews or not; and, knowing that, they are as safe without the blood as with it. When they came to cross the sea, Moses was told to stretch out the rod over the sea, and that its waters would divide. Philosophy would have said: There is nothing in such an act to bring the desired result. When they thirsted for fresh water in the wilderness, and Moses was told to go and smite the rock, or, as afterwards, to speak to the rock, philosophy would have seen no connection between the act commanded and the water that was promised. Afterwards, when they were in the land of Canaan, they were told how to take Jericho; to march around it once every day for six days, and then on the seventh day to march around it seven times; and as they marched they were to blow on trumpets made of ram's horns, and, on completing the last round, they were to give a long, loud blast and a great shout. And the promise was that the wall of the city should fall, and they were to go up into the city, each from the point where he might happen to be. But if philosophy or military skill had directed the matter, the plan would have been different. We find a man from Syria, Captain Naaman, who was told by the prophet of the Lord to go and wash himself seven times in the river Jordan, in order that he might be cleansed from leprosy. At first he was insulted at the thought; but, when his servant reasoned with him, he did what Elisha told him, and was healed.

We must remember, when we come to religious truth, that God is its author, and that it is *His* place to say what the conditions are for the reception of any grace or blessing. Our philosophies may be good in some things, but in the religion of the Bible they amount to but little. "The secret things belong to the Lord our God: the things that are revealed belong to us and to our children forever, that we may do all the words of this law." This is the manner of God's legislation. He has not asked the counsel of the wisest of His people, but held all authority in His own hands, and has, at all times, said what should and what should not be law. One single fact of divine statement must settle any controversy on which it speaks.

(13). *Contrary or negative facts may be used in the establishment of truth.*—"He that *believeth not* shall be damned," is sufficient to show that faith is at least one of the conditions of pardon. Like this is the statement of the Master: "If you do not believe, you shall die in your sins, and where I am you cannot come." This would have the same bearing. "You do not believe, because you cannot hear my words," would be just like saying that hearing His word was one of the conditions of becoming a believer. "You believe not, because you are not of my sheep, as I said to you." His sheep heard His voice and followed Him. Hence, if they had listened to His teachings, and been in the company of those who followed Him, they too would have been believers. "For unless you repent you shall all likewise perish." This is equal to saying "those who do not repent shall perish." This is the negative form of saying that repentance is one of the conditions of salvation. We read of some who "rejected the counsel of God against themselves, not being baptized of John." This is saying in substance that if they had been baptized by John, they would not have rejected the counsel of God against themselves. Hence we have it stated in this negative way that John's baptism was the counsel of God, or at least a part of it. "No man can come to me except the Father who sent me draw him, and I will raise him up at the last day." This is a plain declaration that those who were drawn by the Father could come to Him. This is carried out by the Savior as He continues: "It is written in the prophets, 'And they shall be all taught of God;' every man therefore that has heard and has learned of the Father comes to me." So in this negative way we have opened to us the manner in which sinners could come to Christ, being drawn to Him by the truth of God, by having heard and having learned of the Father. When Jesus was approached by Nicodemus, who seemed to want to be admitted as a disciple without endangering his standing among his people, the Master told him that except a man be born again he could not see the kingdom of God. No teaching could be plainer to this Senator, that, though there might be *other* conditions of seeing the kingdom of God, beyond all question being born again was *one of the conditions*. And though he tried to break the force of the statement by his question, "How can a man be born when he is old?" he finds no way of escape, as the Lord turns upon him with the "Truly, truly I say to you, unless a man is born of water and the Spirit, he cannot enter into the kingdom of God." This is as emphatic as language could make it, and leaves no doubt respecting the requirement that men must be born of water and the Spirit in order to enter the kingdom of God. We might continue this form of affirmation till we should find every duty marked out in this way, both as to the manner of becoming Christians and also as to how to live the Christian life. Indeed, the negative form of the statement is frequently used as a means of emphasis.

A wrong use of this principle is sometimes made by finding a negative, and arguing from that statement that no other quality or deed is demanded for a given purpose *except the one implied in the one statement*. To illustrate: it is said that "without faith it is impossible to please God." From this it is contended that if faith is present, the possessor will please God. Nothing else is regarded as a necessity in order to please Him, simply because it is not referred to in the passage. This is the same blunder that takes it for granted, from an affirmative statement, that *only the one thing mentioned there* can be requisite to the desired blessing; that if anything else were any part of the cause of receiving the blessing, it would have been mentioned in that one text. This is not a weakness of the inductive method, but a mistake in its use. When a truth is taught by the use of the negative, it is the same as if that truth were taught by the use of a direct statement. All that can be found in it is that the cause named is necessary to the result; but *it does not follow that it is the only cause*. We are at liberty to pray, "give us this day our daily bread;" but if we shall depend upon prayer alone for bread, we shall go hungry. While we should pray for food, there are other conditions by which it shall be acquired— finding, then, that any act is for a certain end, is *not* finding that it is the *only* thing necessary to that purpose.

(14). Causes will frequently become obvious by arranging the facts in the order of intensity.

a. Illustrations of this rule.—Physicians sometimes are enabled to diagnose the case by the use of medicine. A small dose of medicine has a given result. The same remedy is increased, and the effect is increased; this is repeated several times, and the conclusion is fairly reached that a certain medicine has a certain result. And, as a certain condition of the system would be necessary in order for that medicine to have that result, the condition is determined upon, and the patient treated accordingly.

Any physician or scientist, finding that the increase of any chemical increased a certain result, would decide at once that such result was produced at least in part by that act, chemical or medicine, as the case might be.

b. If we find in the Scriptures that with the increase of testimony faith becomes stronger, we at once reach the conclusion that faith comes by the medium of testimony. If we find in Christian experience that just as the members of the Church increase their faithfulness in the worship on the Lord's day, their uprightness and integrity is made to grow, everyone reasons from cause to effect, and from the effect back to the cause.

c. On the other hand, if we find that as people have been deprived of the word of God, their faith becomes weak, we learn by a negative rule that faith comes by the word of God. If, among the heathen who have never heard of our Savior, there are none who believe in Him, we conclude that without this word, it is impossible to constitute people believers in Christ.

d. A caution is needed.—We may increase the testimony and not increase the faith, for there may be modifying causes that will remove all disposition to believe, or that will turn people away the from hearing the word of the Lord. Hence, when we are looking for causes by arranging the facts in the order of intensity, we must be sure that there are no modifying forces; at least, that there are no more of them than there were before increasing the supposed power.

(15). A particular fact cannot be learned from a general statement, when something other than the cause mentioned might have produced the result.—If it is ascertained that a gentleman went to the city on a certain day, the fact that he went does not establish the manner of his going, for there are more ways than one by which he might have gone. A murder having been committed, no one man is to be hanged merely from that fact. Indeed, if it should be known that it must have been committed by one of two men, neither one is convicted by the general fact of murder, for it might have been done by the other.

In the case of the conversion of Lydia (Acts 16:13-15), it is said that "the Lord opened her heart, that she attended to the things spoken of Paul." It is easy to jump to the conclusion that this opening of the heart of that woman was by a miracle, for it might have been done in that way. But we are not at liberty to reason so hastily. We must ask, 'Could her heart have been opened in any other way?' And if it shall be determined that her heart could be opened by natural means, and that such force was present, it is not reasonable to conclude that the result was reached by a cause *that was not necessary* and *that was not known to have been present*. If the preaching of the word had been found to be sufficient to open the hearts of other men and women, so that they would accept the gospel of Christ and obey its requirements, and *that power was present*, then there is no reason for the supposition that the abstract power was present, or that it had anything to do with the opening of the heart of that pious Jewish woman. Again, should it be argued that the word *attend* means to *consider, give attention to,* it will be in order to ask, 'Is that necessary meaning?' And if it is found to mean *to do the things* spoken of, then nothing more will be found in the passage than that, hearing the gospel of Christ from this messenger of the Lord, her heart was so enlarged that she was ready at once to accept of Christ in all His demands.

This rule, however, does not interfere with the effort to find the meaning the word may have in any particular occurrence. This is a lawful and just procedure. All we notice in this place is the error of reasoning from a general statement to a particular conclusion.

CHAPTER V:
THE SEVERAL COVENANTS.

Section 37.
THE NEED OF DISCRIMINATING BETWEEN THEM.

(1). No one can understand his duty without knowing to what law he is answerable. God makes a covenant with Noah, and binds him to build an ark of certain dimensions and out of certain timber, and to put into it all kinds of beasts that could not pass the flood without such help. But I am not to learn my duty as a sinner, nor yet as a saint, by reading this covenant. It is not my duty to make an ark of any size. There are neither duties, threats, nor promises to me, respecting anything of the kind.

So it is with all the covenants that God has ever made with man—each covenant is for the man or the men to whom it was given, and for whom it was intended. It belongs to no other man, or men, except extended to them by its Author. In all the individual contracts that God made with the Patriarchs, the demands, duties, and blessings were peculiarly the property of the men to whom the covenants belonged. Abel offered a sacrifice by faith (Heb. 11:4); hence God had required the sacrifice; but it does not follow that I am to go to my flock and prepare an offering, and then come and burn it with fire. He has not required that of me, and therefore I would not be rendering him any service by such worship. So fathers were high priests, and the rulers of the tribes that grew up about them. They not only offered for themselves, but for their children and their children's children. To these men God gave many primary lessons, containing principles that should remain and have a place in the highest worship that would ever be given to the world. But there were also many things that were peculiar to the times and the people to whom these covenants belonged. Abraham was to go into the country of Moriah, and offer up his son, Isaac, on an altar; but the man who regards that as being direction given to *him*, is in a fair way to commit murder. That demand was made of Abraham alone. In like manner, the blessings that came to that man from such acts of obedience were in consequence of the obedience which he rendered. But if any other man should have done that, it would have been a high crime.

It is known in all matters of law among men, that a man is amenable to the law under which he is living. The law of the United Colonies was good, in many respects, but a man would be regarded as bordering on insanity if he should go to it to learn all his duties as a citizen of one of the New England States. No matter if the present law now contains many things that are to be found in the old law, he obeys these demands not because they were found in the law of the Colonies, but *because they are found in the law under which he lives.*

In the Northern States it was once our duty to catch a colored man, and return him to his former owner; but if one should start out now to catch men and return them to the South, there would be some trouble in the matter. Common sense has everywhere been sufficient for this question, except in religion. Only when we come to ask the way to heaven, do we seem to lose our interest in the ordinary forms of intelligence, and gather up and appropriate language, and commands, and promises that do not belong to us. I open the Bible, and read that it is the duty of the parent to circumcise his boy of eight days; and I go about the task at once, but everyone knowing me is shocked. Why? Is it not in the Bible? You say that it belongs to another people, and these rites and ceremonies are not Christian. That is the difference of covenant. That institution belonged to one age and one people, and I belong to another. Not being under that covenant, I am not to observe that commandment, unless I can find it in the covenant to which I do belong.

(2). *Each covenant that God has made with men may have many things in common with all the others, and yet be distinct.* There is nothing more common than to mistake similarity for identity. Several things are the same in both, and therefore it is concluded that they are identical, except that the one is more complete in some particulars than the other. Every covenant that God has ever made with man has contained the thought that God is the supreme and rightful Ruler of the universe, and that it is the highest privilege of mortals to be in harmony with His wish. Hence, the idea of worship and obedience can be found in every covenant between God and man. It may be said, too, that these things are the great essentials of God's dealings with men. And yet these covenants are not the same; they do not require the same acts of obedience, nor do they promise the same things; nor do they belong to the same people. Paul says (Rom. 9:4-5):

> *Who are Israelites; whose is the adoption, and the glory, and the covenants, and the giving of the law, and the service of God, and the promises; whose are the fathers, and of whom is Christ as concerning the flesh, who is over all, God blessed forever.*

Here is a law and several covenants and promises that were peculiar to the people of Israel. Hence the duties required in these several contracts were not obligatory upon other nations and peoples, unless God had made similar covenants with them. But certainly the promises were peculiar to the descendants of Abraham, It was to be through him and his posterity that the Christ should appear. The land of Canaan belonged to them by divine right; the rite of circumcision was peculiar to them; and the law that was given by Moses was for them during the time of their minority, and was only intended to serve as a school-master, or a leader of children, till the Christ should come and establish the faith by which men should be saved (Gal. 3:23-25).

> *And what great nation is there, that has statutes and judgments so righteous as all this law, which I set before you this day? (Deut. 4:8).*

In the mind of Moses, this law belonged especially to them, and was not the property of any other people.

(3). *Language under one covenant may explain duties under another, in those features in which the two are alike.*—Under all forms of divine law men have been required to worship God with a whole heart. Hence we know that the intention has been the same in that respect. Therefore, whatever may be found in any one of these, on that topic, may be used to enforce the thought and stir up the soul to that devotion which the Lord requires. The devotional Psalms may be used by the Christian, that we may understand the frame of mind that should characterize all who serve the God of heaven and earth. Idolatry is a great sin and has been in all ages; hence any condemnation of that iniquity found in the law of Moses may be used as an assistance in Christian study. "You shall worship the Lord your God, and Him only shall you serve," has been endorsed by the Master, and is for us. The two systems are alike in this respect, and therefore the teachings may be used interchangeably, belonging to one as well as to the other.

So it is with the fact that the Lord wishes men to do His will—that He has more delight in obedience than in sacrifice. This being true, it follows that we are at liberty to get illustrations of obedience and disobedience during any dispensation, that will enable us to better understand our duty as the disciples of Christ; not in the thing commanded, but in the fact that strict obedience to the word and will of the Lord is required of us as His servants. We are now not to go to the slaughter of the Amalekites, as was commanded to Saul, or to march around Jericho with Joshua; but we are to do the things which are now required of us, as they were those things required of them. The demands have changed, but the absoluteness of obedience remains the same now as then. The Savior brings a teaching to the disciples regarding the settlement of all difficulties before worship, by referring to the altar service. And though this manner of service has been discontinued, yet before we bring our devotions before God we should first go and be reconciled to our brother, and then come and bring our gift.

(4). *The laws of each covenant are supposed to be complete in themselves.*—This does not indicate that a man would understand Judaism as well without studying the dealings of God with the Patriarchs as he would if he had familiarized himself with that feature of divine history. Nor does it mean that a man can ever be perfectly taught respecting the New Institution, without having had a knowledge of the Law and the Prophets. But it does affirm that if a man had never seen the law given by Moses, he could know all his duty toward God by a careful and thorough study of the New Testament. There were many Gentile congregations which had no knowledge of the law of Moses, and who were entirely dependent upon the teaching of inspired men as they revealed Christ to them. We learn from Christ, and the men He ordained, every precept which we are expected to observe—to hear His sayings and do them, is to do the will of His Father in heaven, and therefore to build on the solid rock. It is not now what "you have heard that it has been said," but the "*I say to you*," that is to control us in the service of God as Christians. If we are to be Jews, then we must study, that we may know the law and keep it. Christ has brought forward every grand feature of truth and right, and every act of piety and benevolence that can be of any assistance to us in the Christian life. Paul could afford to be indifferent about everything else but the law of Christ. He says:

> *And to the Jews I became as a Jew, that I might gain Jews; to them that are under law, as under the law, not being myself under the law, that I might gain them that are under the law; to them that are without law, as without law, not being without law to God, but under law to Christ, that I might gain them that are without law. (1 Cor. 9:20-21)*

The forms of the law he might or might not observe; it was to him a matter of indifference, a question of expediency; and as for morals and the principles of truth and piety, they were all to be found in the law of Christ.

Section 38.
THE SEVERAL COVENANTS.

(1). The covenant made with Adam, will be found in Gen. 1:28, 29:

> *And God blessed them: and God said to them, 'Be fruitful, and multiply, and replenish the earth, and subdue it; and have dominion over the fish of the sea, and over the fowl of the air, and over every living thing that moves upon the earth.' And God said, 'Behold, I have given you every herb yielding seed, which is upon the face of all the earth, and every tree in which is the fruit of the*

tree yielding seed; to you it shall be for food.' (Compare Psa. 8:3-9; Heb. 2:8-10).

Here we have a part of the covenant. The other part of it consists of man's obedience to God. Hence, by a fall, man lost his divine right to be the ruler of the earth, and has to be reinstated in that position by the redemption in Christ. Just what would have been the result of that covenant having been kept, we do not know, but all the glories of the primitive state would certainly have been secured.

(2). *Covenant with Adam and Eve after the fall* (Gen. 3:15-21).— This contains a long struggle between the serpent and the seed of the woman, and the final victory in behalf of humanity. In the meantime the race will have to be purified by toil, and saved by sorrow, from those iniquities which would drown them in their abominations. They had failed to keep the first covenant, but this one they would keep, for *they could not help it.* This is the first promise of a coming Savior, and is found to consist in toils and duties wrung from the inhabitants of the earth on the one side, and the blessed promise of God on the other, that someday there should come a deliverer to the world who would be able to destroy the works of the devil.

(3). The covenant with Noah before the flood (Gen. 6:13-22):

And God said to Noah, 'The end of all flesh is come before me; for the earth is filled with violence through them; and behold, I will destroy them with the earth. Make an ark of gopher wood; you shall make rooms in the ark, and shall pitch it inside and outside with pitch. And this is how you shall make it: the length of the ark shall be three hundred cubits, the breadth of it fifty cubits, and the height of it thirty cubits. You shall make a light to the ark, and to a cubit you shall finish it upward; and the door of the ark you shall set in the side thereof; with lower, second, and third stories you shall make it. And I, behold, I do bring the flood of waters upon the earth, to destroy all flesh, in which is a breath of life, from under heaven; everything that is in the earth shall die. But I will establish my covenant with you; and you shall come into the ark, you, and your sons, and your wife, and your sons' wives with you. And of every living thing of all flesh, two of every sort shall you bring into the ark, to keep them alive with you; they shall be male and female. And you take to you of all food that is eaten, and gather it to yourself; and it shall be for food for you, and for them.' Thus did Noah; according to all that God commanded him, so did he.

Here we have all the features of a covenant revealed. God makes a contract with this man to save him and his family, and requires of them certain conditions to be kept. The ark was to be built, of the timber prescribed, and according to the manner indicated in the contract; the animals were to be gathered as God had ordained. Still more than this is implied. Noah had been selected from the world as the only man who was righteous in his generations, and whose sons were also free from polygamy, which was then the curse of the earth. The sons of God had gone and taken them wives of the daughters of men, thus mingling with the wicked, and becoming as corrupt as the rest of the world. This is the reason that Noah was chosen: he was free from the corruption of the times. Hence it is to be understood that he should remain free from the abominations of the age. So we understand that this man is to keep himself pure, continue to be a worshiper of God, and to do, in building the ark, just what God had commanded him. The salvation of this man is not reckoned as a matter of debt, but the obedience which he rendered was a necessity on his part to accept that mercy that provided for his life and for the lives of his family.

(4). Covenant with Noah after the flood (Gen. 9:8-17):

And God spoke to Noah, and to his sons with him, saying, 'And I, behold, I establish my covenant with you, and with your seed after you; and with every living creature that is with you, the fowl, the cattle, and every beast of the earth with you; of all that go out of the ark, even every beast of the earth. And I will establish my covenant with you; neither shall all flesh be cut off any more by the waters of the flood; neither will there any-

more be a flood to destroy the earth.' And God said, 'This is the token of the covenant which I make between me and you and every living creature that is with you, for perpetual generations; I do set my bow in the cloud, and it shall be for a token of a covenant between me and the earth. And it shall come to pass, when I bring a cloud over the earth, that the bow shall be seen in the cloud, and I will remember my covenant, which is between me and you and every living creature of all flesh; the waters shall no more become a flood to destroy all flesh. And the bow shall be in the cloud; and I will look upon it, that I may remember the everlasting covenant between God and every living creature of all flesh that is upon the earth.' And God said to Noah, 'This is the token of the covenant, which I have established between me and all flesh that is upon the earth.'

We have the Divine side of this covenant thus presented to us, and the human side of it will appear by turning to the eighth chapter and twentieth verse, and reading to the close of the seventh verse of the ninth chapter. This is seen in the offering of Noah, and the pure worship which the Lord had required, and in keeping the commandments which the Lord put upon the race, in showing justice and kindness toward man and beast.

Though duties are exacted only of men, still this covenant is made with all flesh, or it *concerns* all flesh. Thus again we see that the idea of a covenant implies obligations and a contract between two parties. And, as it will be seen hereafter, God's promises will not fail, except by the failure of man by violating the terms. In that case God will cease to regard them, and the covenant will fail by virtue of the failure of the contracting or covenanting party.

(5). The covenant made with Abram respecting Christ (Gen. 12:1-3):

Now the Lord said to Abram, 'Get out of your country, and from your kindred, and from your father's house, to the land that I will show your: and I will make of you a

*great nation, and I will bless you, and make your name
great; and you shall be a blessing: and I will bless them
that bless you, and him that curses you I will curse; and
in you shall all the families of the earth be blessed.'*

In one form or another, this covenant was renewed many times. It
contained two thoughts, seemingly distinct at the first, and yet they
are bound together, as one is the medium through which the other is
fulfilled. Making of Abram a great nation was necessary in order to
bring about the coming of the Christ and the preaching of that truth by
which the world should be saved. God is preparing a receptacle of His
truth—a nation that will guard it, and keep it, and give it to the world.
They must be kept separate from the rest of the world, that God's
promises may be fulfilled, that prophecies may be given and kept, and
that the Christ may be given to the world, through whom the world
may be saved. The following Scriptures contain references to this
covenant: Gen. 18:18; 22:18; 26:4; Gal. 3:8, 16; Acts 3:25; Heb. 11:8,
17, 18.

(6). A covenant made with Abram concerning land (Gen. 13:14-
17):

*And the Lord said to Abram, after Lot was separated
from him, 'Now, lift up your eyes, and look from the
place where you are, northward and southward and
eastward and westward for all the land which you see,
to you will I give it, and to your seed forever. And I will
make your seed as the dust of the earth, so that if a man
can number the dust of the earth, then shall your seed
also be numbered. Arise, walk through the land in the
length of it and in the breadth of it; for to you will I give
it.'*

This covenant was referred to when Abram first came into the
land of Canaan (Gen. 12:7), but it was some time after this that it was
confirmed, as seen in the account above. It was afterward referred to
as having been already made (Gen. 17:8; 24:7). Isaac was assured that
it was because of Abraham's faithfulness that he should inherit the
land (Gen. 26:4-5). And when Moses was taken up to the top of the

mountain and shown the good land, he was reminded that the contract which the Lord had made with Abraham was about to be fulfilled (Deut. 34:4).

Although this covenant is distinct, yet it is based upon the thought contained in the promise made concerning his descendants—that they should become a great nation. Indeed, the land never belonged to Abraham in person; hence the only way in which it could be fulfilled was by the means of establishing his seed in that land. To belong, then, to that covenant, was to have a right in that land, as an owner— as one who has an outright ownership deed.

The human part of it seems more implied than stated. Yet when Isaac is reminded of his inheritance, it is announced to be on account of the righteousness of Abraham. And all the way through the history of the children of Israel, it was understood that the inheritance was dependent on the continued obedience of the people to the will of God. And it was because of a failure in this respect that they were sold into captivity to the Babylonians till they should learn to keep the commandments of the Lord.

(7). The covenant concerning circumcision (Gen. 17:9-14):

> *And God said to Abram, 'And as for you, you shall keep my covenant, you, and your seed after you throughout their generations. This is my covenant which you shall keep, between me and you and your seed after you; every male among you shall be circumcised. And you shall be circumcised in the flesh of your foreskin; and it shall be a token of a covenant between me and you. And he that is eight days old shall be circumcised among you, every male throughout your generations, he that is born in the house, or bought with money of any stranger, which is not of your seed. He that is born in your house, and he that is bought with your money, must needs be circumcised; and my covenant shall be in your flesh for an everlasting covenant. And the uncircumcised male who is not circumcised in the flesh of his foreskin, that*

soul shall be cut off from his people; he has broken my covenant.'

The ordinance was so distinctively Jewish that the apostles used the word *circumcision* many times to denote the *Jews,* and the *uncircumcision* to denote the *Gentiles* (Gal. 2:7, 8).

It has been said by a few, that nearly all ancient nations had this institution. But of this there is no evidence. On the other hand, there is every reason to believe the statement to be untrue.

And again, while we call this a distinct covenant, it remains a fact that it attaches more or less to the covenant by which Israel became a great nation, and were made the owners of the land of Palestine. And again, it may be said that these have some relation to the one great covenant which God made with Abram, that in his seed all the nations of the earth should be blessed. We find this relation between all of them. In order that in the seed of this man the world should have a Savior, his posterity must be separated from the rest of mankind; hence the organization of a nation. And to fence them away from the nations that were round about them, this institution was given. The land of Canaan was donated to the same end. But while these covenants have this much relation to each other, it is entirely improper to speak of them as but one covenant. All the contracts which God has made with the different portions of the race have had some reference to this great salvation in Christ; but that fact does not make them one and the same covenant.

There are many other smaller contracts made with men; but they have nothing to do with the principles of interpretation, nor yet do they throw any particular light on any portion of the Scriptures. God promises to prosper Jacob and bring him back to his father's house in peace, and Jacob agrees, on his part, to tithe himself, in order that God's worship shall be carried forward on the earth. But whether the covenant is between God and any man, or between two or more men, the thought of it is much the same: there are obligations on both sides, understood and agreed to. It is furthermore indicated in all these that if one party shall fail to keep his part of the contract, the other party is freed from all obligation. God has plainly said that He will act in that way.

> *'As I live,' says the Lord God, 'I have no pleasure in the death of the wicked; but that the wicked turn from his way and live. Turn from your evil ways; for why will you die, O house of Israel? And you, son of man, say to the children of your people, the righteousness of the righteous shall not deliver him in the day of his transgression; and as for the wickedness of the wicked, he shall not fall because of it in the day that he turns from his wickedness: neither shall he that is righteous be able to live by it in the day that he sins. When I say to the righteous that he shall surely live: if he trusts in his righteousness, and commits iniquity, none of his righteous deeds shall be remembered; but in his iniquity that he has committed, therein shall he die. Again, when I say to the wicked, you shall surely die, if he turns from his sin, and does that which is lawful and right; if the wicked restore the pledge, give again that which he had taken by robbery, walk in the statutes of life, commit no iniquity; he shall surely live, he shall not die. None of his sins that he has committed shall be remembered against him: he has done that which is lawful and right; he shall surely live.' (Ezek. 33:11-16).*

Now, though this was said under the law, which based a man's salvation on doing the things it required, still this principle is clearly stated, that whatever may have been the agreement between God and any man or men, if they shall forsake that covenant and turn away from Him, the covenant is broken, and He will not regard them. It is a thought that is by no means confined to the Old Testament. In the Covenant of Christ, it is required that those having accepted the salvation thus provided, shall continue steadfast to the end in order to receive the crown.

(8). The covenant with Israel at Mount Sinai (Ex. 20:1-24):

It is sometimes denied that this was a covenant. But this comes from not having any clear view of the meaning of the word. It is not now a covenant made with an individual, but with a nation. And it contains the substance of the covenants of flesh, land, and circumcision. Its purpose was to serve as a school-master during the time of the minority of that people, to prepare them for the Great Teacher that should come from heaven. The purpose of this covenant is indicated to Moses when he was in Egypt, trying to bring the people out from that cruel bondage.

> *'I am Jehovah: and I appeared to Abraham, to Isaac, and to Jacob, as God Almighty, but by my name Jehovah I was not known to them. And I have also established my covenant with them, to give them the land of Canaan, the land of their sojournings, in which they sojourned. And moreover I have heard the groaning of the children of Israel, whom the Egyptians keep in bondage; and I have remembered my covenant. Therefore say to the children of Israel, I am Jehovah, and I will bring you out from under the burdens of the Egyptians, and I will rid you out of their bondage; and I will redeem yon with a stretched out arm, and with great judgments.' (Ex. 6:3-8)*

In this we have the anticipation of the covenant that God intended to make with this people at Mount Sinai, over His own name, Jehovah. No former covenant had been completed in this name, but after this He was to be known to them by this name.

In Exodus 34:27-28, we read:

> *And the Lord said to Moses, 'Write these words, for after the tenor of these words I have made a covenant with you and with Israel.' And he was there with the Lord forty days and forty nights; he did neither eat bread nor drink water. And he wrote upon the tables the words of the covenant, the ten commandments.*

By referring to the giving of the law on Mt. Sinai, it will be seen that it has the form of a covenant—it is given to that people for a guide and a test of obedience, and it is sealed with blood, and enjoined upon them. It was not wholly religious, because the purpose of God in preparing a people ready to receive the Lord when He should come to the world, made it necessary that a government should exist, and that, by the means of a religious nation, He would be able to give a revelation of His will to the world. Hence the law combines the purpose of those covenants of land and flesh, in order that the world may be prepared for Christ (Gal. 3:8, 16-25).

(9). *The covenant of Christ, made by Him and sealed with His own blood* (Jer. 31:31-34; Heb. 8:6-13; 9:15; Matt. 28:26).—This covenant was in view during the former dispensations. Every offering and service foretold of the coming redemption, and every prophet, priest and king typified the coming Savior who should be *the Anointed* of the Lord, representing the Father in His love for the race, in the mercy and justice by which salvation could be possible to those who have sinned, and in the unlimited authority and power and wisdom by which the world could be lifted up and made ready for the heavens. As he is to provide salvation for the race, and extend it to us as a free gift, it belongs to Him, and to Him alone, to say on what terms the blessings of His sacrifice may be enjoyed: hence He is the one Mediator between God and men (1 Tim. 2:5).

Section 39.
THE FUNDAMENTAL DIFFERENCES BETWEEN THE COVENANT MADE WITH ISRAEL AND THE COVENANT MADE BY THE CHRIST.

(1). *The change in the priesthood.*—It has been thought that Christ was a priest under the law, and that He was introduced into that priesthood by John the Baptist. But of this there is no evidence. Christ did not claim to be a priest while on the earth; and if He had been, there would have been a violation of the law, which provided for but one high priest at a time, for no one can think that He would have been a priest in any inferior sense. There were many opportunities for

Him to have affirmed His priesthood, and His failure to do so is sufficient evidence that He did not occupy that position on the earth. It should be noticed, too, that no apostle ever insinuated, in any way, that the Master was high priest while he was here on the earth. Indeed, Paul takes just the opposite view of the matter (Heb. 8:4). He was not of the tribe that had been designated for such honors under the law, nor were any of the services observed by which he should have been initiated into that office. The theory has grown out of a felt need. Men have wanted to conglomerate the law and the gospel in order that they might find some support for various doctrines which could not be sustained in any other way.

(*a*) The high priesthood under that institution belonged to the *tribe of Levi,* the family of *Kohath,* and the particular family of *Aaron,* but in this, it is in the *line of Judah,* of which tribe Moses said nothing concerning priesthood (Heb. 7:14).

(*b*) In that, men were made priests who had infirmity, who needed an offering for themselves first before they officiated for the people; but in this, we have a priest who is holy, harmless, undefiled, and made higher than the heavens (Heb. 7:26-28; 5:1-4).

(*c*) Those priests discontinued by reason of death, but Christ remains a priest forever (Heb. 7:23-24).

(*d*) Under that system one could become a priest without an oath, but Christ was made a priest with an oath (Heb. 7:21).

(*e*) They were made priests by the law of a carnal commandment, but Christ by the power of an endless life (Heb. 7:16).

(*f*) That priesthood belonged to the law of Moses, this to another covenant (Heb. 7:11-13).

(*g*) The high priest under the law was not a ruler, and could have no connection with the government in any matter not connected with religious service, or the cleansing of the people from some disease or legal defilement; but Christ is king as well as priest. He was priest after the order of Melchizedek, who was king and priest at the same time. In Himself, He answers all human needs—He is the prophet to teach the way of God, the priest to remove all sin, and the king to govern and protect all His disciples. So then we have a faithful and merciful high priest in things pertaining to God.

Paul says:

> *Having then a great high priest, who has passed through the heavens, Jesus the Son of God, let us hold fast our confession. For we do not have a high priest that cannot be touched with the feeling of our infirmities; but one that has been in all points tempted like as we are, yet without sin. Let us therefore draw near with boldness to the throne of grace, that we may receive mercy, and may find grace to help us in time of need (Heb. 4:14-16).*

Thus Paul connects the priesthood of Christ with the throne of Christ. Thrones did not belong to the high priest under the law, but in this covenant our high priest is also a king.

In Zech. 6:12-13, Christ is foretold as a righteous Branch, who should sit and rule on His throne, and be a priest on His throne, and that the government, or counsel of peace, should be between them both.

(2). *There was a change in the atonement.*—The covering by the blood of animals could only serve to carry sins forward to the blood of the everlasting Covenant. "It is not possible that the blood of bulls and goats should take away sins" (Heb. 10:4).

From Lev. 23:26-32, we learn that there was an atonement made once a year. It was on the tenth day of the seventh month. At this time there was a remembrance of the sins committed during the year, and those that had been carried forward (Heb. 10:1-4). Take some of the forms of atonement under the law and the difference between the two institutions will appear as distinct as it would be possible for type to differ from antitype. Ex. 30:15-16 gives the atonement by the use of the half shekel. Lev. 8:18-34, in the consecration of Aaron and his sons to the service of the Lord; as they must be pure themselves, there had to be an atonement for them. The whole of the sixteenth chapter of Leviticus is taken up in giving an account of the annual atonement made for the people. In all this we can find abundant features of typology, but the atonement differs—

(*a*) In the time of offering.

(*b*) The priest making the sacrifice.

(*c*) The blood that was offered.

(*d*) The place where the offering was made.

(*e*) And the results of the sacrifice.

(3). *Change respecting limitation.*—The intent of universality of application was never thought of during the times of the law of Moses. In Deut. 4:7-8, Moses says:

> *For what great nation is there, that has a god so near to them, as the Lord our God is whenever we call upon him? And what great nation is there, that has statutes and judgements so righteous as all this law, which I set before you this day?*

The interrogative form in which this matter is presented here is the strongest form in which Moses could put an affirmative statement. It was the equal of saying, "we all know that no nation has a god so near to them as our God is to us, and no nation has this law, nor anything that approximates it."

There are many evidences that the law of Moses was never intended to reach beyond the nation to whom it was given. The Pharisees in later times did make efforts at proselyting, but it was the zeal of sectarianism rather than obedience to any command of God. The stranger that should dwell within their gates should be circumcised, and adhere to the commandments as they were found in that law, but the thought of bringing the world to the acceptance of Judaism was no part of the institution itself. Its forms and ceremonies were to avoid the idolatry of the times—to maintain that people intact, that it might be known in after times that the promise made to Abraham, to bring the Messiah into the world through his posterity, had been kept. But if that seed had been permitted to lose itself in the ocean of human beings, no proof of such faithfulness on the part of God would have been possible. By paying attention to the sanitary provisions of the law, it will be seen that there are commands respecting the clean and the unclean, for which there can be found no reasons except in the fact that food which is proper enough in other lands, is not good for them in that country. Hence, when the gospel of Christ was given, all these appointments were removed.

The New Covenant was intended, from the very inception of it, to be universal. The first feature of the commission is, "Go into all the world and preach the gospel to every creature." All its ordinances are arranged with reference to the universality of its principles. It is intended not for a given period, but for all time; not for a portion of the race, but for the whole human family. It was not to know any difference between Jew or Greek, barbarian, Scythian, bond, or free, for all should be one in Christ Jesus, the Lord of all, who would be alike rich to all that would call upon Him.

(4). They differ in the promises (Heb. 8:6):

But now has he obtained a ministry the more excellent,
by how much also He is the mediator of a better cove-
nant, which has been enacted upon better promises.

When Israel came over the Jordan, and temporary peace came, after conquering Jericho and Ai, the hosts were brought to the place appointed between Ebal and Gerizim, and heard the substance of the law, as it related to the promises. Their righteousness must consist in perfect obedience to all the demands of that law; and if such obedience should be rendered, they would be blessed in the basket and store, and in their flocks and herds, and in all the good things that pertained to this life. And, on the other hand, if they failed, they were to be cursed in all these respects. (See Deut. 28:1; 29:1; Josh. 8:30-35).

Even long before they came into this goodly land, they were made to know that the land which flowed with milk and honey was to be their inheritance, upon the condition that they would perfectly follow out the directions of the Lord. This was the good news that was preached to them in the wilderness, which did not profit (in many cases), not being mixed with faith in them that heard it (Heb. 3:4).

It is not to be denied that those who were devout looked forward to the coming of the Messiah, and to the glorious redemption which He should accomplish for the whole race. But they saw through a glass darkly. Moses endured as seeing Him who is invisible; and Abraham beheld these things from afar, and by faith brought them nigh, so that he could embrace them; and yet it is too much to say that they were a part of the covenant made with them at Sinai, and that belonged to them as a nation.

But the promises in Christ are far better. They are complete pardon, sufficient help, every needed grace and providence, resurrection from the dead, inheritance in the mansions in the heavens prepared by the hands of the Master Himself. No wonder, then, that Paul says that this covenant has been established upon better promises than that one.

(5). The law was written on stones, but the new institution, is put into the minds and the hearts of all who belong to it.

Are we beginning again to commend ourselves? or need we, as do some, epistles of commendation to you or from you? You are our epistle, written in our hearts, known and read of all men; being made manifest that you are an epistle of Christ, ministered by us, written, not with ink, but with the Spirit of the living God; not in tables of stone, but in tables that are hearts of flesh. And such confidence have we through Christ toward God: not that we are sufficient of ourselves, to account anything as from ourselves; but our sufficiency is of God; who also made us sufficient ministers of a new covenant; not of the letter, but of the Spirit: for the letter kills, but the spirit gives life. But if the ministration of death, written and engraved on stones, came with glory, so that the children of Israel could not look steadfastly upon the face of Moses for the glory of his face; which glory was passing away; how shall not rather the ministration of the spirit be with glory? For if the ministration of condemnation be glory, much rather does the ministration of righteousness exceed in glory. For truly that which has been made glorious has not been made glorious in this respect, by reason of the glory that surpasses. For if that which passes away was with glory,

*much more that which remains is in glory" (2 Cor. 3:1-
11).*

When Jeremiah saw the coming of this glorious institution, he announced that it would be unlike the covenant that God had made with
the children of Israel in the day that He took them by the hand to lead
them out of the land of Egypt; but in this new institution He would
write His law in their mind and put it into their inward parts.

That covenant was outward and formal, but this is inward and
spiritual. Those who belonged to that, depended on the figures, types,
and symbols, for their knowledge of the Lord; but in this, the Lord
from heaven has spoken to us in words that are spirit and life.

(6). *All that are to have a place in the new covenant, shall first
know the Lord.*—This is the statement that is made by Jeremiah, when
he foretold of the coming of the Christian institution: "They shall all
know me, from the least of them even to the greatest of them, says the
Lord." Paul quotes this in the eighth chapter of the Hebrew letter, and
applies it to the New Covenant. In the service of God under the law of
Moses, this never could have been said to be true. Into that institution
they were brought when they were born, and therefore there would
always be many of them who did not know the Lord; hence, if they
ever should know the Lord, they would have to be taught to know the
Lord after they were members of the covenant; but in the new institution it should not be so, for the first thing in it was to teach; and when
they should be discipled, or become learners of the Christ, then they
were to be brought into the kingdom.

(7). *Sin shall be remembered no more: when once pardoned, in
the New Covenant they cannot be remembered against the man
again.*—God said: "Their sins and iniquities will I remember no
more." But this was not so under the law of Moses. Sins not having
been perfectly blotted out (Heb. 10:4), there was a remembrance of
sin once every year. It is on this account that David asks God not to
remember against him the sins of his youth. Had he lived under the
reign of Christ, he could have been assured that his sins, having been
pardoned once, could never appear against him anymore. In that, they
were rolled forward a year at a time, and on the day of atonement, the

tenth day of the seventh month, they were called up, and *azazel* sent into the wilderness, that the sins of the people might go into oblivion again for another year. But sins pardoned in Christ once, can never come up again—they are blotted out, and gone forever.

(8). Into the Old Covenant they were born by a birth of their parents, but into the New, they come by a New birth—of water and the Spirit. This was the mistake of Nicodemus. He supposed that as he had been in the service of the Lord all his life, and was even a teacher of that religion, there could be no such demand made of him. He ought to have known better, and is therefore to be blamed for not knowing what he ought to have understood without a teacher. Had he read the law and the prophecies closely, he would have seen that there was coming a spiritual kingdom, in which the law of the Lord should be written in the hearts of all who should constitute its citizenship, hence a new term of membership would be required. But he was disposed to make the same blunder that thousands have made since, in supposing that there is no difference between the two institutions.

(9). *They differ in respect to form and place of worship.*— Sacrifices were once to be brought to the door of the tabernacle, and there offered to the Lord. When the temple was built in Jerusalem, that was the place where offerings were to be made. The Samaritan woman was anxious to know of Jesus which group was right, the Jews or the Samaritans, respecting the place where men ought to worship the Father. One said at Jerusalem, the other on Mt. Gerizim. But Jesus told her that the worship of God did not belong to either locality, but that any place would do, if the worship was in spirit and truth. This was the only essential. This again shows that the old covenant was a national affair, and was never intended to go beyond the precincts of Palestine. The types and shadows then looked forward to the coming Savior; and while they taught that man was a sinner, and had lost his right to life, there would be a sacrifice offered by which his sins and iniquities might be washed away. But the ordinances of the church of Christ get their significance, not from the idea of a coming Savior, but from a Savior having come, and having died and risen from the dead.

(10). *The law has been abolished and the gospel remains.*—This proposition is not readily accepted. During the dark ages Christianity was greatly corrupted. But in no respect did it receive greater injury than in being mixed with other religions. After four centuries of this doctoring, Christianity was little more than baptized heathenism, with lines of Judaism interwoven.

It is well to have the Scriptures clearly before us when we make a statement like this. The world will ask is why we make it, and we must be able to tell.

In Acts 15:5, we have the demand made of the Pharisees, who had accepted the faith of Christians, that unless the Gentiles would be circumcised and keep the law of Moses, they could not be saved. On this question the convention was held, not that they might vote on the subject and determine what it would be politic for them to require, but to ascertain what God had revealed on the subject. They heard from Paul and Barnabas and Simon Peter as to what God had done by them, and then from James, as to his view of the evidence so far adduced, and that it agreed with the word of the Lord already revealed. And the conclusion of the whole matter was that they were not under that law, and therefore they should not require them to observe any such regulations, but only to observe a few necessary things (See vers. 20-29).

Does someone say that this did not free them from the observance of the law, except in the matter of circumcision? That is a mistake. The whole question was before them at the time—being circumcised after the manner of Moses, and keeping the law of Moses. Now, if there was any part of that law that would remain binding on them by virtue of its having a place in that law, surely someone in that audience would have been aware of the fact, and would have made the statement. But nothing of the kind is mentioned. Certain features of the law were all they required them to observe. Hence, if they were then under the law, it is not too much to say that they did not know it. Hence, the man who says they were yet under the law assumes a wisdom which the inspired apostles did not possess.

Paul argues this question all the way through several of his epistles. I must quote from him several statements in their connection, that no mistake may be made:

> *Therefore remember, that aforetime you, the Gentiles in the flesh, who are called uncircumcision by that which is called circumcision in the flesh, made by hands; that you were at that time separate from Christ, alienated from the commonwealth of Israel, and strangers from the covenants of the promise, having no hope and without God in the world. But now in Christ Jesus you that once were far off are made nigh in the blood of Christ. For he is our peace who made both one, and broke down the middle wall of partition, having abolished in his flesh the enmity, even the law of commandments contained in ordinances; that he might create in himself of the two one new man, so making peace; and might reconcile them both in one body to God through the cross, having slain the enmity by it: and he came and preached peace to you who were far off, and peace to those who were near: for through him we both have our access in one Spirit to the Father" (Eph. 2:11-18).*

It would seem impossible to make a statement plainer than this. The Gentiles and Jews have lost all distinction; they are all on the same footing; the law which had served as a partition wall between them had been removed. They were not under the law, but had been brought together in Christ, all differences having been removed.

In Paul's letter to the Galatians, this question is argued at length; in fact, the whole letter is largely occupied with it. In some way, some teacher had bewitched them with the idea that they must keep the law (3:1). To this Paul objects, assuring them that all their religious blessings had come to them through the hearing of faith, and not through the commandments of the law. He urges that the covenant by which they should be saved was by promise, and not by the law, and that all that was valuable in the law had been transferred to the scheme of salvation through the Lord Jesus Christ.

Brethren, I speak after the manner of men: though it be but a man's covenant, yet when it has been confirmed, no one makes it void, or adds to it. Now to Abraham were the promises spoken, and to his seed. He did not say, 'And to seeds,' as of many; but as of one, 'And to your seed,' which is Christ. Now this I say: A covenant confirmed beforehand by God, the law, which came four hundred and thirty years after, does not disannul, so as to make the promise of no effect. For if the inheritance is of the law, it is no more of promise: but God has granted it to Abraham by promise. What then is the law? It was added because of transgressions, till the seed should come to whom the promise had been made; and it was ordained through angels by the hand of a mediator. Now a mediator is not a mediator of one; but God is one. Is the law then against the promises of God? God forbid: for if there had been a law given which could make alive, truly righteousness would have been of the law. Howbeit the Scripture has shut up all things under sin, that the promise by faith in Jesus Christ might be given to them that believe. But before faith came, we were kept inward under the law, shut up to the faith which should afterwards be revealed. So that the law has been our tutor to bring us to Christ, that we might be justified by faith. But now that faith is come, we are no longer under a tutor. For you are all sons of God, through faith in Christ Jesus. For as many of you as were baptized into Christ did put on Christ. There can be neither Jew nor Greek, there can be neither bond nor free, there can be no male and female, for you all are one man in Christ Jesus. And if you are Christ's, then are you Abraham's seed, and heirs according to the promise. (Gal 3:15-29).

This argument cannot be met. Paul has shown it to have been the purpose of God, in giving the law, to furnish the people of Israel with such primary lessons and such government as would, under the circumstances, do them the most good. But that institution was temporal in its purpose. It was intended to lead them during the days of their minority, and prepare them for the great Teacher that should come from God, under whom they were to graduate for the heavens. During the days of their minority they were under this pedagogue, but when the great Teacher is come, they are no longer under the tutor—this law and authority extended no further.

In the fourth chapter of the Galatian letter, verses 21-31, we have full and complete instruction respecting this matter. Here the apostle brings up the question under the form of an allegory, and shows, beyond any doubt, that the law was to be cast out, as well as the bondmaid. And in the third chapter of his second letter to the brethren at Corinth, he treats the subject in the form of antithesis, putting the gospel on one side and the law on the other. During this presentation he repeats it three times that the law is done away, and makes special reference to that part of the law which was written on the two tables of stone.

Then when we go to search for the duty of Christians; because of the lack of an understanding respecting this matter, many theologians have felt unsafe in adopting the plain truth as a rule of Christian life, lest the necessary authority by which proper conduct shall be secured shall be lacking. Some way they feel that they must come before the people with a "you shall," or they will not be able to secure the obedience which the Lord requires. It has been this feeling that has attached the law to the gospel. On this account they have called the first day of the week "*the Sabbath.*" Yet everyone knows that it is never so denominated in the New Testament; and any one acquainted with the early history of the church is aware that it was far advanced in the sixth century before such phraseology was employed by anyone. Both the Ante-Nicene Fathers and the Post-Nicene Fathers speak of the day on which Christians met for worship as the first day of the week, the *eighth day,* which would be the next day after the seventh; *resurrection day;* but most generally they use the very words of the apostle John (Rev. 1:10), "*The Lord's day.*" All have ever admitted that the ceremonial, judicial—the formal and ritual—features of the law were done away in the crucifixion of Christ, but many claim that something they call the moral law was retained. But for this division of the law there is no authority. There is no such division made by any inspired man, for the reason that no one directed by the Spirit of the Living God ever had any such an idea as that. Many parts of the Old Testament are called by the common term law; sometimes it is divided into the Law and the Prophets; But the largest division that is found anywhere is in the twenty-fourth chapter of the Gospel by Luke—the Law, and the Prophets, and the Psalms. Already we have seen that the apostle Paul makes no such difference as that insisted upon by modern theologians, but sums up the whole of the Old Testament institution, and says that it has been abolished.

In Col. 2:13-17, Paul settles that question of the continuance of the Law as a rule by which Christians should live. He says:

> And you, being dead through your trespasses and the uncircumcision of your flesh, you, I say, he did quicken together with him, having forgiven us all our trespasses; having blotted out the bond written in ordinances that was against us, which was contrary to us: and he has taken it out of the way, nailing it to the cross; having put off from himself the principalities and the powers, he made a show of them openly, triumphing over them in it. Therefore, let no man judge you in meat, or in drink, or in respect of a feast day or a new moon or a sabbath day which are a shadow of the things to come; but the body is Christ's.

Let us realize, then, that the institution of Christ is distinct, and that if we would know our duty to God in this dispensation, we must learn it from this covenant, not from the old.

Section 40.

HOW CAN WE KNOW WHEN THE COVENANT OF CHRIST BEGAN?

This is a question of no little importance. Even those who agree as to the difference between that made with Israel at Mt. Sinai and that made by the Savior, are not sure respecting the exact time when the one was removed and the other began. We have learned, in many ways, that this covenant was not that which was made with Adam, or Noah, or Abraham, or the nation of Israel; but just when it did begin and just when all men ought to have yielded obedience to its requirements, is not so easily determined. We have a few facts, however, that may be of importance in determining this matter.

(1). *Christ lived and died a Jew:* he walked in obedience to that law; he even went so far as to say:

> *Do not think that I came to destroy the law or the prophets; I did not come to destroy, but to fulfill. For truly I say to you, Till heaven and earth pass away, one jot or one tittle shall in no way pass away from the law, till all things are accomplished. Therefore whoever shall break one of these least commandments, and shall teach men so, shall be called least in the kingdom of heaven: but whoever shall do and teach them, he shall be called great in the kingdom of heaven. (Matt. 5:17-19)*

It is impossible to think that Jesus at that time had an independent kingdom, or to suppose that He lived in any way indifferent to the demands of the Law that had been given by Moses. Whatever there was in that Law, He proposed to keep it—God was its Author, and men should observe it.

(2). During His life, His kingdom, was spoken of as being present, at hand, as if it had not yet been established, but would be in the near future.—When John came preaching in the wilderness of Judea, he said, "Repent, for the kingdom of heaven is at hand" (Matt. 3:2). And when Jesus went forth into Galilee, he preached "the gospel of the kingdom of God, and saying, The time is fulfilled, and the kingdom of God is at hand: repent, and believe the gospel" (Mark. 1:14-15).

Again, when the Savior was about to begin the third tour throughout all Galilee, He called to Him His apostles, and appointed them to go into other places in this country, and said to them: "As you go, preach, saying, The kingdom of heaven is at hand."

Then again, just before His transfiguration, he said:

> *Truly I say to you, There are some of them that stand here, who shall in no way taste of death, till they see the Son of man coming in his kingdom. (Matt. 16:28)*

Once more, when he was nearing Jerusalem, for the last time; He is at Jericho; is at the house of Zacchaeus; and teaching them that the Son of man had come to seek and save that which was lost.

> *And as they heard these things, he added and spoke a parable, because he was near to Jerusalem, and because they supposed that the kingdom of God was immediately to appear. Therefore, He said, 'A certain nobleman went into a far country, to receive for himself a kingdom, and to return.' (Luke 19:11-13)*

And when the parable is spoken, there remains no question in the mind of any reader that it relates to himself—that he was going into a far country to receive for himself a kingdom, and to return again, that He might reckon with His servants.

Hence He did not begin by establishing his kingdom; it was not established for Him; it was not in existence at the time of His going up to Jerusalem to be put to death.

And supposing that His disciples were even tolerably well informed, the kingdom was not yet established when He ascended into the heavens.

> *They therefore, when they were come together, asked him, saying, Lord, will you at this time restore the kingdom to Israel? (Acts. 1:6)*

The answer that follows shows that if the kingdom was then in being, the Savior did not care to inform them on that point. Indeed, He indicates that it was yet future, and that they should be His agents in the presentation of His claims; but that the time had not yet arrived for the work to begin. They must tarry at Jerusalem for the heavenly endowment; and when that should be received, the work might begin.

(3). The kingdom was presented by the Savior as having so come that men could press into it.

> *The law and the prophets were until John: from that time the gospel of the kingdom of God is preached, and every man enters violently into it. (Luke 16:16)*

There is a difficulty in the minds of many in these statements. In a number of texts we are taught that the kingdom of heaven was not established while the Savior was on the earth; and now we come to an affirmation that men were pressing into it during even the lifetime of John. And as it would be absurd to maintain that men could enter that which had no existence, it is demanded that the kingdom be understood to have been in existence after the preaching of John the Baptist. This difficulty is more apparent than real. The word *kingdom* in itself does not always have the same meaning. It implies: (1) a king; (2) laws; (3) subjects; (4) penalties for disobedience, and rewards for faithfulness; (5) a throne and power for the king. Any one of these may be put for the word itself, according to a figure yet to be considered. Also, like the word *gospel*, or good news, it may refer to the time of its coming or to a time when it shall assemble the world for judgment, or any time between these. But what is the meaning in this place? One thing must be conceded at the beginning of the investigation—the Scriptures must not be made to contradict. It will be impossible to make more or less of the texts that we have cited. This fact prepares us to understand the use of the word in question in an unusual sense. But what sense? This question will be best answered by determining after what plan John performed his work. Did he come to establish the kingdom or church of the Christ?

Gabriel tells Zacharias that John was to "Go before *his* face in the spirit and power of Elijah, to turn the hearts of the fathers to the children, and the disobedient *to walk* in the wisdom of the just; to make ready for the Lord a people prepared *for him*" (Luke 1:17). In verses

76 and 77 of the same chapter, we have Zacharias saying, when the Lord had opened his mouth:

> *Yes, and you, child, shall be called the prophet of the*
> *Most High: for you shall go before the face of the Lord*
> *to make ready his ways; to give knowledge of salvation*
> *to his people in the remission of their sins.*

It is evident from all this that John did not come to set up a kingdom, but to introduce the King, and prepare a people for His reception. In harmony with this thought, he preached the approach of the kingdom; and that, in view of that fact, men ought to repent, to turn to God, and do works suitable for repentance. Then, when the kingdom was preached in the days of John, it was preached not as having come, but coming—near at hand. Hence, when men *pressed into it* as if by violence, they pressed into that prepared condition which it was John's work to direct.

While this is the evident meaning of the language, it makes complete harmony with every other statement on the subject.

(4). While there was a gospel in the sense of good news respecting coming events, there could be no gospel in the complete sense till Christ had come and been put to death, and had risen from the dead (1 Cor. 15:1-4). Whatever else there may be in the word gospel, the record of the death and the resurrection of the Savior was certainly a part of it. We cannot think of the kingdom or church of Christ as having come, and the gospel not yet preached in its fullness. And yet it would have been impossible for any man to have preached it before His resurrection. The apostles did not know that He was to rise from the dead. And if they had, they could not have preached that He had so risen till He had been redeemed from death. Hence we conclude that it would have been impossible for the church to have been instituted before the crucifixion of the Savior.

(5). *The limits of Judaism were upon the disciples during the days of the Savior.*—In the tenth chapter of Matthew we have the Master sending out the twelve into the towns and villages of Galilee, but strictly charging them not to go into any road that would lead to the

Gentiles, nor into any village of the Samaritans, but to go only to the lost sheep of the house of Israel.

But when he gave them the great commission, after He had risen from the dead, all restriction is removed. It no longer contains promises for the Jew which are not also to the Gentiles. Then they were to be witnesses to Him in Judea, in Samaria, and to the uttermost parts of the earth. Then they were to go into all the world and preach the gospel to every creature; they were to go and make disciples of all the nations. This could not be done while the bonds of Judaism were upon them. Hence the kingdom of Messiah could not have been in existence till the limitations of the Jews' religion were taken out of the way.

(6). *The law and the priesthood were changed at the same time.*— This we have already seen, and only refer to it here by way of remembrance (Heb. 7:11, 12; 8:4). We have also seen that Christ was not a priest upon the earth; hence that the law was not changed till He came into that everlasting priesthood after the order of Melchizedek; and this He did not do till He ascended into the heavens, to make an atonement for the sins of the whole world.

(7). The new law of the kingdom of the Christ should go forth from Zion, and the word of the Lord from Jerusalem.

The word that Isaiah the son of Amoz saw concerning Judah and Jerusalem. And it shall come to pass in the latter days, that the mountain of the Lord's house shall be established in the top of the mountains, and shall be exalted above the hills; and all nations shall flow to it. And many peoples shall go and say, Come, and let us go up to the mountain of the Lord, to the house of the God of Jacob; and he will teach us of his ways, and we will walk in his paths; for out of Zion shall go forth the law and the word of the Lord from Jerusalem. (Isaiah 2:1-3).

Micah 4:1-2, contains the substance of the foregoing. This precludes the possibility of the law of Christ going forth from Jordan. But it has been objected that this does not refer to anything that could have taken place in the days of the apostles, as it relates to the last or latter days. But the last days of what? If Isaiah was prophesying about the world, then it would refer to the latter times of its history or being. But he starts to tell what awaits Judah and Jerusalem in the latter times. Hence this prophecy relates to the latter times of that city and people; before the Jews should be finally dispersed, and their city destroyed, the law should go forth. Those changes came in the year 70 A. D., and hence the law went forth before that time.

(8). *The apostles had the keys of the kingdom* (Matt. 16:13-19), but they were not at liberty to use them till after the first Pentecost succeeding the resurrection of the Savior.

> *And he said to them, 'These are my words which I spoke to you, while I was yet with you, how that all things must needs be fulfilled, which are written in the law of Moses, and the prophets, and the Psalms, concerning me. Then he opened their mind, that they might understand the Scriptures; and he said to them, Thus it is written, that the Christ should suffer, and rise again from the dead the third day; and that repentance and remission of sins should be preached in his name to all the nations, beginning from Jerusalem. You are witnesses of these things. And behold, I send forth the promise of my Father upon you: but tarry in the city, until you are clothed with power from on high. (Luke 24:44-49)*

In the appeal of the Savior to the "thus it is written," reference is made to the language of Isaiah and Micah, for these alone tell of this new law of salvation going forth from Jerusalem. Just after the Savior had risen from the dead, the fulfillment of that prediction was near, but it must wait till the heavenly endowment should first come. Thus again we see the impossibility of this law of salvation going forth from any other place, or at any other time than that indicated in the interpretation of the prophecies given by the Savior himself.

(9). No covenant could be in force till it was ratified by the death of the sacrifice appointed to that end.

*For where a testament is, there must of necessity be the
death of him that made it. For a testament is of force
where there has been death; for does it ever avail while
he that made it lives? (Heb. 9:16, 17)*

It would be impossible, then, for the new covenant, or testament,
to be in force while Christ, who had been appointed as the covenant
sacrifice, was living.

A mistake is sometimes indulged here in maintaining that nothing
can be regarded as a part of this testament except that which had already been given by the Savior. This, of course, would render all the
writings of the apostles worthless, and rule them out from being part
of the New Testament. This is to push the meaning of the language
entirely beyond its import. All that is bound in a covenant may not
have been mentioned at the time of sealing it with the people. At the
time that Moses took the book and sprinkled it with blood, and enjoined it to the people, but little more than the ten commandments had
been stated. The whole of the priesthood and the law of sacrifices had
to come afterward. They covenanted not simply with items of law, but
with Him who had made the law, and, therefore, bound themselves to
all that necessarily adhered in this law. So with the covenant of
Christ. He gave them the great principles of the New Institution. But
at the time He left them there were lessons which they could not
learn. He had these things to say to them, but they could not bear
them then. Hence the Holy Spirit had to be given to these men to lead
them into all truth, to teach them all things, to bring all things to their
remembrance that He had taught them before, to receive the things
that belonged to Him and deliver to them. But it would be idle to say
that these things that came to the apostles after the ascension of the
Savior were no part of that Institution, or that they were not confirmed to them when the Lord made the atonement for the sins of the
people. The one article of the Christian's creed being accepted, everything belonging to it is accepted with it. When men confess that they
believe with all their heart that Jesus is the Christ, the Son of the Living God, they have accepted everything of which He is the author.

The order, then, of making a covenant, is to present the matter clearly before those who are to be parties to the contract, and then seal it with a proper sacrifice. So the great feature of the New Testament was clearly stated, and when sealed with the blood of the appropriate sacrifice, there is bound upon all who accept the Christ, all of which He is clearly the author. But Paul's reasoning on the subject remains intact—that it could not have been of force till after the death of Him who made it.

(10). *Christ is the corner stone.*—In Acts 4:11, 12, Peter says:

He is the stone which was set at naught by you the builders, which was made the head of the corner. And in none other is there salvation: for neither is there any other name under heaven, that is given among men, wherein we must be saved.

In 1 Cor. 3:11, Paul says:

For other foundation can no man lay than that which is laid, which is Jesus Christ.

And again in Eph. 2:19-21, he says:

So then you are no more strangers and sojourners, but you are fellow citizens with the saints, and of the household of God, being built upon the foundation of the apostles and prophets, Christ Jesus himself being the chief cornerstone; in whom each building, fitly framed together, grows into a holy temple in the Lord; in whom you also are built together for a habitation of God in the Spirit."

In every figure in which the church of Christ is contemplated as a building, Christ is regarded as the chief corner stone. It is not necessary to say that those who have constructed this figure did not have it in their minds that the building could be erected first, and the cornerstone afterwards. It is received without argument that they supposed the building was erected *after* the cornerstone was laid, and *could not be built before that.*

(11). *In all mentions of the kingdom, after the day of Pentecost, it is spoken of as if it were in existence.*—A single exception is found in those passages in which the kingdom is spoken of in its triumphant state, in the period of the judgment and everlasting reward. In those the saints are waiting for the kingdom of God; not for its establishment upon the earth, but for the rewards for services rendered. A few of the affirmations of the inspired apostles upon this point will not be out of place. But before giving them, we wish to remind the reader of the statements that were made while the Savior was living. Then everywhere it was said that the kingdom was at hand. If now it is said to have come, to be in existence, the impression will be unavoidable that it was established in the meantime.

> *To the end that you should walk worthily of God, who calls you into his own kingdom and glory. (1 Thess. 2:12)*

> *Giving thanks to the Father, who made us suited to be partakers of the inheritance of the saints in light; who delivered us out of the power of darkness, and translated us into the kingdom of the Son of his love. (Col. 1:12)*

There is nothing found in the connection in which these texts occur to lessen the full force that should ordinarily be given to the words that are used. Hence we feel duty bound to receive them in their full importance.

> *Let not then your good be evil spoken of: for the kingdom of God is not eating and drinking, but righteousness and peace and joy in the Holy Ghost. (Rom. 14:16-17)*

While Paul is not aiming to define the word in this text, he certainly does indicate that the kingdom with which they had to do was in existence.

In Rev. 1:5, John says that Christ was the ruler of the princes of this world, and in the ninth verse he says:

> *I John, your brother and partaker with you in the tribulation and kingdom and patience which are in Jesus,*

was in the isle that is called Patmos, for the word of God and the testimony of Jesus.

Sometimes the church of God, of Christ, is employed to express the same thought; for instance, in Matt. 16, the words *church* and *kingdom* are used interchangeably—"On this rock I will build my church;" "to you do I deliver the keys of the kingdom." In the use of these terms He is expressing the same thought. No one denies that the church of Christ came and was fully established on the Pentecost next after the ascension of the Savior. Hence whatever was the law by which His people should be governed till His return to us again, was sent forth at that time. This was the law of the Lord that should go forth from Zion, and the word of the Lord from Jerusalem. It is that divine law by which all the people of God shall live, and contains the terms upon which sinners may be accepted in the name of the Lord Jesus Christ. Before this time the Master said, *"I will build my church;"* after that time, they all speak of the church and the kingdom as being in existence.

(12). *The kingdom of Christ was set up on the day of Pentecost next succeeding His ascension.*—This statement is the result of the investigation already given. And while on this we might rest the case, it is still in order to give it further consideration, for there are other Scriptures which will throw light on the subject. We wish now to examine the subject as if we were hunting the beginning of a section corner. We have certain field notes, and so many chains and links in one direction will give us a hidden stone which will serve as a witness. And a certain number of chains and links in another direction will give us a tree with a certain mark, which shall be another witness. So in this case, there are prophetic utterances and teachings of the Savior which will serve as witnesses in the matter.

We have already heard from Jer. 31:31-34, with Paul's assurance that it referred to the New Covenant (Heb. 8:6-13). Hence it marks the time when the law ceased to be the power that controlled the people, and when they became free in Christ.

We have also heard from Isa. 2:1-3, and Micah 4:1-2, and have been informed by them that the New Law should go forth from Zion, and the word of the Lord from Jerusalem. And upon these texts we have had the comment of the Savior, in Luke 24. After his resurrection, these passages had not been fulfilled, but would be in the near future, when repentance and remission of sins should be preached in His name among all nations, beginning at Jerusalem. Also, it is well to be reminded that the Savior promised the fulfillment of all this when His apostles should be endued from on high. The endowment, too, is pointed out as the promise of the Father which they had heard. And now it is left for us to see what this promise of the Father was, and then find its fulfillment. In doing this we will, beyond all question, find the going forth of that new law spoken by the prophets and the Savior himself.

> *And it shall come to pass afterward, that I will pour out my Spirit upon all flesh; and your sons and your daughters shall prophesy, your old men shall dream dreams, your young men shall see visions: and also upon the servants and upon the handmaids in those days will I pour out my spirit. (Joel 2:28-29)*

The Savior announces the fulfillment of this prophecy in John 14:15-17, when he promises another comforter, who should abide with them. But in the following chapters (15-16), the promise is made still clearer, and the duty that will then follow:

> *But when the Comforter has come, whom I will send to you from the Father, even the Spirit of truth, which proceeds from the Father, he shall bear witness of me: and you also bear witness, because you have been with me from the beginning.*

Notice, that when the Spirit of truth should come and bear witness, the apostles should also bear witness. In chap. 16:12-14, this promise is made still clearer:

> *I have yet many things to say to you, but you cannot bear them now. Howbeit when he, the Spirit of truth, is come, he shall guide you into all the truth: for he shall not speak from himself; but whatever things he shall*

hear, these shall he speak, and he shall declare to you
the things that are to come.

Before the apostles would be qualified for the testimony which they should bear concerning Jesus, they would need this heavenly Comforter and Director, that they might be freed from any weakness in the discharge of the duties that would then devolve upon them. The Master had been more than three years in giving them this new law, by which men should have the remission of their sins and be admitted into that grace in which they would be regarded as the sons of the Living God. Still there were truths that they did not understand while the Lord was with them, and they could not, for their views concerning the Messiah were so erroneous that their minds were blinded. But when the Master had suffered death and had risen again, they were in a better condition to learn. So the Spirit is sent to complete their education, and fully qualify them for their work as the ministers of the gospel of Christ, to give the law of the kingdom to all the nations.

According to Luke, in his gospel (24:47-48) and Acts 1:4, the Lord re-announced the commission just before leaving them for the heavens, but forbade them going out till they should receive the promise of the Father, that is, the heavenly Comforter, the Holy Spirit. When he should come to guide them into all truth, then should their work, as indicated in the great commission, begin at Jerusalem; they should then tell to the world the way of life through the Lord Jesus Christ, who is clothed with all authority in heaven and in earth.

To find this beginning of the way of life in Christ, we have only to find when the Spirit came into the world according to all these promises. We have not long to wait for the fulfillment. Within ten days after the Savior ascended, the Spirit came. And with His coming all that had been promised was fulfilled, in their endowment and the witness that was borne by the Spirit and by the apostles.

And when the day of Pentecost was now come, they
were all together in one place. And suddenly there came
from heaven a sound as of the rushing of a mighty wind,
and it filled all the house where they were sitting. And
there appeared to them tongues, parting asunder, like as

of fire; and it sat upon each one of them. And they were all filled with the Holy Spirit, and began to speak with other tongues as the Spirit gave them utterance. (Acts 2:1-4)

This has all the appearance of the fulfillment of the prediction of the prophet Joel, and the promise of the Savior. When Joel wrote, it was a long way off; but when the Savior spoke, it was near. But Isaiah and Micah had also their minds fixed on the attendance at that time. They said that all nations should flow to it; from which we understand that all nations should be represented at Jerusalem at that time. And so it is stated by the historian (Acts 2:5). "Now there were dwelling at Jerusalem Jews, devout men, from every nation under heaven."

We are ready to decide in our own minds that the time has come for the work to be done which had been entrusted to the hands of the apostles—to give to the world the new Law of the kingdom. But it is better for us to have the opinion of an inspired man on the subject.

But Peter, standing up with the eleven, lifted up his voice, and spoke forth to them, saying, 'You men of Judea, and all you that dwell at Jerusalem, be this known to you, and give ear to my words. For these are not drunken, as you suppose; seeing it is but the third hour of the day; but this is that which has been spoken by the prophet Joel;

And it shall be in the last days, says God,
I will pour forth of my Spirit upon all flesh:
And your sons and your daughters shall prophesy,
And your young men shall see visions,
And your old men shall dream dreams
Yes and on my servants and on my handmaidens in those days
I will pour forth of my Spirit; and they shall prophesy (Acts 2:14-18).

So, then, we have not been mistaken in the appearance of things. Inspired authority declares that this is the fulfillment of the prophecy of Joel. But this is not all—they understood now that the promise of the Father had come, and that at that time they were to declare *all the words of this life* in the name of the new King. And Peter therefore continues to announce that Jesus has been raised from the dead, and made to be both the Lord and the anointed One. And when the people ask what they are to do, he tells them to submit to that same Jesus whom they had crucified, that they might be saved. This they did. After this, when Peter had been to the house of Cornelius and preached the gospel of the Christ to them, he was taken to account for it by the brethren who were at Jerusalem. He recounted the whole matter in order, telling them all things that had occurred in his call to that place and the work he did.

> *And as I began to speak, the Holy Spirit fell on them, even as on us at the beginning. (Acts 11:15)*

Now there are a number of things that it will be well for us to note:

1. This new covenant should be unlike the old one (Jer. 31; Heb. 8).
2. It should go forth from Jerusalem (Isa. 2; Micah 4; Luke 24).
3. All nations should be represented there at that time (Isaiah, Micah, Luke, in Acts 2:5).
4. The Holy Spirit should be present at that time, and give them supernatural power (Joel, John, Luke, Acts).
5. The Holy Spirit and the apostles should bear witness at that time (John and The Acts).
6. The demonstration should be at the beginning of the gospel plan of saving men (Luke 24:44-49; Acts 2:4; 11:15).

Surely this is enough. One who will not be able to see from this induction of facts that the kingdom of the Christ was set up on the day of Pentecost, is either unable or unwilling to see the plainest truth.

But against this there is an objection; it is this: If this is so, then there was fifty days that the world was without any authorized law. If the law was taken out of the way and nailed to the cross of Christ, and yet His law did not go forth till the Pentecost, which was fifty days later, then there was no law during the interregnum. Yet all men believe that the law did end with the crucifixion of the Savior; that from that time there was no more offering for sin or other service in the temple according to divine appointment. And the simple truth is that all men were amenable to God according to the light which they had. Those who had been the disciples of Christ and knew His requirements, were under obligations to obey them; and those who did not have these advantages, were amenable to God for such light as they did possess. In any age of the world, when any man has done the best that be knows and could know, he has been free from iniquity in the sight of God. And it was then the same that it has ever been in that respect.

From that time the world was not under law to Moses, nor according to Moses, but under law to Christ (1 Cor. 9:21). It is not now the law that was given to the patriarchs, nor to the people of the Jews at Mt. Sinai; but we are to be the servants of God by accepting Christ and doing His will, as found in the New Testament. Every truth that will make for our spiritual good is to be found in it. Every sin is there condemned; hence it is to us the perfect rule of life.

Someone again objects that the early Christians did not have the New Testament, and therefore were without the law necessary to perfect Christian character. But they had the apostles and direct inspiration, and this was all that they could have needed. The Lord's will was the same then that it is now, and it was revealed to them then as they needed the knowledge.

Section 41.
THE TRIAL AS TO THE TIME OF THE ESTABLISH-MENT OF THE KINGDOM.

We have already seen that any theory which is opposed by any known fact cannot be true. Hence we desire to have our theories tried by the facts that have been induced.

(1). If the kingdom of the Christ was in existence during the time of John the Baptist, then there were two Laws in force at the same time.—As it is impossible for God to be the author of such a state of things as that, it seems unreasonable to contend that John introduced it.

(2). Those texts which place the establishment of the kingdom later than the time of John upon the earth cannot be true if the church began during his life. It was after he was dead that the Savior sent out men to preach that the kingdom was at hand.

(3). *The Jewish limits or restrictions* that were upon the apostles would be incomprehensible upon the hypothesis that kingdom of the Messiah was then in existence. There could be no such limitation to the institution of which Christ was the author, for His was intended to go to the ends of the earth.

(4). *If Christ had been king while on earth,* then he would have been priest as well for he became a priest after the order of Melchizedek, who was king and priest at the same time. And if he had been priest on the earth, he would certainly have been high priest, for no one can think of the Savior taking an inferior rank. And if he had been high priest on the earth, then they would have had two high priests at the same time, and that, too, by divine authority. Paul says, "If he were on earth, he would not be a priest."

(5). If John instituted the kingdom by the baptism of Jesus then it was not set up at Jerusalem, according to the prophetic promise, and according to the clear teaching of the Savior Himself.

(6). If the kingdom had been established at a time prior to the resurrection of the Savior, then it could not have been unlocked by the keys held by Peter, for neither he nor any other apostle was at liberty to use such authority till the coming of the heavenly endowment.

(7). If the church came into being prior to the death of the Savior, then it was built before the laying of the cornerstone. We have already seen that Christ was, and is, the chief cornerstone; and the idea of building the church before the laying of the cornerstone is preposterous.

(8). If the Covenant of Christ was in force while the Savior was yet alive then Paul's illustration must pass for nothing. He thought that a covenant was of force after the death of him that made it, not before.

(9). We have also seen that if the kingdom was established before the ascension of the Lord, then it was established without the apostles knowing it. If they had committed such a blunder as that, it is unaccountable that the Master did not correct them.

(10). We have already seen that the gospel in its fullness was not and could not be preached till Christ had died and risen again from the dead. Hence, if the church was established before that time, it was in existence before the gospel was, or could be, preached.

CHAPTER VI:
THE VALUE AND USE OF HISTORY AND BI-OGRAPHY
IN THE INTERPRETATION OF THE SCRIP-TURES.

Section 42.
WHO WAS THE WRITER?

That is about the first question on opening any book. If we know not its author, we shall be quite in the dark, much of the time, while trying to interpret its pages. Large and small, there are a great many questions we may ask about the writer or the speaker that will assist in the interpretation of what has been said. We don't have the space to devote to their discussion, and will leave it to the genius of the exegete. But there are a few questions that we must ask.

(1). *Was he an inspired man?*—Is God the author of the communication? Did He direct the wording of the letter, or the speech? Or did He give the writer or speaker the ideas and then leave him to his own selection of words and manner of speech, in presenting these ideas to the people? It is evident to every careful student of the Bible that both of these plans have been followed. Generally God gives the inspiration, and leaves the man to present the thought in the words he chooses. But at other times it was impossible for men to hold the thoughts that God had to communicate. Under such circumstances He gave the words, for man could not be trusted with any part of it. At such times they spoke as the Spirit of God gave them utterance. But it is fair to say that the most of the Bible has been given by men who were inspired, but who were left to do the work according to their own methods of expression. This will account for the difference that may be found between almost any two of the writers of the Old and New Testaments. Matthew is not like John, nor is James like Paul, nor is the style of Isaiah the same as that of Jeremiah.

(2). *Was the author an educated man?*—If we could know that the writer has been left to himself in the selection and use of terms, we should deal with him as we do with any other writer in the use of grammar. If the writer was scholarly, we may be assured that the laws of the language in which he wrote are not violated, and the strictest rules of its grammar should be applied in the interpretation. But a less scholarly person may be held less firmly by such rules of interpretation. Most of the prophets seem to have been speaking men, and their sayings and predictions were gathered up by others, and recorded. But Isaiah was a writing prophet, and his language may be regarded, for the time, as strictly classical. He differs from Jeremiah, in that his figures are completed according to rule, while those of the latter are frequently broken off at their height, and the communication concluded in literal language.

Knowing first that Luke was a physician prepares us to anticipate the marks of his profession on his writings. All through his account of the teachings and doings of Jesus he has left the shades of his culture. The orderliness of his record is that of a student. This is true, not only of his gospel, but of Acts of the Apostles. When the other writers say that a man having the leprosy said to the Master, "If you wish, you can make me whole"; and He said, "I do wish, be whole." Luke reports the man as "*full of leprosy.*" By that expression he indicates that the man was in the third stage of that disease, and therefore incurable. The others say that "*Simon's wife's mother lay sick of a fever,*" but Luke says that she was "held by a *great fever.*" Thus he gives the extent of the trouble—she was bedfast, held, or bound down. When a man in the synagogue, whose hand was withered, was healed by the Savior, Luke is particular and says it was his *right hand.* And so it is all the way through the narrative—he enters into all the details, both in describing the diseases and the manner in which they were healed. To a physician, these would seem to be matters of importance; but they would not impress others in that way. His profession appears clearly in his statement of the prayer of Jesus in the garden (Luke 22:44-45): "And being in agony, he prayed more earnestly: and his *sweat became as it were great drops of blood falling down upon the ground.* And when he rose up from his prayer, he came to the disciples, and found them *sleeping for sorrow.*"

It would not have been apparent to another man that they were asleep because of sorrow. Even most of the theologians of the present time have charged upon these men an indifference to the occurrence of the hour. But Luke has redeemed them from that imputation. He could understand how the undefined sadness of that awful night could so entirely overcome these strong men, that as an infant cries itself to sleep, so they were exhausted by sorrow, and slept. It would be his place, too, to describe the bloody sweat, which would, to him, indicate the near approach of death. But for the angel that appeared to strengthen the Savior, the sorrow of the night would have been too much for him, and He would have been dead before the morning.

Knowing this man's culture beforehand, we are ready to enter with him into all the details, and understand him.

(3). *What religious bias or prejudice?*—We have before seen that God has not always directed the very words of the men through whom He has made a revelation of His will. And it is not too much to say that they had feelings like other men; and the fact that their speech partakes more or less of these feelings is evident to every careful reader. Sometimes these men write history, and were in need of no guidance from the Lord, being competent to tell very clearly the facts in the case. When we find that Isaiah would not speak to Pekah in a respectful way; that he does not call him king, nor even speak of him by his own name but as *"that son of Remalia,"* we would think it strange to find that he has embellished the qualities of the man. When Elisha speaks of the king of Israel as *"that son of a murderer,"* we expect him to be fairly explicit in stating the faults of the man. But while we feel compelled to say this much, even respecting men who were divinely employed to reveal the will of the Lord, we must remember that many of the characters of the Bible were not inspired, and did not claim to be. Hence their words are to be understood in the light of their prejudices, and allowances should be made on that score, just as if we were reading an account of their sayings in any other book.

The Bible is responsible for nothing but a faithful record of what was said and done. The language of the worst men that have ever lived is to be found in the Bible. The sons of Belial have had their say, and even Satan himself has given his falsehood in his most attractive manner. Hence we should know who speaks, and especially his heart condition. It is unreasonable to quote the language of Job's comforters as containing the will of God perfectly, for God condemns their views, and the men themselves. It is just a little more in order to quote Job himself. And yet he undertook to speak of things of which he had no knowledge. The Lord reduces the sage somewhat, and Job confesses that he had presumed on intelligence that he did not possess.

(4). *What of the style?*—That speakers and writers greatly differ in their manner of composition, no one calls in question. Two men may have the same thing to say, but the *manner* of saying it will show all the difference of mental temperament and skill. One presents his thought by the use of florid rhetoric, while another proceeds by the shortest lines known to the art of communication. Some are closely logical, while others pay but little attention to any relation between premise and conclusion. The logical mind will follow one topic, with another having direct relation with the preceding and succeeding statements. Others are haphazard, and put many strange things in juxtaposition. And these peculiarities are not removed by inspiration.

The eight writers of the New Testament exhibit many styles of composition. Some of these writings are in short sections, so that no particular violence will be done if the usual method of verse interpretation should be followed. But most of them have a subject that must be considered as a whole, or the meaning will never be gathered. Paul is peculiar for his logical acumen. It never forsakes him. Commonly, when a writer or speaker reaches the lofty heights of exultation, all signs of logic drop out of sight. But not so with Paul. From first to last he is severely logical. It was his mental nature, and any inspired thought that will come to us through him must assume that form. Even his rhapsodies are finely inwrought with syllogism. Not only so, but he starts out with the purpose which cannot be accomplished with a single verse or chapter. He ordinarily presents his topic, directly or indirectly, and divides and subdivides, and brings out all the truth that relates to the matter in hand, and reaches his conclusions by a careful induction of the facts. Not only so, but he anticipates the objections that may arise in the minds of his readers, and shows that they are not well founded, or, in the nature of the case, the conclusions they have reached are untrue.

Now, what I insist upon is that each writer shall be studied as to his manner of composition, for not until we shall understand the writer will we comprehend the writing.

Paul is not only a logical writer but a very versatile writer. He seems to have a large vocabulary from which to make his selections of terms. Hence, even when he is presenting an antithesis he will likely change the terms on both sides every time he makes the comparison. The best illustration that now occurs to the mind is in 2 Cor. 3:6-12. There the Law and the Gospel are referred to by so many different terms, that one who has not paid attention to the style of the writer, in this respect, is very liable to miss the meaning altogether.

(5). *A writer usually condemns the evils which appear the most dangerous to him.*—Hence, if he has been converted from any particular doctrine, he is likely to regard that as the prince of evils, and give his time largely to opposing it.

The fact just mentioned will account, in part, for the great space that Paul gives in efforts to show that Christianity and Judaism were distinct, and that we are not now under the Law, but under the Gospel of Christ. To know the history of the man, therefore, will greatly assist in understanding him.

Section 43.
WE SHOULD KNOW TO WHOM THE WRITING IS ADDRESSED.

(1). *What is their history?*—Where have they been? What have they done? From whom have they descended? A reference being made to such matters would be quite unintelligible to one who knew nothing of their antecedents. If they had been *Gentiles, carried away to dumb idols,* we should know it, and all about the character of that worship in which they had been engaged. *If they had been Jews,* raised and trained in the *Law* and the *traditions* of the times, we need to know that also, for these things may be referred to, and leave us in doubt as to their importance without such previous intelligence.

(2). *We need to know their education.*—It is presumed, at least, that every wise author will speak in the language of the people. Hence the words he uses, if they have any unusual signification, it will be because of the people to whom the words are employed. When Jesus said to the thief on the cross: "Today you will be with me in paradise," He certainly employed the word 'paradise' in the sense in which the thief and the people of that day would understand the term. Hence, the best dictionary that can be had respecting that word will be found by referring to the use of the word made by the people. The Sadducees did not employ the term at all, but the Pharisees did, and meant by it, *a place of abode for righteous spirits between death and the resurrection.* Hence, unless He deceived the man, and that intentionally (for He knew in what sense the thief would understand it), He employed the word in its common or accepted sense. This rule is usually, if not universally, agreed to, that, in finding the meaning of the word, we must know the meaning given to the word by those to whom it was spoken.

(3). *It is very necessary to know their customs.*—Many references to such things may be made which we cannot comprehend, unless we have been first informed in these things. Not only this: there may be prudential measures adopted, concerning which there is no divine command, and yet an apostle may recommend a certain course. And without attention to this matter, these prudential recommendations have been elevated into divinely directed rules of life. It might be a shame for a woman in the city of Corinth to be unveiled. And under such circumstances Paul would have her wear a veil; but it would not follow that every woman in the world must wear a veil, or be regarded as unChristian. So also would he advise respecting meats that had been offered to idols. If there is any danger of leading any one into idolatry by eating such meats, then he should refrain. It would be better to do without the needed food than to endanger the salvation of one for whom Christ died. In the same way, it would be better for the gospel to be preached only by a portion of the church than to give such offense to the community that the people could not be had to hear the claims of Christ.

(4). *We should also know what are the sins to which they have been addicted.*—In the city of Corinth, a member of the church had taken his father's wife, and was living with her as if she were his own. Now we ought to know why it was that they were not humbled, but rather puffed up, on that account.

(5). *To what temptations were they subject?*—Were they exposed to Grecian philosophy, or to the arguments of Jews, or half-converted Christians, who were more Jews than disciples, and who were trying to bring them again into the bondage of the Law? Were they exposed to that subtle philosophy that claims to have received the good of all systems of religion and philosophy, and to have thrown away the evil and retained all that was valuable, and would therefore lead them into a conglomerate system made up of Judaism and heathenism, baptized in the name of Christ? Were they surrounded with the deceitful claims of the Nicolaitans, and urged to believe that a Christian cannot sin in doing his own pleasure—having been begotten of the Father, and His seed remaining in him, it would be proper to follow his promptings, as they would be the result of the divine seed, or regeneration? Were there men among them who claimed to be apostles, and who would readily make merchandise of them? Were there false teachers among them, as there had been false prophets before them? The prophets had many a tilt with false teachers who claimed that God was the Author of what they said. And the disciples were troubled with those grievous wolves who rose up to head parties in their own interests. There were foolish and vain talkers whose mouths had to be stopped. They withstood the teaching of the apostles, as *Jannes and Jambres* had withstood Moses, when before the court of Pharaoh. For such contention, men had to be prepared, and many a lesson was given for that purpose.

But false doctrine was not the only temptation that was in the pathway of the early Christians. Persecutions were before them, and for these they must be prepared. When the Savior sent out the twelve and the seventy, He felt that they should be prepared to stand up against the persecutions that awaited them. And Paul, knowing the trials of the Hebrew brethren, tried to arm them for the conflict, so that they might endure to the end. To know these trials, through which they were passing, will greatly assist in the interpretation of those Scriptures.

Section 44.
WHO ARE SPOKEN OF?

Knowledge of these is not as essential as in the other cases, and yet many references will be much more easily understood by having the same question asked and answered as in the previous inquiry. Though less absolutely demanded, the same questions ought to be answered to enable the reader to know the strength and point of the remark. We read many times in the New Testament of Herod, of Herod the king, of Herod the tetrarch. But who these Herods are, or if they are all just one Herod, many readers do not know. Their characters and power should be in the mind of the reader, for without such knowledge the point of many things said will not be apparent. One will be greatly assisted in reading the Gospels and Acts, by knowing the characters that figure in government. So it will be in order to inquire about Pontius Pilate, Felix, Festus, Ananias, Agrippa. When the Master was in Perea, they came and told him that it would be better to depart out of the coast, as Herod would try to put him to death. He answered: "Go and tell that fox," etc. The point of that remark is not seen without a knowledge of the character of this ruler. So it is, all the way through the Scriptures—their meaning will be much more apparent after a careful study of the persons spoken of.

Section 45.

THE CHARACTER OF THE WRITINGS, OR THE KIND OF COMPOSITION.

In the Scriptures we have history, biography, law, prophecy, praise, poetry, words of anger and of exultation. If we were reading any other book, we would not think of using the same rules for the interpretation of those several different kinds of composition. While the historian or the biographer may deal in splendid rhetoric and occasionally embellish with a highly wrought figure of speech, yet we know that it is his aim to present us with a number of facts. And we interpret in light of the work he was trying to accomplish. Generally, however, such writers deal in the plainest words and easiest sentences.

If law is being interpreted, we do not expect to find a single figurative expression. The author has evidently tried to be severely plain and definite. The very purpose of law precludes the thought of anything in the composition but the plainest and most direct form of speech. It has been the intent of him who gave the law to have his will carried out by the people. Hence we expect him to use every precaution to prevent any misunderstanding.

But when we come to condemnation, or exhortation, or any words prompted by mental ecstasy, we naturally look for the overflowing of all the lower grounds of thought and communication.

Poetry, whether found in the Bible or elsewhere, is granted a license of extravagance. It is supposed to have a right to play upon words for their sound. It is the style suited to strong imagination. It will tell the story of the dreamer or of the pathetic lover in language suitable to the mentality that employs it. No one thinks of interpreting the language of the poet as he does that of the essayist. And yet a very large portion of the Bible is in poetry. The simile, the metaphor, the allegory, the hyperbole, furnish gorgeous chariots for the conveyance of the rhythmic mind. All of the Psalms, most of the book of Job, and a very large portion of the prophecies, are in poetry. It is, then, of as much importance to regard the different kinds of composition while reading the Bible, as in reading any other book. The Oriental figure of speech should have as much latitude as the modern rhyme. For instance, in Job 29:16-30:31, when the good man of Uz compared his former, with his present condition, his words are very strong. He shows his honor, as compared with the very low condition of those who then mocked him, in true poetic style. The very occasion seemed to be poetic, and the atmosphere was burdened with hyperbole. There is no danger of being deceived by this, if we are aware of the kind of composition.

Section 46.

WHEN WRITTEN?

At first thought, this is a question of no importance. But when we think again, understanding that by it we will determine under what law or dispensation the writing or speaking was done, it becomes of great importance. If a man should ask what he should do to be saved, during the existence of that law of Moses, everyone would expect an answer that would harmonize with the demands of that law. Its righteousness consisted in doing, perfectly, the things which it required. And if the inquiry was, 'What will it profit a man if he shall do the things which the law demands?' he would be answered by anyone informed in the matter, that he should be blessed in the basket, and in the store, and in his cattle, etc., etc. But no one at all acquainted with the teaching of the New Testament would think of giving these answers to these questions. It is seen, then, that it makes a great difference as to the time that the writing or the speaking was done. No one should, then, go to the Old Institution to learn how a sinner can become a Christian, for the two covenants are radically different in that respect. In *that,* they were saved by the deeds of the law; in *this,* by faith in the Lord Jesus Christ. When the rich young ruler came to the Savior and said, "Good Master, what good thing shall I do, that I may inherit eternal life?" the Master directed him to the practical features of the Law. But when He sent out His disciples to go to the end of the earth and preach the gospel to every creature, He said that "he that believes and is baptized shall be saved, and he that does not believe shall be damned." The difference in these answers is due to the difference in time and the change in covenants that has taken place.

"My Spirit shall not always strive with man," is quoted again and again as if it related to the present hour. Many would no doubt look for it in the New Testament. And yet it was spoken before the flood, of the wicked antediluvians, and concerning the one hundred and twenty years that yet remained before the world should be carried away with a flood. About as apt as this is the quotation generally indulged, *"Yet I loved Jacob, and I hated Esau."* It seems to be supposed that God did actually hate Esau before he was born, and love Jacob at the same time, for no other reason than that He *could.* But those who stop and ask when this was said, are enabled to see that the language was employed by Malachi, the last of the Old Testament writers, when both Jacob and Esau had been dead for twelve hundred years. Hence the language was not spoken concerning these men *when they were infants*, nor when they were come to maturity, but concerning their descendants; and hence it was selected by the apostle Paul to prove that God was no respecter of persons—that He had selected Jacob, because He knew that his people would be superior to the descendants of the older brother. Their violence to Jacob, as Israel came out of Egypt, and God's hatred of them for it, proved that they were an unworthy stock, and that God did well in selecting Jacob, whose descendants were a much better people.

The language of the thief, and of Jesus to the thief, is not understood by many persons, on account of not noticing under what covenant they were yet living.

It should be borne in mind, too, that time brings a change of circumstances, and that with such a change customs, thoughts, and feelings change also. Hence, with such difference, all prudential matters will correspondingly differ. While faith and obedience will ever remain the same, there are things which are neither right nor wrong in themselves, and are of no interest, except as they are wise or unwise methods of carrying forward the will and work of the Lord. They are merely the circumstantial or local details, and would not be proposed beyond the conditions that made them valuable.

Section 47.
THE PLACE OF WRITING OR SPEAKING.

If we could always know the surroundings, we would know very much of the intention of the speaker. An illustration will be clearer to the mind of the reader when he can be made to see the things referred to by the writer or speaker. And to have that knowledge, sometimes, it is necessary to know where the author was at the time of speaking. When Jeremiah stands in the gate of Jerusalem and preaches to that people, there is peculiar significance in the place in which he was at the time of the address. If King Uzziah or Azariah was ordered out of the temple, one must know why he was not at liberty to remain, and where he was, that he was profaning the house of God. Much of the life of the Savior is not understood because the reader does not know where He and His disciples were at the time. There is a careless way of reading the Scriptures that marks nothing, and knows nothing of the passing events. If the reader of the Gospels would read each of the evangelists, so as to get the order of the events of the Savior's life, he would then know the things which preceded and the language which he is investigating. One of these writers has not told all the occurrences, but the others have filled out the account, and, from the whole story, the truth of any particular part of it can be better understood. Perhaps the meaning of the sixteenth chapter of Matthew, verses 13-19, would not have been in doubt if the people knew where they were at the time that Jesus said, "Upon this rock I will build my church." If we could see the disciples with their Lord in the coasts of Caesarea Philippi, and, therefore, looking into that city, we could easily see the illustration of the Master. There was a city built upon the rock, and Jesus intended to build His church on a foundation just as solid as that. And when He proposed to give the keys into the hands of Peter, He intended to make him a gatekeeper—give to him a post of honor, such as was probably held by someone plainly in sight. With this in mind, no one would think of Peter being the rock on which the city was to be built. How a gate-keeper might serve in the capacity of a rock foundation on which the city itself should rest, would never be seen by any one.

When Jesus gave His disciples the figure of the vine (John 15), it should be borne in mind that they had been in Jerusalem, and that they had just gone out into the Mount of Olives; and hence, at the time of giving this figure, they were on the hillside east of the city, and were looking down at those who were raking together the withered and dismembered branches, and burning them in the night when they would not be liable to set fire to anything else; or that they were then passing through the midst of such scenes on their *way out of the city*. In either case the illustration becomes very forceful. There was the vine, the keeper, the pruner, the withered branches beings raked into heaps and burned, and there were also the living vines which would likely bear much fruit, being purged for their good.

It is the same when the Lord gave His disciples the allegory of the good shepherd. It was at the "feast of dedication, and it was winter." During the winter season the shepherd put the flock into the fold at night, and took it out in the morning. Hence He presents Himself in the light of a true shepherd, and also the door of the sheep. These have a common thought, and were offered to make them understand their relation to Him, and His care for them. If they would accept Him as their teacher and guide, they should find food and protection at all times, for He loved them to the point that He would even lay down his life for them.

CHAPTER VII:
RULES FOR THE INTERPRETATION OF WORDS AND SENTENCES.

Section 48.
RULES FOR THE INTERPRETATION OF SENTENCES.

It seems out of place that we should consider the question of sentences before that of words, for it is certain that if we don't know the meaning of the words used in the construction of the sentence, it will be impossible for us to know what the sentence means. And yet, it is taken for granted that enough of the meaning of the words will be in the mind to assist very greatly in the basic knowledge, at least, of the purpose and thought of the sentence. And then, from that knowledge, it will be comparatively easy to return and examine each word in detail as to its particular place and purpose in that sentence.

Rule 1. *Always interpret according to the known purpose of the author.*—But this, of course, presupposes that the reader can know, at the time of the investigation, what that purpose was. This may not be perfectly understood. Indeed, the sentence under consideration may be an essential feature of the investigation. Still, it is sometimes the case that an author's purpose has been stated, either directly or indirectly. If this knowledge is in the possession of the exegete at the time of such investigation, then the sentence under consideration must be interpreted in the light of that purpose. This is one of the weaknesses of many commentaries. The critic has commented on single verses. He has known nothing of the general purpose of the author, and therefore many times applies the language to topics not at all in the mind of the writer. This is a wrong that we would not tolerate in the use of any other book. It would be as well to take a description of some part of Asia and apply it to the United States, as to employ the language of any of the writers of the Scriptures to a subject other than that which was in his mind at the time when the words and sentences under consideration were employed. We would, in that way, compel the writer to say just the things which he did not intend to say. The work of the exegete is to bring out the meaning of the writing, which must be the meaning the author intended to put into it.

In the interpretation of law, this rule is of very great value. If there are sections or passages in the law, the meaning of which are doubtful, then recourse may be had by going to the intent of the legislators who made it. Sometimes it happens that in the framing of the platform of a political party, a doubt arises as to the meaning that ought to be given to a particular resolution. If the men can be found who framed the resolution, and any reasonable means furnished by which to know in what sense the convention understood it, then their understanding of the resolution must interpret the passage in doubt.

We ought to treat the Bible with as much respect as we do the words of men. Hence the greatest possible care should be taken that every writer in the book divine should be made to mean just what he wished to be understood to say. It is not *what we can compel the Bible to say*, that we are to seek, but *what it was employed to say*, what the writer meant when he said what he did.

It is a kind of common rule to make out of the temptation or the transfiguration of the Savior whatever the genius of the interpreter is competent to invent, and not what the writers themselves meant by what they said. No man can read the account of the temptation of the Savior without reaching the conclusion that the writers were trying to tell just what, in their opinion, really occurred; and so it is with the transfiguration. Now, if anyone wants to dissent from the opinions of these men, that is another question; but as an exegete, his work is done when he has found that meaning which the author intended to convey. Hence this general purpose of the writer having been first obtained, no interpretation should follow that is not in perfect accord with it.

There is an apparent exception to the rule which we have just considered. An author frequently makes an incidental remark. It may or it may not be essential to his argument or the record which he is making. When such statement or remark has been made, it has all the force that any other affirmation could have, coming from that writer. A fact may be referred to by way of illustration, and this might be our only means of knowing of the existence of that fact, and yet that reference will be sufficient to establish the existence of it. We might not know that the salt of Palestine could lose its savor but for the remark made by the Savior, *"If the salt have lost its savor."* His purpose in employing the illustration was to show that the disciples should be the means of purifying and saving the world, but the illustration brings out a fact incidentally. Paul says, "As *Jannes and Jambres withstood Moses,"* and we learn that these were the names of two of the magicians with whom he and Aaron had to contend. Paul was called *Mercury* or *Hermes,* because he was the chief speaker. From this we would learn that Mercury was a god of eloquence, at least as compared with Jupiter (Zeus), who was supposed to be represented by the less talkative Barnabas. The chief captain or *chiliarch* at Jerusalem asked Paul if he were a Roman citizen, and when he said he was, the captain remarked that he had purchased that honor with a great sum of money, to which Paul replied that he was born free. While this is merely incidental, still it tells its own story respecting Roman citizenship at that time.

It is in this way that many of the ancient customs have come to be known at the present time. We may not know just what their beds were like, but, when Jesus commands a man, "Take up your bed and walk," we learn something about it. When the Master healed the blind man at Bethsaida, and by the first application he was made to see a little, and said, "I see men as trees walking," it reveals the fact that the man had seen trees before, and hence had not been born blind. The question of Nathaniel, "Can any good thing come out of Nazareth?" assures us that the place was not held in very high esteem. That Jesus came to a fig tree, "if haply he might find figs," shows that figs might be found at that season of the year, for He knew the country and the time of the ripening of the fruits. It was not the purpose of the writer to enlighten us on the subject of figs, and yet we do gain just that much in an incidental way. Paul writes to the brethren at Rome and also at Colossae, and to show that they were so completely separated from sin that they could not think of returning again to its practice, says that they had been buried with Christ in baptism (Rom. 6:3-4; Col. 2:12). He was not writing on the manner and action of baptism; but, from the illustration, we learn that when they were baptized they were buried.

But in all this there is nothing that causes the mind to part company with the author, or to cause the interpreter to fail in any way to follow the author into all the purposes of writing, or to interpret anything contrary to that intent.

Section 49.
HOW MAY WE KNOW THE PURPOSE OF THE AUTHOR?

Rule 1. *The speaker or writer sometimes states just what he wanted to accomplish by speaking.*—If we were in doubt as to the purpose of the two parables beginning the eighteenth chapter of Luke, we would only have to turn and read again the first verse, which declares that the Lord spoke these for the purpose of teaching "that men ought to always pray and not to faint." If we did not know the purpose of the three parables of the fifteenth chapter of Luke, the first and second verses would suffice, for we are there informed that it was to answer those who objected to Him because He received sinners and ate with them. He gave a parable respecting the distribution of pounds when he was at Jericho, not simply for the lesson of responsibility and judgment, but because they were nigh to Jerusalem, and many of them were thinking that when He should arrive there the kingdom would be established. The parable was first that they might not be deceived in that very important matter. It is clear that Isaiah writes concerning Judah and Jerusalem. Hence, while he utters words of warning and takes up burdens for the kingdoms of the earth, he does so because of their connection with the main subject in hand. This we learn from the direct statement of the prophet himself (1:1-2). Luke states to the most excellent Theophilus the exact purpose had in mind when he began to write (Luke 1:1-4). The apostle John tells us his purpose in writing the book known by his name (20:30-31). And Paul is quite as explicit in the announcement of his topic when he begins his letter to "the saints that are in Rome" (1:16-17).

But the intention of the writer is not always so easily known. Many times we are left to examine the contents of all the sections in the book in order that we may know certainly just what the writer meant to accomplish by the writing.

If the language under consideration was spoken, not written, then we may have to ask those who heard the speech what they understood by it. If there was any particular meaning in the *manner of pronunciation,* or *in the tone of the voice,* those who heard the speech may be interrogated with propriety. When Micaiah was called forth to tell Ahab whether he should go up against Ramoth in Gilead, the prophet said, "Go, and prosper" (1 Kings 22:15, 16). And for all we could tell, from this distance, he meant for him to go, and to feel assured that his campaign would be successful. But Ahab, who heard him, knew from the manner in which he spoke that he did not mean it, and asked him to tell him nothing but the truth. Then the prophet told him just what would come of the campaign. Similarly, on the day of Pentecost, when the multitude asked what they should do, we might be in doubt as to the meaning of the question. 'Do about what?' might be queried. But Peter, standing by, understood the meaning of the language, and in the answer to their inquiry gives us the meaning contained in their words. No one doubts that he answered the question which he understood them to ask. Hence, in his answer, we get the purpose of their inquiry (Acts 2:37-38).

Rule 2. *Carefully consider the immediate context.* The purpose of this is to ascertain the immediate purpose of the author. It is not enough to know the main object in view, for there are a great variety of ways by which this end might be attained. We might know, therefore, what particular argument was offered, or what fact was being stated that might bear on the main subject. When we have the statement on each side of the doubtful sentence, we could almost supply the sentence if it were blotted out. We fill ellipses with *words,* and we could fill them with *sentences,* with only a little more difficulty. Certainly, then, a knowledge of the context will greatly assist in the exegesis of any doubtful passage.

But it doesn't seem to be known that there is also *a context of conduct.* What was done and said at the time may throw much light on the meaning of the words in question. Pilate said to Jesus, "*What is truth?*" and then arose and went out. He gives the Master no time to answer the question; and his actions show that he did not expect any answer to what he had said. The *conduct* of this ruler precludes us from considering him an inquirer after truth, but he appears a mere caviler, and his query has no more in it than "Humph! What do you know about truth? The wisest philosophers of the earth are not agreed as to a standard by which it is to be measured; therefore you have presented a subject that you know nothing about." This, too, will show in what estimation Pilate, at that time, regarded the Savior. He thought him to be a harmless crank—a man of no glaring faults that would render him worthy of death, but quite out of place when trying to lead the people into new truth which the world at that time did not know.

Many times, in the study of the gospels, we would be greatly assisted in the interpretation of difficult passages if we knew what was done at the time that the sentence in question was employed. Jesus said to Peter and Andrew, and to James and John, "Follow me, and I will make you fishers of men." This has peculiar significance to us when we know of the miracle which had been wrought. Also in the twenty-first chapter of John, when the Master said, "Do you love me more than these?" we should know what had been done. To get the meaning, we must keep in view the toil of the night, and their failure to catch anything. Christ gave them abundance of fish, and then asks to know where their affections are: for the fishing of the former days, or the following of Jesus, which they claimed to have left all to do. Sometimes the gospel writer in the New Testament has not recorded the occurrences at the time; and, in that case, it is wise to inquire of the others for the needed facts in the case.

Rule 3. *The Bible, being the truth of God, must harmonize with itself.*—Sometimes the doctrine is proposed, and then the proofs and counter-proofs are sought for; and if the proofs are more numerous than the counterproofs, the doctrine is regarded as being sustained. But in that case there are some counter-proofs that must be thrown aside as uninspired statements. If they had been inspired, they would have been on the other side of the question. Being uninspired, they are false, for they claim inspiration as their source. Infidelity feeds and fattens on this kind of interpretation. Let it be remembered that no doctrine can be true if it is opposed to any clear statement of the word of God. Perhaps these differences of proof and counter-proof have been extorted from the Bible, by applying its statements to subjects that were not before the minds of the writers; and therefore the whole war has been conducted in the absence of any teaching of the Scriptures whatever. But if the exegetes had been taught that the word of God harmonizes with itself, and must never be so interpreted as to bring its statements into collision, this work of fighting Scripture with Scripture would have been discontinued long ago.

But the unbeliever says, "You are not qualified to interpret the Bible, for you start out with an assumption that it is of God, whereas *it may not be from that source.*" In answer to this, we say that we do not start out as exegetes of this kind till the primary question of authorship has been fixed. That should, indeed, be the first purpose of investigation—*is this the book which God has given?* But if that question be answered in the affirmative, after a fair examination, then our rule applies.

We might turn aside, however, long enough to say that the unbeliever is the last man that ought to complain, for all his examinations are for the purpose of *finding,* or *creating,* some flaw in this divine communication. He starts, too, generally, without any previous consideration of its contents. We say then, 'Examine first the claims of the Bible in respect to authorship. When the mind is at rest on that question, then proceed with the rules we have arranged, as they are adopted for consideration of the contents of all other books.'

Rule 4. *Light may be thrown upon, a doubtful or difficult passage by comparing it with other statements of the author on the same subject.*—In several epistles of Paul, he dwells more or less on the same subject. In some of these he has treated the subject fully; in some of them he has merely referred to it. Now, from a slight reference, the reader may not be able to gather the meaning of the writer; but by turning to where he has treated the same subject more at length, the difficult passage will be fully explained. In the Ephesian and Galatian letters he shows that the law given by Moses was no longer a rule for them; that it had been taken out of the way and nailed to the cross; that it had served as a partition wall to separate Jew and Gentile, but that when Christ was put to death on the cross, that partition wall was broken down, so that they might be united in one body. And while that language could not be misunderstood by those for whom it was directly intended, at that time, it is by some doubted whether Paul has in his mind some particular portion of the law, or all of it. But in the Colossian letter (2:14-18), and in the second letter to the Corinthians (3:6-14), where he has written more fully on that particular point, he leaves no doubt as to his views on that subject. If we would understand him perfectly concerning our duty toward those who are not fully instructed in the gospel, it would be well to compare 1 Corinthians 8:1-13 with Romans 14: So it is with the officers in the Church by the appointment of the apostles. If we expect a complete and perfect statement in any one passage on that subject, we shall be disappointed; but if we will gather up all that we find from the same writer, we can understand his view on the subject.

Rule 5. *Help may be had in the interpretation of sentences by examining the statements of other writers on the same subject, who are of equal authority.*—If we say that all the apostles were inspired, then all that they have all said concerning any one thing must be true. If we will know certainly all that the Savior said in the great Commission, it will be well for us to read what all the writers have said about it. Matthew, Mark, and Luke have spoken, at any rate, purposely in the matter. They have not used the same terms in making their several records. But we may be sure that they mean the same thing. At the time when they wrote, their brief statements on that subject were ample; and now, if we will admit all that all have said, we shall evidently get the entire commission of the Master to the twelve. So when we ask

Paul as to his views concerning salvation in Christ without the deeds of the law, it is in order for us to also ask James as to the need of the obedience of faith. For the parties for whom they wrote, there was no need of a more complete statement; and to us there will be perfect instruction when we have the two compared. 1 Pet. 2:13-15 will he better understood if read in conjunction with Rom. 13:1-7. They both treat of our duty towards civil government; and by the comparison we get the sum of wisdom on that subject.

Rule 6. *The use of common sense respecting the things which we know, of ourselves.*—This takes for granted that there is knowledge in men—that, after all, it may be said that we do know some things. We have consciousness of being, of thinking and willing, and of being able to act according to our wills. Any theology that denies the power to do any of these things is rejected at once, and will recommit the matter to the exegete, assuring him that, as it is impossible for God to lie, he has made a mistake in the interpretation of God's book. The theory that no man can, of himself, think a good thought or perform a good deed, has made all thinking men either doubt the Bible or the interpretation that sustains that theology. Common sense says: "I know the theory is not true, hence I know if the Bible supports it, that God is not the Author of it."

Caution in the use of this rule.—While there are many things which we can know, whether we have ever seen a Bible or not, we must be careful that we do not array our whims against the word of God. There are things that we know, and there are things which we do not know. We are not at liberty to assert an opinion as a standard. It must amount to absolute knowledge. Then, so far as it exists, we can use it as facts gained in any other way.

Rule 7. *That which, is figurative, must be interpreted according to the laws that govern figurative speech.*—Literal language is not to be interpreted by figures, but figures are to be interpreted by that which is literal. Almost any theory can be supported by the Scriptures, if the exegete shall be at liberty to assume his positions and catch the sound of words from highly wrought figures, and compel them to do service as didactic agents. In this way men have sustained all the doctrines that genius could originate. David declares that he is a worm, and not man; Job declares that man lies down, and rises not till the heavens are no more. In this way the Jews made the Savior say that the temple which had been so long in construction, if it were destroyed, He would rebuild it in three days. They knew better, but they could make the play on His words, and that answered their purpose. It would seem now that men feel that they are at liberty to turn the Scriptures into a curiosity shop, where men of cunning may show their skill in the maintenance of strange doctrines, in disregard of all the rules by which other books are interpreted.

Section 50.
RULES BY WHICH THE MEANING OF WORDS SHALL BE ASCERTAINED.

Rule 1. *All words are to be understood in their literal sense, unless the evident meaning of the context forbids.*—Figures are the exception, literal language the rule; hence we are not to regard anything as figurative until we feel compelled to do so by the evident meaning of the passage. And even here, great caution should be observed. We are very apt to regard contexts as teaching some theory which we have in our minds. And having so determined, anything to the contrary will be regarded as a mistaken interpretation; hence, if the literal meaning of the words shall be found to oppose our speculations, we are ready to give to the words in question some figurative importance that will better agree with our preconceived opinions. Let us be sure that the meaning of the author has demanded that the language be regarded in a figurative sense, and that it is not our theory which has made the necessity.

Rule 2. *Commands generally, and ordinances always, are to be understood in a literal sense.*—Commands are rarely issued in figurative language. The general who would issue orders in figurative language would certainly be misunderstood many times. This would defeat his aim. Hence, if he ever delivers an order in language that is not plainly literal, he will do so with the greatest precaution, assuring himself first, that it will be impossible for his words to be misinterpreted.

The Savior does say, "Let your light so shine," etc., which is an order in a figurative use of words. But in that case there is no probability of any one failing to catch the exact thought. He also said to Nicodemus, that a man "must be born again;" but He does not leave any room for doubt as to the meaning of the words employed. For a man to be born of water and of the Spirit would never be mistaken by such a man as this ruler of the Jews.

But at all times, in giving a law with ordinances, nothing but the plainest use of words is to be expected.

Rule 3. *The literal meaning of a word is that meaning which is given it by those to whom it as addressed.*—It is always to be supposed that when an author has written to a people, knowing in what sense they would certainly understand his words, he has had the good sense to use the words in that signification. Or if, at any time, he has seen proper to use the words in a better sense than that in which the people did, he has given their meaning in some other way. In writing an account of the Savior's life, His words are sometimes employed in a sense that was not common to the people. But the apostles have immediately given the meaning that the words have in that place. If He said, "Destroy this temple, and in three days I will raise it up again," the writer says He referred to the temple of His body. Or again, when He said if anyone would come to Him and believe in Him, out of his belly should flow rivers of water, to prevent any misapplication of the language, the writer says that He said it of the Holy Spirit, that should be given to His disciples after He should be glorified.

How shall we know what the words meant or in what sense the People understood them?—This may be known by the use made of the word by the writer. He probably employs the word several times in the communication, and in one of these he will have so surrounded it that its meaning is clear. Again, it may be determined by other writers who have lived at the same time and among the same people. Indeed, it may be that one of the people to whom the language was addressed has indicated the meaning they gave to it. If so, his use of the word will determine the meaning beyond any question. But if the writer has not made any use of the word that will clearly designate its meaning, and if no one of the people of that age has employed the word in question, and especially from among that people, then we are bound up to the classic use of the word—for the classic use of a word may be assumed to be its import, unless, because of the known education of the people to whom it was employed there should be some good reason for departing from that signification. If good dictionaries can be had, they should be regarded as of great value. But the classics are of greater authority, for they are the source from which the lexicographers have gathered their meanings.

Rule 4. *The Scriptures are supposed to give to some words meanings which they do not have in the classics, and therefore the Bible becomes a dictionary of itself.*—This statement is entirely too broad, and yet it is proper that the scriptural use of a word should be examined. For instance, the word 'elder' occurs several times, with an official importance. But what office is intended by the word must be learned by the use of the word. By reference to 1 Pet. 5:1-2; Acts 20:17-28; Titus 3:5-6; 1 Tim. 3:1-8, 5:17, we discover that the office of bishop or overseer is intended, when the word 'elder' occurs as indicative of office.

But it has not been found that any word of the Scriptures has been used in a sense contrary to the classic use. In every case, where you have a word that needs to be defined by the nomenclature of the Bible, you have a word that may be employed differently without violation of any authority. Nor does it follow from searching for the scriptural use of a word, that it is always to be understood in the same sense—in any case, in which more than one meaning is possible to the word. The word 'tempt,' many times, occurs in the sense of induce to do wrong, but generally it has the meaning of to *try,* or *prove.* Thus it is said that God tempted Abraham, and yet an inspired apostle says that "God cannot be tempted by evil, neither does he tempt any man." Unless we shall allow the two meanings of the word in the Bible, as elsewhere, we are confronted with a contradiction in the word of the Lord. But it is sometimes the case that an author has a favorite expression, and his use of it differs from that which is generally made of it. Phrases in the Bible are somewhat peculiar to the men who use them. A favorite expression of Isaiah was "rush and palm branch." When we have become acquainted with him and his writings, his meaning is very plain. It is a metaphor that stands for all the people. If they were to be carried away *"rush and palm branch,"* then they were all to be taken. He uses head and tail for the same purpose. "Thou hast said," for an affirmation, is of the same kind. Almost every people will be found to use words and phrases in this way.

Rule 5. Words of definite action can have but one meaning.—That is, they can have but one meaning that relates to action. If they could have more than one meaning in this respect, they would not be words of definite action. Jump, walk, run, sit, chop, clip, sprinkle, pour, shoot, hang, strike, etc., are definite, and therefore but one meaning is possible to any one of them. Hence, when action is ordered by any one of them, it cannot be obeyed by doing any other thing than that which is the meaning of the word employed. As to the result, or con-sequence, however, it is not so. To shoot may mean to kill, but it may mean to wound. To hang may differ in results, sometimes having one effect and sometimes another. The same is true with all the other words.

Rule 6. The writer's explanation is the best definition that can be found.—He is supposed to know, better than anyone else, just what meaning he wished to put into the word. Hence if he has told us in words that admit of no doubt, that is the end of all query in the matter. *Immanuel* means 'God with us.' *Rabbi* means 'master,' or 'teacher.' Ordinarily, *Rabbi* meant great, but in this instance it means master; and this, too, is the meaning which is in the word in all its New Tes-tament use. When Paul represents the Savior as having opened for us a new and living way into the Holiest of all, he means, 'by His death it was accomplished through the *vail of His flesh.*' But as this will oc-cur again in the rules by which figurative language is to be under-stood, we leave it for that place.

Rule 7. *The proper definition of a word may be used in the place of the word.*—If the trial be made in this way, and the definition is wrong, the sense of the passage will be so destroyed as to make it apparent. It need only to be stated that the true meaning of a word will give the same sense that the word would give; hence, to remove the word and replace it with the definition is easily done, and is a valuable method.

Rule 8. *By antithesis.*—Many times two positions are matched one against the other. The best illustration known to me is found in the second letter to the Corinthians (3:6-14). Paul here changes the terms several times on both sides; but by this rule we trace his meaning without any possibility of being mistaken. In his two double allegories (Gal. 4:22-31, and Rom. 11:16-26), these opposites serve a valuable end. By proper attention to them, neither one can be lost sight of, nor be misunderstood. But as this will be treated as a figure of speech, we dismiss it from further consideration at present.

Rule 9. *By the general and special scope.*—By the general scope, we mean the general range of mental vision, or the main purpose in the mind of the writer. By the special scope, we mean any sub-purpose having reference to any particular part of the general discussion. To illustrate: Paul wished to make it clear to the saints that were in Rome, that the gospel was the only system by which men could reasonably hope for salvation. He embraces this in his thesis (1:16-17). But to find that this proposition was true, it was necessary to show that men are lost. There could not be a system of salvation if there was nothing to save; hence he starts out to show that all men are lost. This again has to be divided, that he may approach the subject in a way that would not give offense. So he shows that the Gentiles were sinners. But in doing this, it was still necessary to divide the subject in hand and show (1) that they were responsible in that they once knew God; that they could know of God by his works in nature; and that in history, or in His dealings with the children of men He had revealed His wrath against all ungodliness. (2) That they began to fall by the neglect of their devotions, and continued by becoming vain or filthy in their imaginations; by changing God into the likeness of men, and four-footed beasts and creeping things; that the stages of their fall were: leaving God, becoming corrupt in themselves, and then becoming immoral towards men, or evil affected towards men. A second subdivision is to show that the Jews were in no better condition than the Gentiles; hence that they were also in need of salvation. This, again, is subdivided into two different lines of argument: their history, or an examination of the facts in the case, and also the statements of their own Scriptures. But, having gained the first point in the argument, he next proceeds to show that they could not save themselves. That accomplished, he must show them that the gospel could do what could not be accomplished in any other way.

But now there are new lines of thought that must needs be investigated, such as the extent and results of this salvation, and whether there has been any injustice on the part of God in arranging this plan of saving men. Also, when man has been redeemed from a state of sin, he must needs be placed under some system by which he will be kept from sin, and made to be the kind of man that he ought to be. To develop the man, should he be placed under the law that Moses gave, or will the gospel of Christ furnish him with those directions and helps which he most needs? And even then it was left to know if the redemption in Christ was full and complete, or if it saved the spirit and left the body to rot in the grave. In this way Paul conducts the argument, following each proposition with another which connected with it.

Having the main purpose of this letter in the mind, and the particular purpose in view in the section from which the words come, the interpretation is easy and safe. Instead of this safe rule of interpretation, there has ever been a tendency to ignore the topic under discussion, and find first what the word under some circumstances might be made to mean, and to conclude that such must be its meaning in the passage in question. Though no one interprets any other book in that way, yet there seems to be a willingness to compel the Bible to submit to such treatment.

Rule 10. *Etymological construction will many times tell the meaning of the word.*—Nearly all the names of the ancients had meanings, and, when they are constructed of more than one syllable, the meanings of the several syllables will give the meaning of the whole word or name. *Beersheba,* from *beer* (wells), and *sebiah* (seven), would be seven wells; *Bethel,* house of God—these are specimens of the meanings that attached to the names of places. If we analyze our English words, we find that they were made of patchwork, and came into being with the meaning of the added patches. It should be confessed, however, that the rule does not always work, as some words have changed their meanings entirely since they were first made.

Rule 11. *The meaning of a word is frequently known by the words used in the construction with it.*—In this way we could first determine what part of speech it was. We could tell whether it indicated action or transition. If a verb is used at any time in any unusual sense, or a preposition, the words around it will reveal the fact. This is especially true when we know the manner of the writer.

Rule 12. *We may have sometimes to study the history of a word in order to get its meaning at any particular time.*—It has occurred, in the history of some words, that they have changed their meanings a number of times. Hence, if we are asked what such a word means, we must answer according to the time and place of its use. 'Let' once meant to hinder; 'prevent' once meant to come before (pre-event).

On this subject Mr. Terry, in his work on Biblical Hermeneutics, says:

> *Words, being the conventional signs and representatives of ideas, are changeable in both form and meaning by reason of the changes constantly taking place in human society. In process of time the same word will be applied to a variety of uses, and come to have a variety of meanings. Thus, the name **board**, another form of the word **broad**, was originally applied to a piece of timber, hewed or sawed, so as to form a wide, thin plank. It was also applied to a table on which food was placed, and it became common to speak of gathering around the festive **board**. By a similar association, the word was also applied to a body of men who were wont to gather*

around a table to transact business, and hence we have board of trustees, board of commissioners. The word is also used for the deck of a vessel; hence the terms **on board**, **overboard**, *and some other less common nautical expressions. Thus it often happens that the original meaning of a word falls into disuse and is forgotten, while later meanings become current, and find a multitude or variety of applications. But, while a single word may thus come to have many meanings, it also happens that a number of different words are used to designate the same, or nearly the same, thing.*

All living languages are subject to such changes as those which have just been mentioned. Hence the necessity of carefully attending to the question of history when the meaning of a word is under consideration.

Rule 13. *Illustrations or parables may give the peculiar sense in which a word is to be understood in the Scriptures.*—The young lawyer conceded that to love God and to love one's neighbor were the great commandments of the law. But, to excuse himself, he was anxious to avoid knowing who was his neighbor. This, the Savior brought out by the parable of the Good Samaritan, so that the man himself assented that to do kindness was to be neighborly. And, like the Samaritan, race prejudice was to be forgotten in the face of need, and human sympathy was to have its rightful control.

Rule 14. *In defining definitions, nothing but primary meanings are to be used.*—I will illustrate by the introduction of a few of the most common words:

To eat, means literally to *chew and swallow.* Hence, if this word shall be translated into any other language, the word containing that thought must be used, and no other. Then it may be translated again from that into a third, if the same precaution be used, and no change occur. But let us see what will become of the word in case we should be permitted to use secondary words in translating or defining. *To eat* means secondarily to *corrode,* to *consume,* to *enjoy,* to *rub* or *fret,* to *wear away by degrees,* to *prey upon,* to *impair. To consume* means to *waste away slowly,* to *be exhausted,* to *squander.* Now, as *to eat* means *to consume,* and fire consumes, or *to burn* is *to consume,* therefore to eat and to burn are the same thing! Yet everyone knows *that* it is not true!

To walk is to move slowly on the feet in such a way as to permit the heels to touch the ground. But secondarily the word means *to appear as a spectre,* to *act* on any occasion, to *be in, motion,* as a clamorous tongue—"their tongue walks through the land"—to *live, act, behave.* Men who have no feet can live and walk with God, that is, they can worship and obey God. Now you can see in this way we can prove that to walk does not mean any action, either on the feet or any other way, but simply to worship.

To shoot means to discharge with force, to germinate, to sprout, to begin to vegetate, as a plant or its seed. As a result, *to shoot* means *to kill;* but to hang means to kill, therefore a man may be shot by being hung! But who believes such nonsense?

In this way we might continue till we should have examined every word of definite action, and in each case we will find that very ordinary skill would be equal to the removal of the meaning of any word in English, or in any other language. Unless this rule is observed, there is no safety in translating from one language into another, or in defining definition in any language.

The story is told of a Welsh minister who preached for two churches, one a Welsh speaking and the other an English speaking people. Someone asked him how he supplied sermons in both languages. He said he took the Bishop's sermons and translated them into Welsh, and read them to his flock. "But," said the querist, "how then do you supply the other congregation?" "Oh," said the ingenious divine, "I translate them back into English, and the Bishop himself would not recognize them by that time." If this free translation stopped with the sermons of men it would be a small matter, but the Bible is treated in the same way.

CHAPTER VIII:
FIGURATIVE LANGUAGE.

We have already seen that much of the Scriptures was written in language that was highly figurative; that its poetry and prophecy, and very much of its prose, contain the loftiest of Oriental hyperbole. It behooves us, then, to acquaint ourselves with the rules governing this kind of speech. We know that if we shall interpret literal language as if it were figurative, or figurative as if it were literal, we will certainly miss the meaning.

Section 51.
HOW CAN WE KNOW FIGURATIVE LANGUAGE?

Rule 1. The sense of the context will indicate it.—As before said, nothing should be regarded as figurative unless such a demand is made by the meaning of the immediate context, or by the evident meaning of the passage as a whole.

Rule 2. A word or sentence is figurative when the literal meaning involves an impossibility.—In Jer. 1:18 it is said:

> *For, behold, I have made you this day a defensed city,*
> *and an iron pillar, and brazen walls against the whole*
> *land*

Literally, we know that such was not the fact. God had made this man to resemble these things in some respects: he should be strong and immovable like them, hence the comparison.

> *The Lord is my rock, and my fortress, and my deliverer;*
> *my God, my strong rock, in him will I trust; my shield,*
> *and the horn of my salvation, my high tower. (Psa.*
> *18:2).*

Literally, it is impossible for God to be a rock, a tower, or a horn. It is evident to everyone, at first sight, that the author did not expect to be understood as indicating such a thing as that God was a literal rock, etc.

Leave the dead to bury their own dead. (Matt. 8:22).

Those who were literally dead could not have buried any one. Hence we are bound to regard the dead in this phrase as not literally dead.

And the stars of the heaven fell to the earth, as a fig tree casts her unripe figs, when she is shaken by a great wind. (Rev. 6:13).

Of course John did not see the literal stars fall to the earth. There are millions of these bodies, most of which are many times the size of the earth.

This is my body; . . . this is my blood (Matt. 26:26-28).

It was a literal impossibility. Metaphorically it was true, but literally it was not true.

Great caution must be used in the application of this rule; otherwise we will have all the ignorance of self-constituted critics arrayed against the statements of the word of God. We must pause long enough to know that impossibilities are really confronting us before we make the demand that the passage shall be regarded as figurative.

Rule 3. The language of Scripture may be regarded as figurative, if the literal interpretation will cause one passage to contradict another.—That is, if we have two passages, and the literal interpretation of both makes one to contradict the other, we are at liberty to regard the language of one, at least, as figurative. There is one possible exception. We have some words that are used in more than one meaning. Hence the word in one place may have one meaning, and in another it may depart from that thought.

The fool and the brutish together perish. (Psa. 49:10).

For, behold, they that are far from you shall perish. (Psa. 73:27).

All the wicked will he destroy. (Psa. 145:20).

Not only do the wicked perish, but the righteous also.

There is a righteous man that perishes in his righteousness. (Eccl, 7:15).

The righteous perishes, and no man lays it to heart. (Isa. 57:1).

The godly man is perished out of the earth. (Micah 7:2).

But it is easy to have all this contradicted by using a literal interpretation in each case.

For as in Adam all die, so also in Christ shall all be made alive. (1 Cor. 15:22).

The Lord knows how to deliver the godly out of temptation, and to keep the unrighteous under punishment to the day of judgment. (2 Pet. 2:9).

Not only will God reserve the wicked as well as the righteous in the intermediate state, but He will send the one away into everlasting life and the other into everlasting punishment. See Matt. 25:46.

Jesus said to her, I am the resurrection and the life: he that believes in me, though he dies, yet he shall live: and whoever lives and believes in me shall never die. (John 11:25-26).

Take all these passages in a literal sense, and contradiction is inevitable.

It would be easy to prove, in this way, that the dead are unconscious, that they know not anything, and just as easy to show that living men were in the same condition. Indeed, we can find that the two hundred men who followed Absalom, who were the statesmen and counselors of David, "knew not anything." In this way we can make the word of God contradict itself, and say what we all know to be false. Let no one say that this is the fault of the Bible, for the same thing can be done with any other book. The trouble that is usually experienced in these contradictions is deciding which text is to be understood figuratively. This, however, will be explained when we come to give the rules for the interpretation of figurative language.

Rule 4. When the Scriptures are made to demand actions that are wrong or forbid those that are good, they are supposed to be figurative.

> *And if your hand or your foot causes you to stumble, cut*
> *it off, and cast it from you: it is good for you to enter in-*
> *to life maimed or halt, rather than having two hands or*
> *two feet to be cast into the eternal fire. And if your eye*
> *causes you to stumble, pluck it out, and cast it from you:*
> *it is good for you to enter into life with one eye, rather*
> *than, having two eyes, to be cast into the hell of fire.*
> *(Matt. 18:8, 9).*

Perhaps a few have understood this to direct actual physical prun-
ing, but it is sufficient to say that ninety-nine out of every hundred, at
least, have understood it to be figurative. Indeed, it is not right for a
man to dissect himself in any such a manner. Hence the language is
figurative.

> *If any man comes to me, and does not hate his own fa-*
> *ther, and mother, and wife, and children, and brethren,*
> *and sisters, yes, and his own life also, he cannot be my*
> *disciple. (Luke 14:26).*

Except those who have wished to find something in the Bible that
is repugnant to all our knowledge of right and wrong, none have regarded this as literal speech. The command to honor father and mother would be violated directly, by the authority of the Savior, in de-
manding a literal interpretation.

> *And you shall say to them, 'Thus says the Lord of hosts,*
> *the God of Israel: drink, and be drunken and spew, and*
> *fall and rise no more, because of the sword which I will*
> *send among you.' And it shall be, if they refuse to take*
> *the cup from your hand to drink, then shall you say to*
> *them, 'Thus says the Lord of hosts: You shall surely*
> *drink.' (Jer. 25:27-28).*

We cannot think of anything being commanded by the devil that
would be worse than what a literal interpretation would make Jehovah
require of His own people. But when we come to know that God was
using their own conduct as a symbol of the destruction that was coming upon them because of these very crimes, and that He is presenting

their faults before their minds by the strongest use of irony, the case becomes very different.

Rule 5. When it is said to be figurative.—The author would know whether the language was figurative or not: and hence, if he says it is, we have nothing to add.

John 2:18-22 gives the statement of the Master that if they should destroy this temple He would raise it up again in three days. They thought, or at least they pretended to think, that He referred to the temple in the city of Jerusalem; but the writer says He spoke concerning the temple of His body.

> *Now on the last day, the great day of the feast, Jesus stood and cried, saying, 'If any man thirst, let him come to me and drink. He that believes on me, as the Scripture has said, out of his belly shall flow rivers of living water.' But he spoke this of the Spirit, which they that believed on him were to receive: for the Spirit was not yet given; because Jesus was not yet glorified. (John 7:37-39).*

In John 10:6 it is stated that Jesus spoke a parable to them. In Luke 18:1; 19:1, it is expressly stated that He was speaking in parables. In Gal. 4:24 Paul speaks of "things [which] contain an allegory."

Rule 6. When the definite is put for the indefinite.—This is many times the case in the Scriptures. Day, hour, year; ten, one hundred, one thousand, ten thousand, and ten thousand times ten thousand. Such expressions occur frequently. They are rarely supposed to refer to that exact number or period.

> *His goods shall flow away in the day of his wrath. (Job 20:28).*

> *In the day of temptation in the wilderness, when your fathers tempted me, proved me, and saw my works forty years. (Psa. 95:8; Heb. 3:8).*

> *Do not hide your face from me in the day of my distress. (Psa, 102:2).*

Your people offer themselves willingly in the day of your power. (Psa. 110:3).

In the day that I took them by the hand, to bring them out of the land of Egypt. (Jer. 31:31, 32).

Glorify God in the day of visitation. (1 Pet. 2:12).

To proclaim the acceptable year of the Lord, and the day of vengeance of our God. (Isa. 61:2; Luke 4:19).

We will . . . continue there a year, and buy and sell, and get gain. (James 4:13).

Changed my wages ten times. (Gen. 31:7, 41).

And in every matter of wisdom and understanding, concerning which the king inquired of them, he found them ten times better than all the magicians and enchanters that were in all his realm. (Dan. 1:20).

We leave the other numbers for the present, as they will be called up in the rules for such figures of speech.

Rule 7. When said in mockery.—Men have always had the habit of using words to convey a thought quite different from that which a literal interpretation would indicate.

And it came to pass at noon, that Elijah mocked them, and said,' Cry aloud: for he is a god; either he is musing, or he is gone aside, or he is in a journey, or peradventure he is sleeping, and must be awakened. (1 Ki. 18:27)

No one has ever supposed that Elijah meant to say that Baal was actually a god, for he said it mockingly.

But others mocking said, 'They are filled with new wine.' (Acts 2:13)

New wine, or sweet wine, would not make any one drunk, and all knew it, and they meant to say just what we do, when we say of a man that he has *taken too much tea.* We do not mean to assert that tea would make him drunk, but in mockery we use one word for another.

And the rulers also scoffed at him, saying, 'He saved others; let him save himself, if this is the Christ of God, his chosen.' (Luke 23:35)

They do not mean to concede that he saved others; but that he had *claimed* to save them, and that his hypocrisy was at last revealed in the fact that He could not save Himself, assuming that, if He could not save Himself, He had not saved others.

In Acts 23:5, Paul seems to deny that he knew that Ananias was high priest. But that is impossible. It is easier understood as sarcasm, as if he had said: "Pardon me, friends; I would not have known that he was high priest if you had not informed me; he has acted more like a leader of a mob than a high priest."

Rule 8. *Common sense.*—Figures of speech sometimes occur when we have to depend on the things we know, in order to decide if the language is figurative or literal.

We have many statements in the Scriptures that are in excess of the facts. We do not need to be told that they are figurative; we know it. And yet no untruth is told if we keep the hyperbole in view. It is used for the purpose of intensification, and, with the purpose in mind, there is no danger of being misled. When God says that He will make His "arrows drunk with blood," or Paul declares that he is less than the least of all saints, there is nothing deceptive to those who will employ their common sense in the interpretation.

Jesus answered and said to her, If you knew the gift of God, and who it is that says to you, 'Give me to drink'; you would have asked of him, and he would have given you living water. The women says to him, 'Sir, you have nothing to draw with, and the well is deep: from where did you get this living water? Are you greater than our father Jacob, who gave us the well, and drank from it himself, and his sons, and his cattle?' Jesus answered and said to her, 'Everyone that drinks of this water shall thirst again: but whoever drinks of the water that I shall give him, shall never thirst; but the water that I shall give him shall become in him a well of water springing

*up to eternal life.' The woman says to him, Sir, give me
this water, that I do not thirst, neither come all the way
here to draw. (John 4:10-16)*

We are safe in saying that this was a low-minded woman. Her
mistake in interpreting the language of the Savior was because she
was not competent to lift her mind into the realm of spiritual thought.
Even after the Master had given her a view of His blessing, she was
thinking of the water she had come to carry home in her pitcher.

In Matt. 20:22-23, the Savior tells the disciples that He had a cup
to drink, and a baptism to be baptized with, and asks the ambitious
James and John if they were able to endure these things; and they said
they were able. Now, we have no direct rule that will reach the case,
except that of common sense. By that rule we know that the language
was figurative.

*They are drunk, but not with wine; they stagger, but not
with strong drink. (Isa. 29:9)*

The Lord has given us water of gall to drink. (Jer. 8:14)

*Babylon has been a golden cup in the Lord's hand, that
made all the earth drunk; the nations have drunk of her
wine; therefore the nations are mad. (Jer. 51:7)*

*And I trod down the people in mine anger, and made
them drunk in my fury, and I poured out their lifeblood
on the earth. (Isa. 63:6)*

*With whom the kings of the earth committed fornication,
and they that dwell in the earth were made drunk with
the wine of her fornication. (Rev. 17:2)*

*I fed you with milk, not with meat; for you were not able
to bear it. (1 Cor. 3:2)*

We might continue till we would weary the reader with those
Scriptures that everyone knows to be figurative; and yet we have
scarcely a rule for determining that fact, nor do we need any. We do
not conduct the investigation of such passages by tardy rules; through
common sense all readers know them to be figurative.

Section 51.
RULES FOR THE INTERPRETATION OF FIGURATIVE LANGUAGE.

We shall find that many of the rules which applied to didactic speech will be applicable here, and we shall depend upon the reader to keep those rules in mind. But some of them we shall feel obliged to mention, because of their peculiar use and value in the interpretation of figurative language. We also find that there are additional rules necessary to a full understanding of this kind of speech. Hence the section now introduced.

Rule 1. *Let the author give his own interpretation.* This, of course, applies as well to literal as to figurative language. But it is very seldom that an author has thought it necessary to interpret language that was strictly literal. Generally he would not be able to do better by the second effort. But many times, when the language is highly figurative, the writer feels that some explanation is needed. It is always safe to take his definition of the speech he has made. He certainly knows more than anyone else could know respecting his meaning. As simple as this rule is, and as certainly correct as it is, it is still greatly neglected. Many have proceeded as if their calling was to correct the blunders of the author. They show their ability as exegetes in making out of the figures employed a great many things that the writers never thought of.

When Ezekiel saw his vision of the valley of dry bones (ch. 37), he gave the world of interpreters a vast field for the employment of 'genius.' Men have made many things out of that vision; in fact, there are not many things they have *not* found in that chapter. And yet, in the eleventh verse, the prophet says it referred to the house of Israel—that as they were away from home, and seemingly neglected, they were ready to give up all hope of returning. But in this vision, it was made known that they should return to their land again. Scattered as they were, God could bring them together, and bring them out, and plant them in their own land again.

In Jer. 18:1-10, we have another abused passage. When the prophet went down to the potter's to see a work wrought on the wheel, a vessel of honor was made, but it became marred in the hand of the potter, and he made it into another and less honorable vessel; and then the man of God has the application, "So are you in my hand, O house of Israel." God had done well enough by them, but they became marred in His hand; and as the potter had power over the clay to make of the "*same lump*" a vessel to honor, and then one to dishonor, so He could and would do with Israel—if they would not be the people that they ought to be, He would give them a place of less importance and glory.

John 2:14-22 has an explanation by the writer. Jesus would raise up His *body* in three days—not the *temple* in Jerusalem.

In Matt. 13:18-23, the Master explains the meaning of the parable of the sower. We have several explanations of the Master by which His parables are made clear to the mind of all disciples.

Rule 2. The interpretation should be according to the general and special scope.—As this is one of the rules for the interpretation of literal language, little now needs to be said. If the rule is necessary to a right understanding of that which was meant to be plain, certainly it is of great importance in the exegesis of that which is confessedly difficult.

> *The law of the Lord is perfect, restoring the soul. (Psa. 19:7)*

In the interpretation of this passage we must not lose sight of the topic under consideration. God's ways are not as our ways; He employs silent forces for mighty ends. In His handiwork can be seen the evidence of His wisdom and goodness, and in His law is that power by which the souls of men are turned around from the wrong to the right. This does not mean to say that God had nothing to add to this law; it was perfect *for the purpose for which it had been given*. We learn afterwards, from Paul, that it was a school-master to bring men to Christ. But David does not teach differently when he is studied in the light of the purpose before his mind.

Ezek. 36:23-29: In this passage we have some splendid figures, but when studied in the light of the purpose of the writer, they are very easy of interpretation. He presents the children of Israel, in re-

180

turning from their long captivity in Babylon, as being cleansed from their filthiness and their idolatry. As a man in the camp of Israel would have to go out of the camp, and have a clean person sprinkle on him the water of purifying, on the third day and on the seventh day (Num. 19), and on the seventh day at evening wash his clothes and bathe his flesh in water, God represents Himself as undertaking their cleansing by sprinkling this clean—or cleansing—water on them, that they may be clean.

Matt. 5:13-15 is regarded as an easy figure, and yet it can be removed from its purpose by a failure to keep in mind the topic before the mind of the Savior. You are the light of the world and the salt of the earth. Let your light so shine, etc. Christ's disciples are to guide the world into truth and duty, and exercise a saving power in behalf of the race.

Rule 3. Compare the figurative with literal accounts or statements of the same things.—In doing this, it will be seen that you cannot make the figurative contradict the literal. It may add beauty and strength to the literal statement, but it cannot teach differently.

"And it shall come to pass afterward, that I will pour out my Spirit upon all flesh; and your sons and your daughters shall prophesy, your old men shall dream dreams, your young men shall see visions: and also upon the servants and upon the handmaids in those days will I pour out my Spirit" (Joel 2:28, 29).

When we have carefully read the Scriptures respecting the Holy Spirit, we are sure that God is meant. Regardless of whether we shall adopt the language of the Nicene Creed, speaking of 'God the Holy Ghost', or not—when we speak of the Spirit of the Lord, we speak of God. But how shall we think of God being poured out as if He were water? His gifts may be given without limit, in such abundance as to justify the figure in the mouth of a poet, but no one expects to find anything that will seem like a literal pouring out of God on men and women.

The Savior tells of the same occurrence, but in very different style. His words are prophetic, but they are plain.

> *But when the Comforter is come, whom I will send to you from the Father, even the Spirit of truth, which proceeds from the Father, he shall testify of me. (John 15:26)*

In the account of the fulfillment of this prophecy we have all the facts brought out.

> *And when the day of Pentecost was now come, they were all together in one place. And suddenly there came from heaven a sound like the rushing of a mighty wind, and it filled the whole house where they were sitting. And there appeared to them tongues parting asunder, like as of fire; and it sat upon each one of them. And they were all filled with the Holy Spirit, and began to speak with other tongues, as the Spirit gave them utterance. (Acts 2:1-4)*

By these literal statements, then, we have the figure of the Spirit of God being poured out. He came to the earth to make His residence with the disciples of the Master; He came with splendid gifts, and assumed the work which had been assigned Him—that of comforting all disciples, and guiding the apostles into all truth.

The Savior says (John 7:37-38) that out of believers should flow rivers of living water. And this figure He used to indicate what the Holy Spirit would do when He would come. But to know just what was meant by such a figure, we need only read the accounts of the work accomplished by the disciples, for in this way we certainly know what was referred to by the Lord. This promise was fulfilled. What did the disciples do when they fulfilled it? Learning that information, we have a full answer to the query, and the correct exegesis.

No one expects any literal flowing, and nothing like that is seen in the history of the men who are the fulfillment of the prediction. Being full of the Spirit, they went and preached everywhere.

Rule 4. *By the resemblance of things compared.*—Christ is represented as a lamb slain from the foundation of the earth; and in His trial and crucifixion is presented to us as a sheep before her shearer and a lamb taken to the slaughter. When we have considered the characteristics of a lamb, we are not at any loss to see the force and beauty of the figure. But in the Revelation, He is also called the *Lion* of the tribe of Judah. How is He both a lion and a lamb? This last figure sends us back to look for other qualities in the Savior than those of gentleness and innocence. He is mighty as well as meek.

In Gen. 49 we have the patriarch Jacob telling his sons what should come to pass in the latter times. Beginning with the eldest, he continues till he has told their characteristics. But the figurative language in which this is done makes it necessary for us to study each one of the tribes, that we may have the true interpretation of this prophetic blessing. Reuben is the excellence of dignity, and yet as unstable as water; Simeon and Levi were instruments of cruelty, and should be divided in Jacob and scattered in Israel. Judah was a lion's whelp, and his hand should be on the neck of his enemies, and should hold the sceptre till the Shiloh should come. He should wash his garments in wine and his vesture in the blood of grapes. His eyes should be red with wine and his teeth white with milk. Here is Judah's character as a tribe, and the history of the people. Continue making a diligent search for the features of likeness between the symbols and the facts, and there will be little difficulty in the interpretation.

> *But you do not believe, because you are not of my sheep. (John 10:26)*

It is not difficult to add a little to this statement, and make out the idea that because they had not been foreordained from the foundation of the world to be saved, they were unable to believe. The Savior did not have that subject before Him at the time. Still, the language can be *pressed* into that thought. If "sheep" here stands for the disciples, then they had to believe in order to become His disciples; and the language would be, in substance, *"you do not believe, because you do not believe."* This would be so perfectly meaningless that it cannot be admitted for a moment. In verse 16, He says, "Other sheep I have, which are not of this fold." All admit that this reference is to the Gentiles. But certainly they were not believers then, for they had never heard of Him. By reading verses 3 and 4, we have the peculiarities that made the metaphor appropriate. They heard Him, they followed

Him; they were therefore of that willing mind that made them ready to hear and receive the truth. It was this unsuspecting quality in them that marked the difference between them and those Jews who refused to consider the evidence of His divinity, and therefore remained in unbelief.

In Matt. 23 we have some of the strongest metaphors in any language. In verses 27 and 28 we have a simile and its interpretation, which makes it valuable:

> *Woe to you, scribes and Pharisees, hypocrites! for you are like whitewashed tombs, which outwardly appear beautiful, but inwardly are full of dead men's bones, and of all uncleanness. Even so you also outwardly appear righteous to men, but inwardly you are full of hypocrisy and iniquity.*

If the Savior had not interpreted this figure for us, its meaning would still have been clear by using the rule just laid down. But in the use of this rule, we must be careful not to compare accidental qualities, those for which the figure was not employed. A very ingenious interpretation of Psalm 1:3 draws all attention to the fact that the tree was *planted* by the streams of water. It did not grow there of its own accord; and reaches a conclusion that was never in the mind of the author. Whether the doctrine of foreordination (the source to this "exegesis") be true or not, it is certain that David was not discussing any such fine theology. His contrast was simply between righteousness and ungodliness—righteousness prospered and iniquity cursed. The righteous man was like a tree planted by the rivers of water, getting moisture in the time of drought, and therefore bringing forth his fruit in his season.

Rule 5. The facts of history and biography may be made to assist in the interpretation of figurative language.—If we can know certainly to what the man of God has referred, then by an acquaintance with that person or thing, we can certainly find the point and power of the figure of speech.

In Jeremiah 1, the enemies that were to come against the land of Judah were pictured as a boiling caldron, with its mouth from the north. Thus, it was about to overflow them, and scald them to death, The coming and destruction of the Babylonians, related in the history of the nations, enables us to see the meaning and force of the figure employed by the man of God.

> Then said the Lord to Isaiah, Go forth now to meet Ahaz, you, and Shear-jashub your son, at the end of the conduit of the upper pool, in the high way of the fuller's field; and say to him, 'Take heed, and be quiet; fear not, neither let your heart be faint, because of these two tails of smoking firebrands, for the fierce anger of Rezin and Syria, and of the son of Remaliah.' (Isa. 7:3-4)

Now, to get the meaning that the prophet put into this figure, one needs to study the character and condition of the two kings who had made a league against Judah. *Pekah,* king of the ten tribes, had formed an alliance with *Rezin,* the king of Damascus, in which they had agreed to combine against Judah, and place a vassal king on that throne, the son of Tabeel. But the force of these two men was nearly spent, and hence the prophet represents them as two smoking fire-brands that need not to be feared.

When Jesus was on the east side of the river Jordan, they came and told Him that it would be better for Him to depart out of the coasts, lest Herod should kill Him. He said: "Go and tell that fox," etc. We should study the character of Herod Antipas, in order to see the strength of the metaphor.

When we have a people drunk, but not with wine, staggering, but not from strong drink, it is important to learn of their condition to assure ourselves of the exact purpose of the figure. It is valuable, in the exegesis of any speech, to have before the mind just what was under contemplation when the speech was made.

If we could be in Jerusalem in the winter, and see the shepherds of that region bring their sheep to the cotes at night, and give them shelter, and then lead them out in the morning to some place of grazing, and guard them during the day, we would better understand the two allegories of the Savior in John 10, which were designed to teach the same lesson—that He was a sufficient protection by day and night, in life or in death. But without this knowledge or attention to these facts, we are liable to abuse the passage, as has been generally done. Christ is not the door of the church, but of the sheep; He had no church at that time. He is the way, or the *through*—the *narrow opening* that leads to protection and rest—for all the disciples.

And in the study of the allegory of John 15, we must understand the vineyard, the trimming, burning dead branches, fruit bearing, etc. Indeed, if we could go with the Savior and the disciples across the Kidron, and sit down with them on the side of the Mount of Olives, and look at the vineyards on the other hillside, by the lights made by the burning of the piles of dead branches, then the allegory would be all the more impressive.

In the interpretation of prophecy especially, it is of great importance to be well acquainted with the facts of history. They tell of the destruction of many cities and countries in language that is highly figurative; and, without any knowledge of the historic facts in the case, we may form an incorrect view of the teaching. Many prophecies will never be understood till they shall have been fulfilled, and then they will be grand evidences of the inspiration of the prophets. The destruction of Babylon, as foretold by Jeremiah and Isaiah, can be easily understood in the light of the events that have occurred. We can now go and stand with Isaiah on the walls of Babylon, in the vision, and see the two lines of smoke, or dust, rising from the East, and listen to the wail from within the city, and see well enough the two lines of the approaching army of Medes and Persians. The many statements of the prophet Isaiah concerning the destruction to be wrought by the hands of Sennacherib, the king of Assyria, are all clear after the events. The language that was dark to us before reading the account of their fulfillment, because of the highly wrought imagery, is very plain in view of the history.

Rule 6. *Any inspired interpretation, or use of the figure, in an argument or teaching, will decide its meaning.*—In Rule 1 we have the author's interpretation, which, of course, must be admitted by everyone. But this is based upon the same principle. If we concede that the writers of the New Testament were inspired of God, then we must accept any application of Scripture that they have made. To deny their exegesis of any passage is to deny the authority by which they spoke.

Isa. 6:9-10 is applied by the Savior in Matt. 13:14-15. And though we may say that this had been the condition of that people for many centuries, certainly the Master's use of the language was correct.

In 1 Cor. 10:1-8, we have an application of some Old Testament typology that is very instructive—Israel fleeing from bondage; being baptized into Moses; and that rock following them representing Christ.

Likewise in the fourth chapter of the Hebrew letter, there is a typology of the Sabbath given that would not have been understood, except for the teaching of the apostle Paul or the instruction of some other inspired man. Also his use of Sarah and Hagar and their sons, found in Gal. 4:21-32: "These are an allegory." And he not only announces that they are an allegory, but he tells what they mean. The one stands for the Old Institution, and the other for the New. We belong to the New, and not to the Old. The son of the bondwoman shall not be heir with the son of the free. The one Institution results in bondage, while the other brings freedom.

Isaiah 29:14 is employed by Paul in Acts 13:40-41. By this use of the passage we learn of its Messianic import.

In this way Psalm 41:9 has been shown to refer typically to Judas, who was guide to them who took Jesus: "My own familiar friend . . . has lifted up his heel against me." In Acts 1:15-18, Peter quotes several Scriptures, the meaning of which would not have appeared to us except for the use he makes of them; after this it is clear enough that they refer to Judas, and that another should take his place as a witness for the Savior. I think we might have read these texts a great many times without ever once suspecting their meaning—if we did not have the assistance thus rendered by the New Testament's use of them.

There seems to be a lurking suspicion that the apostles used the Old Testament Scriptures with too great a freedom, and quoted them rather for the sound than for their actual meaning. But this criticism is not begotten by faith in the inspiration of these men.

Rule 7. *We must be careful not to demand too many points of analogy.*—Many have proceeded in the interpretation of figurative language as if it was their privilege, or rather their calling, to invent as many features of similarity as their genius could originate, and then demand a corresponding thought and purpose for each. If they could know certainly that the man who is used as a type had a wart on his nose, or a mole on his ear, the wart or mole would have to come in for a hearing—they would see some typical intention in the whole affair. You see, it would have been just as easy for the Lord to select one without these features as with them, and therefore He must have had some divine reason for such a selection. By these interpreters, every occurrence of Old Testament times is supposed to have some feature of typology. And in the interpretation of these types and symbols, every peculiarity in the type must have some antitypical thought. Perhaps the very purpose, for which the type was employed, is lost sight of in the haste to identify small and unimportant features that act no part in the revelation of God to men. Sometimes the apostles have taken up some portion of Old Testament history and used it for the purpose of illustrating some truth in hand; but it does not follow that it was intended as a feature of typology. Paul says, "Do not harden your hearts as in the provocation, in the day of temptation in the wilderness, when your fathers tempted me, and proved me, and saw my works forty years." It does not follow, from this, that all this stubbornness was intended as a type of anything in the New Testament time. A man is said to have found, in the sheep being placed on the right hand of the Master in the day of judgment, evidence that all the colored people would be saved, as their hair is similar to wool. But while we are disposed to smile at the quaint interpretation, it is no more ludicrous than many that are given at the present time. Very much harm is done to the word of God by over-interpretation. Men sometimes bombard the Bible—they plant their batteries on some eminence, and see how many bombs they can shoot into it.

Rule 8. *It must be remembered that figures are not always used with the same meaning.*—A lion may not always symbolize the same thought, nor need a sheep, water, or fire always be employed for the purpose of expressing the same calamity or blessing.

There is a very grave error among an untaught class of exegetes in compelling every word that has, at any time, been used figuratively, to always represent the same thought as in that passage. To follow out this plan, we would have nothing left in the Scriptures of a literal character. It is about impossible to find any word that has not, at some time, been employed in a figurative sense; and nearly every animate and inanimate object has been used to represent some thought other than that which would simply state its being or action. This comes from a wrong method of interpretation, or from not having any method. Many seem disposed to regard themselves as at liberty to make anything out of the Bible which their theology may demand or their whims require. And if, at any time, they find a passage that will not harmonize with that view, then the next thing is to find one or more words in the text used elsewhere in a figurative sense, and then demand that such use be the Biblical dictionary on the meaning of that word, and hence that it must be the meaning in that place. Because the term *Logos* is employed in speaking of the Christ, therefore it must always have that meaning; and it is even carried so far as to say that the *Word,* either in the Old or New Testament, must always refer to the Savior. And yet ten minutes' use of a good concordance and the Bible would convince any thinking person that it is a fearful blunder. Oil and water have been employed to represent the Holy Spirit; therefore they always have that meaning! Because metaphors have been used in the Scriptures, therefore everything is a metaphor!

It is a kind of standing rule with a certain class of prophets, who are prophesying now, and trying to get the old prophets to agree with them, that if, at any time, a figure has been employed under circumstances in which its meaning is doubtful, if some other prophet has used that symbol, in a manner that removes doubt as to its meaning in *that* place, then take that use as a dictionary for the purpose of the figure in the doubtful passage. If this should be adopted as a rule, the exceptions will be found to be so numerous that the rule will be found of no value. If, at any time, it is found that two prophets are describing the same thing and employing the same figure for that purpose, it is possible that one of them has been clearer in the use of the figure than the other; and, in that way, there can be found a definition of the text that would otherwise have remained in doubt. But under almost any other circumstances the rule will not do.

Because Jesus said He was the bread from heaven, it does not follow that the word *bread* must always refer to Him. He used the word leaven to represent teaching and influence both, and yet these are the figurative uses. It does not mean that the leaven that the Israelites were to put out of their camps before the feast of the Passover, was influence or doctrine. Nor because the word leaven, when used as a symbol, must always mean something bad, because it usually has that signification, for Jesus says that the "kingdom of heaven is like leaven that a women took and hid in three measures of meal till the whole was leavened"—surely the kingdom of heaven is not something that is to be shunned. Fermentation is not the only quality of leaven: its ability to gradually and quietly extend its power is one of its features, and is that one for which the Master employs it in the passage quoted (Matt. 13:33).

Water is many times used as the symbol of blessing among the ancients: it stands many times for almost any kind of refreshment. In Deut. 23:4, Moses remembers the Moabites and the Ammonites in their unkindness in not meeting Israel with bread and water. In 1 Sam. 25:11, we have the churlish Nabal refusing to give bread and flesh and water to the servants of David. In 1 Cor. 3:6, Paul uses it as a symbol of Christian culture. In John 7:38-39, the Savior symbolizes the Holy Spirit by its use; and in 4:10, He uses it in a more extended sense of spiritual blessings, including eternal life. But water has not only the power to bless, but the power to injure; hence it has been employed for that purpose, or to symbolize that thought. In Psa. 69:1, David says; "Save me, O God; for the waters are come in to my soul." Isa. 30:20 speaks of the water of affliction. This power of water to deluge and drown, gives signification to Matt. 20:22: "I have a baptism to be baptized with."

The word *sheep* is many times used as the symbol of innocence, because a sheep is less offensive and defensive than any other of the domestic animals. In metaphor, therefore, they represent the people of God, while the goat is the symbol for the children of the wicked one, (Matt. 25). And yet a ram is a sheep. He is the symbol of a kingdom, and is offensive. Many times sheep go astray. Isa. 53:6: "All we like sheep have gone astray." Jer. 50:6-17: Israel was scattered and lost. Ezek. 34:6-11: Israel had fled to the mountains, and were scattered abroad, and needed to be hunted up.

Fire has more nearly always the same metaphorical import than any other word I know of in the Scriptures. It is a good servant and a cruel master. But its only Scriptural use is in view of its burning. It is never the symbol of blessing, except as trials and pains result in reformation and purity. Our faith may have to be tried in the fire, and we may be said to be salted with fire, and all this may work for us the peaceable fruits of righteousness; but at the time of this purification it did not seem to be very joyous. If we are made to pass through the furnace of affliction or persecution, it may do us good; but fire has all the time been employed as the figure of that which causes pain. Though it remove our dross, yet it does so by burning, and not by any soothing process. God's word is as a refiner's fire, in that it separates a man's sins from him, or the man from his wickedness.

It is true that some writers have favorite illustrations, and when we have become familiar with their use, we have a dictionary that will fairly define them. It is also true that one inspired man copies from another. Finding that another has said the same things that the Lord wishes him to say, it is right and proper that the same things should be said again; and he is right in saying them again. If, at any time, we can be sure that one is a copy in whole or in part of the other, and the ore is clearer than the other, it is proper that the clearer language should aid us in the exegesis of that which is doubtful. But beyond this we may be very wary of compelling figures to mean the same thing.

Rule 9. *Parables may explain parables.*—We have seen that any figure of speech may be explained by the writer, or any other inspired writer, by literal language. We have also seen that a figure may be adopted by another writer in whole or in part, and, in such cases, that which is free from doubt as to its meaning may be employed to make known that which is not clear. This rule only carries that thought a little farther, and shows that a parable, or other figure of speech, may be legitimately made to assist in the interpretation of another figure of speech.

In the first verse of the tenth chapter of John, the Savior begins an allegory that closes in the sixth verse. In this He introduces the thought of a shepherd, faithful in all his work, to illustrate His relation to them. "But they did not understand the things which he spoke to them."

He therefore began another allegory, to give them this thought. This time he takes the door, or the open space into the sheepcote, to assure them that His help and protection would be sufficient (verses 7-18).

One of these illustrates the same thought that the other does, and therefore the one assists us in comprehending the meaning of the other.

In Matt. 13, we have seven parables for the purpose of causing the disciples to understand the nature of Christ's kingdom. This is a large number on one topic, and yet Luke and Mark add three more to this list. They do not all of them cover exactly the same point, and yet they were all employed to assist in understanding the things concerning the kingdom of God. And many of the same points were covered several times. Christ was intent on removing a fundamental mistake. They supposed that when the kingdom of the Messiah would come, it would be like the other great kingdoms of the world—it would be temporal, and therefore it would come in much the same way. But He wished them to know that such was not the nature of His kingdom, and that it would not come by an army, but by the power of truth—the truth being sown into the hearts of men would cause them to be subject to Him.

I have no doubt that a number of the sayings of Jesus were repeated in many places. Even the prayer which He taught His disciples,

was repeated. In Luke 15 there are three parables for the same purpose. He had been eating with publicans and sinners, and the Pharisees blamed Him for it. He showed them, by the parable of the lost
sheep, and the lost piece of money, and the lost boy, that they were
the last persons in the world who should find any fault with it. Indeed,
they should rejoice that these then were returning home. The Master
gave several parables on the subject of the use and abuse of riches.
Any one of these can be rightfully employed in the interpretation of
another. That rich fool that said, "I will pull down my barns, and build
greater; and there will I store all my corn and my goods. And I will
say to my soul, 'Soul, you have much goods laid up for many years;
take your ease,'" etc., gives us the stupidity of the silly man who will
plan as if this life was all that is for him. In the parable of the rich
man and Lazarus, we have not only the foolishness of thus giving
one's mind to the accumulation of wealth, but the corrupting influence on the mind and heart of him who possesses it. While they have
something of different ends in view, in several features they are quite
the same, and may render much assistance each in the interpretation
of the other.

Rule 10. *The type and the antitype are frequently both in view at
the same time.*—It is common to say that a type is made of material
things, and the antitype is always a spiritual thought or fact. The
anointing with oil prefigured the anointing of the Holy Spirit; the
anointing of the prophet, priest, and king of the patriarchal and Jewish
times, told of Him who should be our Prophet, Priest, and King; that
the washing under the law symbolized the spiritual purity that should
be in all the people of God. The wilderness of wandering represented
the journey of life, with its many dangers, toils, and trials; the Jordan
told them of the death that was to be before the land of promise; and
passing it prefigured the resurrection of the dead; and then, when they
should enter the promised land, they had a type of heaven itself. All
this we can admit. Indeed, I think it is quite true. And yet several figures and types have been employed to represent the same antitype and
several of these may be seen at the same time; and even the mind of

the prophet may be fixed not only on several types, but on the antitype as well.

We may say that the bondage of Israel, in Egypt, symbolized our bondage in sin—that when they left Pharaoh we have a figure of the necessity of repenting and turning away from sin;—but just there we come up to what seems to be the introduction of another thought, for the apostle Paul uses the passage through the Red Sea as a type of our baptism into Christ. Their Sabbath was a type of Christian rest in Christ (Heb. 4:1-10); but it had also in view that which the Christian is looking for—the eternal rest that remains for the people of God. Here, then, we have one spiritual thought symbolizing another of greater extent and duration. 1 Pet. 3:16-21 uses the flood of Noah and the salvation of the righteous family as typical of our baptism. This is not strange, when we know that these are two symbols for the same safety in God.

Many of the prophecies of Isaiah are inexplicable on any other hypothesis. In nearly all the latter part of his vision, he is carried away to Babylon, and is looking into the future from the time of the captivity. Hence he frequently sees the children of Judah and Benjamin returning home. And the joy of the man of God becomes so great that everything seems to him to be ecstatic—the very land of Canaan itself is glad: its hills are frisking about like lambs, and its mountains are skipping like rams; and the cedars of Lebanon are clapping their hands for joy. But in that ecstasy of mind the prophet is sure to see the still greater redemption in Christ. Here are the type and the antitype both in prophecy. Nor is this all: this type and antitype are like two hills in a line, the smaller one being the nearer. There may be a long distance between the two, but they look as if they were only one hill. Hence, after one line of prophetic history is described, which runs through the type and antitype, it is in order for the prophet to return and bring forward another. But this makes him refer to the type immediately after mentioning the antitype. Many commentators have lost their star here. Having seen one prophecy relating to the return from Babylon, and then the clear and certain reference to the coming of the Christ and the work of redemption which He should accomplish, and then another mention of return to the Holy Land, they take it for granted that it must now relate to some final return of the Jews to that country. But let us remember that these men were telling what they saw, and that in the range of their mental vision there are both type and antitype, and the trouble is removed.

There has been a great deal of misunderstanding of Matt. 24 on this account. Some have seen in it nothing but the destruction of Jerusalem. Beyond any question, the Savior did refer to the destruction of that city. But others find in it language that must refer to the final judgment of the world, and then hasten to the conclusion that it cannot refer to the destruction of Jerusalem at all, but that it must all relate to the coming of the Lord and the end of the world. But when we find that both of these things were before the mind of the Master at the same time, the trouble is taken out of the passage, for we have in these two events all that the language demands.

CHAPTER IX:
THE VARIOUS FIGURES OF THE BIBLE.

We have done more in the separation of all figurative language into families of figurative speech than any other people. Among the ancients there were but few designations. In the Scriptures we have the parable, the proverb, the type, and the allegory named. We also have the fable used, but not named. Under these headings they crowded all we know of figurative language. They were free in the *use* of figures, but not in *definitions* of them. We must, therefore, be permitted to bring to the task everything we can get by which to understand the kinds of figurative language they employed, and the laws that govern each of these classes. The parable, at that time, contained all that we today put into the parable and the simile and the similitude—and sometimes the parable and the proverb were used interchangeably. At other times it means a type. This seems strange to us, for they are so unlike, as we speak of them. But we will give the reasons for this further along in the work. We do not stop to blame the Orientals[2] for not distinguishing between one figure and another, for modern writers, with all the advantages of our schools, do not always succeed. Our works of rhetoric are not well agreed as to the exact office of the several figures that are now in common use; and there are many writers on types, and metaphors, and parables, and allegories, who do not seem to have taken any advantage of our works of rhetoric. But when we have exhausted the list of figures found in our modern books on interpretation, we have not yet found all the figures that are used in the Scriptures. It has seemed necessary to either enlarge some of the figures we have now, or invent terms by which to indicate the character and power of other forms of speech found in the Bible.

---

[2] This is a term used to describe the people of the Middle East, specifically the Jews in this context.

Section 53.
THE PARABLE.

This is from the two Greek words, *para,* beside, and *ballein,* to throw; hence it means 'placing beside or together, a comparing, comparison: a story by which something real in life is used as a means of presenting a moral thought.' The actors in a parable are real—human beings are the actors, and they do nothing which they could not do in reality; things were not stated which could not be accomplished by the agencies employed.

The parable is the oldest and most common of all the figures of speech. The Old Testament contains many of them, and the Savior taught almost constantly by that medium of illustration.

There seem to have been several reasons for its use in the teaching of the Master.

> *And the disciples came, and said to him, 'Why do you speak to them in parables?' And he answered them, 'To you it is given to know the mysteries of the kingdom of heaven, but to them it is not given. For whoever has, to him shall be given, and he shall have abundance: but whoever does not have, from him shall be taken away even that which he has. Therefore I speak to them in parables; because seeing they see not, and hearing they hear not, neither do they understand.' (Matt. 13:10-13)*

Now, in this declaration of purpose the Savior seems to have in view the teaching of one part of the crowd, and preventing the other part of it from understanding what was being said. His reason for not giving them the truth was that they would not receive it nor follow it.

And yet when we have read the Scriptures through, the parables seem to have been employed, for the most part at least, for the purpose of making clear that which would not otherwise have been understood. That purpose of the parable is so patent that it is the only view that the people generally have of it.

The allegories which the Savior employed in John 6 seem to have been to hide the truth from those who would abuse the light if it were furnished. And yet at the same time the teaching became more power-ful to those who came to Him afterwards, and had it explained to them. And I think there is every reason to believe that the parable was used for the same purpose—that of embalming the truth, that it might never be forgotten. These story illustrations of the Savior were not only a means of making truth to be understood, but to cause it to be remembered. Those who heard His stories of illustration never forgot them.

Again, we find a purpose in the use of this figure that is quite in addition to any others yet mentioned: it was to present a truth to the mind, and yet keep the person for whom it was intended from seeing the point till the mind had assented to the truth that was taught by it. To proceed by the use of statement and argument would cause the person to array himself against the force of the truth being presented. Nathan came to David with a very pitiful story about some man who went and took the ewe lamb, the only one his poor neighbor had, and killed it for the friend who stopped with him, while he had plenty of flocks of his own (2 Sam. 12:1-6). David could easily see the mean-ness of such conduct, and he became so enraged that he determined to have the man put to death—he was too mean to live. Nathan had not made the application. But when he said, "You are that man," David was soon made to see the force of the truth. He could not have been made to understand his sin in any other way—at least, not so clearly.

In 2 Sam. 14:1-24, we have the account of a parable arranged by Joab, and told to David by the woman of Tekoah, to have the king send for Absalom from the land of Geshur. She came looking very heartbroken, and told the king of her two sons who strove, and one having killed the other; the people were trying to kill him, and that would quench her coal, or extinguish her family. This so wrought up-on the feelings of David that he said he would protect her son. Then she asked why he did not cause his own son to return home. The point was gained, and Absalom came home to his own possessions.

An illustration of this use of the parable will be found in the teaching of the Savior on the fourth day of the week of crucifixion. It is commonly called the parable of the vineyard, and will be read in

198

full in Matt. 21:33-46; Mark 12:1-12; and Luke 20:9-19. To get this lesson properly before the mind of the reader, I will make a condensed reading from the three records:

> And he began to speak this parable to the people. "There was a master of a house that planted a vineyard, and set a hedge around it, and digged in it a winepress, and built a tower, and let it out to vine-dressers, and went into another country, and was absent from home a long time. And when the time of the fruit drew near, he sent his servants to the vine-dressers to receive the fruits of it. And the vine-dressers took his servants and scourged one, and killed another, and stoned another, wounding him in the head. Again he sent other servants more than the first: and they treated them in like manner. And the owner of the vineyard said: 'What shall I do? Having one son, my beloved, I will send him; perhaps when they see him, they will reverence him.' But when the vine-dressers saw him, they reasoned among themselves, saying: 'This is the heir; come, let us kill him, and the inheritance will be ours.' And they took him and drove him out of the vineyard, and killed him. Therefore, when the owner of the vineyard comes, what will he do to those wicked vine-dressers?" They said to him, "He will miserably destroy those wicked men, and let his vineyard to other vine-dressers, who will give him the fruits in their seasons." "Yes," said Jesus, "He will come and destroy those vine-dressers, and will give his vineyard to others."
>
> And when they heard it (perceiving that he had spoken the parable against them), they said, "Let it not be!" And Jesus looked on them, and said to them: "Did you never read in the Scriptures: 'The stone which the builders rejected has become the head of the corner? This was from the Lord, and it is wondrous in our eyes.' For this reason, I say to you, 'The kingdom of God shall

be taken from you and given to a nation that will bring forth the fruits of it. And he that falls upon this stone shall be dashed to pieces: but him on whom it shall fall, it will make him like chaff for the wind.'" And when the chief priests and Pharisees heard his parables, they sought to lay hold on him, but they feared the multitude, because they regarded him as a prophet.

This is the form of the parable, and its results which come by reading the account in all of the evangelists. If we have not read amiss, then Jesus did for them what Nathan did for David—He came up on the blind side of those men, and presented them truth so that they assented to it, before they saw that it meant *them*.

I think, then, we are at liberty to say that parables were used for the following purposes—(1), To reveal truth: making the people to understand the unknown by a comparison with the known. (2) For the purpose of concealing truth from the minds of those who had no right to it, or who would abuse it if it were given to them. (3) They were made the means of embalming truth. (4) For the purpose of causing men to assent to truth before they could know it certainly meant them.

While we are ready to regard the parable as the most apt mode of instruction, and the easiest and safest manner of enforcing conviction, yet it is the most difficult of all figures to construct. It is easy to rehearse a story for illustration, but to construct a parable is not so easy.

In 1 Kings 20:35-43, we have a parable in which Ahab is condemned for permitting Benhadad to go free, when it was his duty to destroy him:

And a certain man of the sons of the prophets said to his fellow by the word of the Lord, 'Smite me, I beg you.' And the man refused to smite him. Then he said to him, 'Because you have not obeyed the voice of the Lord, behold, as soon as you are departed from me, a lion shall slay you.' And as soon as he was departed from him, a lion found him, and slew him. Then he found another man, and said, 'Smite me, I beg you.' And the man smote him, smiting and wounding him. So the prophet departed, and waited for the king by the road, and disguised himself with his head-band over his eyes. And as the king passed by, he cried to the king: and said, 'Your servant went into the midst of the battle; and, behold, a man turned aside, and brought a man to me, and said, Keep this man: if by any means he be missing, then shall your life be for his life, or else you shall pay a talent of silver. And as your servant was busy here and there, he was gone.' And the king of Israel said to him, So shall your judgement be; you have decided it.' And he hasted, and took the head-band away from his eyes; and the king of Israel discerned him that he was of the prophets. And he said to him, 'Thus says the Lord, Because you have let go out of your hand the man whom I had devoted to destruction, therefore your life shall go for his life, and your people for his people.' And the king of Israel went to his house heavy and displeased, and came to Samaria.

The purpose of this parable is clear to everyone. The king was to be condemned by himself. David had been led to do that; and the Master had caused the Jews to pass judgment against themselves by the use of a parable.

The parables of the New Testament are quite clear. A few of them were explained by the Savior, but most of them were so clear that no one would miss the meaning who wanted to know the truth. And yet some of these have been very strangely interpreted. The three parables in Luke 15 are so plain that it would seem impossible for anyone to miss their importance. And yet many things have been deduced from them that were not in the Savior's mind. The first and second verses give the key to all of them:

Now all the tax collectors and sinners were drawing near to him so that they could hear him. And both the Pharisees and the scribes murmured, saying, 'This man receives sinners, and eats with them.'

Then, to show them the unreasonableness of such a complaint, He gave them the three parables that followed—the lost sheep, the lost piece of money, and the lost boy. By these He taught them that they ought to forget the better class, for the time, in their earnest endeavor to save sinners.

The parable of the sower (Matt. 13:1-9) is explained in verses 10-23; and the parable of the good seed and the tares (Matt. 13:24-30) is explained in verses 36-43. Although these are exceedingly plain in themselves, and the explanation is as clear as language could be, still they have been made to teach almost everything that genius could imagine. Quite a common interpretation of the good seed and the tares is that there can be no withdrawal of fellowship, for the wicked and the righteous shall grow together till the end of the world. It is nothing to these exegetes that the Scriptures teach in several places that they must withdraw from all that walk disorderly, and that the man that will not hear his brethren nor the church should be to them as heathen and a publican. Nor does it change the matter for them that the Master says the *field is the world,* and the harvest is the *end of the world.* Some way they have fixed it in their minds that the kingdom and the church are the same, and therefore the field is *not the world, but the church.* It is strange that they do not see that Christ is Ruler of the kings of the earth, and that all authority in heaven and earth was given into His hands.

The rest of the parables spoken at the time that Jesus was in the boat at Capernaum, are easily explained as similes or similitudes. They differ from what we now denominate a parable, in that they are not stories, but statements of truth or fact, with which statement the unknown truth is compared. But of this in its own place.

The parable of the great supper (Luke 14:16-24) has several points to present to the mind: (1) The greatness of the feast being prepared. (2) The unreasonableness of apologies that were made for not attending it. (3) The ease with which all could attend. (4) The sin of slighting honor and favor, and the punishment that would come to such persons. (5) And that the places that had been reserved for those first bidden would be given to others who would accept. Of course it is easy to see that the Jews had been favored with this first invitation, and that, refusing it, they would be cast aside, to make room for those who would receive an invitation as a great honor.

The parable in Luke 16:19-31, of the rich man and the poor man, has been made to mean almost everything within the range of theological speculation. And yet, if one will turn and read ver. 14, it will be easily seen that it was for the purpose of showing them the results of wealth on the mind that would yield to its influence and control. The Master had said that it was impossible to serve God and Mammon both; but there were wealthy Pharisees present who derided Him.

To show the result of the course they preferred, the parable is recited:

> *Now there was a certain rich man, and he was clothed in purple and fine linen, faring sumptuously every day: and a certain beggar named Lazarus was laid, full of sores, at his gate, desiring to be fed with the crumbs that fell from the rich man's table. Yes, even the dogs came and licked his sores. And it came to pass, that the beggar died, and that he was carried away by the angels into Abraham's bosom: and the rich man also died, and was buried. And in Hades he lifted up his eyes, being in torments, and saw Abraham afar off, and Lazarus in his bosom. And he cried and said, 'Father Abraham, have mercy on me, and send Lazarus that he may dip the tip of his finger in water, and cool my tongue; for I am in anguish in this flame.' But Abraham said, 'Son, remember that you in your lifetime received your good things, and Lazarus in like manner evil things: but now here he is comforted, and you art in anguish. And besides all this, between us and you there is a great gulf fixed, that they which want to pass from here to you may not be able, and that none may cross over from there to us.' And he said, 'I beg you therefore, father, that you would send him to my father's house; for I have five brothers; that he may testify to them, lest they also come*

into this place of torment.' But Abraham said, 'They have Moses and the prophets; let them hear them.' And he said, 'No, father Abraham: but if one goes to them from the dead, they will repent.' And he said to him, 'If they will not hear Moses and the prophets, neither will they be persuaded, if one rise from the dead.'

No one asked that this parable should be explained. Its meaning was clear to those to whom it was spoken. But modern theology is opposed to its teaching, and it is doubtful, even if the Savior had explained it, if the interpretation would be any better received.

Some have been heard to say, "It is nothing but a parable." Well, what of that? It is not said to be a parable, and yet there is much evidence that it was. But does that fact lessen the importance of its teaching?

Another way of removing the offensive truth is to say it refers to the Jews and the Gentiles. But why say that? There has been no reference to any such a topic in the connection—no evidence that the Master had these nationalities before Him. Here are a few reasons why it can have no such meaning:

1. It was not stated, nor even hinted, as being any purpose in giving the parable. There is neither statement before nor afterwards, that would lead to such a conclusion; nor is there the slightest hint in the presentation of the parable that it had that thought for them.

2. The purpose is clearly indicated, as before shown, to be to show the dangers of wealth.

3. The Jews have never seen the Gentiles in a condition such that they regarded them as in Abraham's bosom and themselves shut out.

4. They have never believed themselves delivered over to torment.

5. They have never asked that the Gentiles should come to their relief by administering comforts that were beyond their reach.

6. There has never been any impassable gulf fixed between these peoples, so that one may not pass over to the other.

7. The Gentiles were never laid at the gate of the Jewish nation, asking crumbs that were falling from their table.

8. Neither nation has gone into another state of being, or into non-existence, as some critics would have death to signify.

9. If the Jewish nation had died, it would not have five brothers remaining yet in the world, who might be warned against its fate.

10. To try this interpretation of the parable by removing the word and inserting the definition, we would have nothing but nonsense made of the whole figure. If *rich man* means Jewish nation, then remove rich man and insert *Jewish nation;* and so for the *beggar* insert *Gentile nation.* Now read the parable, inserting these definitions, and nothing but nonsense is left in it.

Then there is no reason for the interpretation, and every reason why it cannot be correct.

The real neabubg of the figure may be easily gathered by anyone at all interested in knowing the teaching of the Master:

1. It is not possible to serve two masters (13-14).

2. After death, the conditions cannot be changed. If men are not in a safe condition then, it will be impossible for them to be prayed out of that purgatorial condition, or for any relief to come to them.

3. Praying to saints is of no value.

4. Men are expected to prepare to meet God by the light of the revelation which He has furnished.

5. There are no warnings to come back to us from the Spirit land.

6. There is consciousness between death and the resurrection from the dead.

7. There is an intermediate state between death and the resurrection. This scene is laid on a condition that comes after death. It was before the resurrection, for there will be none on the earth to warn after the resurrection shall have taken place. But someone will say that the eternal state of these men being fixed, the judgment is passed with them, and therefore the resurrection, in their cases, has been accomplished. This is not true. Lazarus going back would be regarded as one going to them from the dead; and this could not be said of any one in the resurrection state.

We have chosen to give this much space to this one parable, first, because of its own worth; and second, because of the many wrong views that have been taken of it. Many of the things to be gained from it have been taken for granted by the Savior. He uses the words of the Pharisees, and evidently in the same sense in which they employed them.

In Luke 18:1-74, we have two parables on the subject of prayer. In that of the importunate widow we have perseverance in prayer taught, and in the second, relating to the Pharisee and publican, the humility necessary to acceptance before God. These are the only lessons contained in them. The quality of the unjust judge in no way represents anything that is true with God; and the parable was not instituted for that purpose, but simply to show that men ought always to pray, and not to faint.

Jesus taught a young lawyer how to be neighbor by the use of the parable of the Good Samaritan (Luke 10:25-37). We are not able to say if this case ever occurred, nor do we care: the lesson is perfect. Having agreed that to love God with all his heart and his neighbor as himself, were the duties of men, he wished to excuse himself with a pretense of ignorance about who his neighbor was. So the Master has a Jew, who was hated by all Samaritans, to fall among robbers and to be left in need of help; and while the priest and the Levite passed without noticing him, looking on the other side, the Samaritan took him to an inn and paid his expenses. And, having presented the case, He said: *"Go and do likewise."* There could be no question asked respecting the meaning of this parable, for only one was possible—that the Samaritan was made to know that the Jew was his neighbor, and that he must do him good. Hence, if this man will love his neighbor as himself, he must do as that man did.

It would seem impossible for anyone to misunderstand the parable of the Good Samaritan. And yet Bishop Heber has a sermonic exegesis of it in which the traveler represents the human race; his leaving Jerusalem is made to symbolize man's departure from God; Jericho is the symbol for temptations; the robbers are the devil and his angels; the priest signifies the sacrifices of the Old Testament; the Levite represents the law of Moses, and the Samaritan typifies the Savior. And yet it is candidly asserted that the Bishop was a man of good sense! I think he might have gone further, and made the inn represent the church of Christ; the oil and the wine the blood of the atonement and the gift of the Holy Spirit; the two pieces of money the two ordinances left till the Savior shall come again; and the promised return of this man, to stand for the second coming of the Savior to the world. Then it would be too bad to leave out the ass on which the man had ridden. The beast might symbolize the feeling of self-sufficiency on which the world rides away from God. It is high time that we were done with such foolishness. And yet almost every figure of the whole Bible has been rendered about as ludicrous as this, by someone who was regarded as brilliant.

The Savior's parable concerning the feature of rewards in the kingdom of heaven (Matt. 20:1-16), has suffered more from interpreters than the woman with an issue of blood during a period of twelve years had from the physicians. There was never any reason for all this, except that men have wished to find some apology for delinquency, or to exhibit skill in exegesis possessed by no one else.

This householder went out in the first, hour, and in the third hour; also the sixth, ninth, and the eleventh. Each time he found men waiting for someone to employ them. In the evening he had his steward to pay them all alike—a penny.

Many have seen in this parable that the Lord is holding out encouragement for those who come late in life to begin in the service of the Lord. They have lived, perhaps, in the light and blaze of Christian truth, and now, when the dying hour has come, and they have no further strength with which to serve the devil, they repent, and are to be preached into the highest heavens, because there were some contortions when they came face to face with death.

Others have shown skill in the work of interpretation by supposing that the Lord referred to different ages of the world by the several hours at which servants were employed. For instance, the Lord employed men in the Adamic period; then in the time of Noah, Abraham, Moses, John, Jesus. If this arrangement does not suit the particular fancy, then some other can be fixed upon that will show an equal amount of dexterity. It is not interpretation, however, but injection.

Nothing like either of these was in the mind of the Master. The chapter begins with: *"For the kingdom of heaven is like."* Its beginning word is the sign of a logical conclusion, and hence the parable that follows is to illustrate a statement already made. Turning to the last verse of the previous chapter, the remark that needs to be carried out is: "But many shall be last that are first; and first that are last." And then, when the parable has been recited, that point is supposed to have been gained, for He says: "So the last shall be first, and the first last" (20:16).

By reference to the previous chapter, and the twenty-seventh verse, the reason for the remark appears to be the danger of Peter, and perhaps others of His early disciples, taking too much glory to themselves. He said, "We have left all, to follow you." The Master says that all who had left houses, etc., to follow Him, should be rewarded; but it is not a question of having had the first opportunities to know Him, for all those who would unite their fortunes with Him should receive the same reward. There is no thought about any being acceptable to God who had wasted their lives in the service of the enemy, when they had a chance to know the will of the Savior; nor is there the slightest reference to the different ages of the world. The parable is beautiful, when employed as the Master gave it.

The parable of the ten virgins is one of the clearest in all the New Testament. Its one point—the need of watchfulness, in view of the coming of the Lord—is apparent to every reader. And yet this parable has suffered much from over-interpretation. Men have seen that the Lord will come when the world will be indifferent, or sound asleep— *it is midnight;* that He will come with a crowd of attendants—or *with all His holy angels;* that the supply of *the Holy Spirit* will be wanting with those who do not renew frequently. Some have found that all the virgins slept before the Lord's coming, and therefore He must refer to *the time of the resurrection of the dead.* But all of this is a work of supererogation. The whole thought of the figure is that they should always be ready; for the Lord will come at a time when men do not expect Him, and they must be ready to enter with Him, or they will not be able to enter at all. There will be no opportunity to prepare, then, for entering into the wedding.

The parable of the unjust steward (Luke 16:1-13) has, perhaps, given more difficulty to critics and commentators than any other. Many strange translations have been proposed to get rid of the imaginary troubles of the figure. It is maintained by some that the rendering generally given makes the Savior recommend the dishonesty and theft of this man; whereas, instead of being held up as a model, he ought to be regarded as the most extreme of knaves. Hence, instead of the common translation of verse 9, "Make to yourselves friends of the mammon of unrighteousness," it should read, "Make to yourselves friends *without* the mammon of unrighteousness." They think that it was the Savior's purpose to direct them to do just the opposite of what this wicked steward did: he made friends with money, or wealth, and they should make friends without it. And this thought is supposed to be enforced by the fact that He said this to His disciples, who were without this mammon.

I shall not stop to criticize the translation proposed, but suppose that the language may be so rendered. The way to settle the question is not, however, by the possibilities of translation. The Lord never presented a figure that He made to depend upon any renditional gymnastics. The truth is much easier than that. When we learn that there may be many things in a parable that are merely incidental, and are no part of the lesson to be learned, we will be ready to search, first of all, for the purpose for which the figure was employed. Learning this, the interpretation will be easy. No one can suppose, for a moment, that the Savior had in His mind any sanction for the robbery perpetrated by this man (11-13). Several questions need to be settled, in order to assure ourselves that we know exactly the purpose of the parable:

Who constituted His hearers?—It will be answered, "*His disciples.*" But who are meant by that term? From the word "also" (verse 1), we suppose it to be the crowd that He had addressed in the previous chapter. And we know that they are a mixed assembly—publicans and sinners, Pharisees and scribes. We learn from 16:14 that these Pharisees were lovers of money, and that they heard this parable, and scoffed at Him for speaking it. Hence, if the word *disciple* must be limited to the apostles, yet it remains a fact that, as the sermon on the mount was delivered in the hearing of the multitude, and much of it *for* the multitude, so it was in this case. And yet it is more probable that Luke uses the term to indicate no more than *those who were learning of Him at that time.* These publicans were very much in need of something on the money question that would check their avarice and theft. It is seen that the Pharisees were in no better condition.

What did He intend to accomplish by the parable?—They understood Him to condemn them for giving their hearts and lives in the acquisition of wealth. The closing of this parable and the institution of the next (19-31), show that such was His purpose.

Where, then, is the lesson?—The wisdom of using the things of this life that we may have a home provided in the life that is to come. The Savior does not commend the wrong that the steward did, but the wisdom of looking ahead far enough to secure a home when he should be cast out of this one. Hence they were not to be so wedded to their money that they would fail to make a good use of it; and to give their hearts to its acquisition would prevent that service of God which would be necessary to secure for them a home beyond this life.

The seven parables of Balaam are difficult, because they are *not what we call parables.* There are in them similes, similitudes, and clear prophetic statements. See Num. 23:7-10, 18-24; 24:3-9, 15-19; 20:21, 22, 23-25. Each time it is said in the beginning that Balaam "*took up his parable.*" I understand this to mean, he spoke by inspiration in figurative language. Some of these are beautiful similes, but there is not what we now denominate a parable.

There are a number of parables in the New Testament that will be treated under the head of similes, because they belong in that line of figure. As we said before, they had but few figures, or but few names for figures of speech in Bible terms. We have now separated these, and given to them names by which we can understand definitely just what we have to deal with. There are also many parables which we have not mentioned; they are in the order in which parables are presented, but we have not the space to devote to them. Besides, there will not be found any difficulty in their interpretation.

Section 54.
THE FABLE.

This is often confounded with the parable. Yet there is a clear distinction. Webster says of a fable:

> 1. *A feigned story or tale; a fictitious narration, intended to enforce some useful truth or precept; an apologue. 'Jotham's fable of the trees is the oldest extant, and as beautiful as any made since.'—ADDISON.*

> 2. *The plot, or connected series of events, forming the subject of an epic or dramatic poem. 'The moral is the first business of the poet: this being formed, he contrives such a design or fable as may be most suitable to the moral.'—DRYDEN.*

> 3. *Fiction; untruth; falsehood. 'It would look like a fable to report that this gentleman gives away a great fortune by secret methods.'—ADDISON.*

If we take the fables of Aesop as a guide, a fable is an illustration made by attributing human qualities to animate and inanimate beings. The truth or moral to be enforced may be of a very high order, but the actors are selected from those beings which are incompetent to do such things. Like a parable, it is put into a form of a story; but unlike the parable, its actors are unreal, while the parable is made from the actual occurrences of life, and no one is made to act a fictitious part.

The fable is better suited to indicate some blunder made by men, and to serve the purpose of amusing criticism, than to illustrate any high moral truth. Hence it is little used in the Scriptures.

> *And all the men of Shechem assembled themselves together, and all the house of Millo, and went and made Abimelech king by the oak of the pillar that was in Shechem. And when they told it to Jotham, he went and stood in the top of Mount Gerizim, and lifted up his*

voice, and cried, and said to them, "Hearken to me, you men of Shechem, that God may hearken to you. The trees went forth, once upon a time, to anoint a king over them; and they said to the olive tree, 'Reign over us.' But the olive tree said to them, 'Should I leave my fatness, with which, by me, they honor God and man, and go to wave to and fro over the trees?' And the trees said to the fig tree, 'You come and reign over us.' But the fig tree said to them, 'Should I leave my sweetness, and my good fruit, and go to wave to and fro over the trees?' And the trees said to the vine, 'You come and reign over us.' And the vine said to them, 'Should I leave my wine, which cheers God and man, and go to wave to and fro over the trees?' Then all the trees said to the bramble, 'You come and reign over us.' And the bramble said to the trees, 'If you truly anoint me king over you, then come and put your trust in my shadow; and if not, let fire come out of the bramble, and devour the cedars of Lebanon.' Now therefore, if you have dealt truly and uprightly, in that you have made Abimelech king, and if you have dealt well with Jerubbaal and his house, and have done to him according to that which his hands deserve: (for my father fought for you, and adventured his life, and delivered you out of the hand of Midian: and you have risen up against my father's house this day, and have slain his sons, seventy persons, upon one stone, and have made Abimelech, the son of his maidservant, king over the men of Shechem, because he is your brother): if you then have dealt truly and uprightly with Jerubbaal and with his house this day, then rejoice in Abimelech, and let him also rejoice in you: but if not, let fire come out from Abimelech, and devour the men of Shechem, and the house of Millo; and let fire come out from the men of Shechem, and the house of Millo, and devour Abimelech." And Jotham ran away, and fled,

and went to Beer, and dwelt there, for fear of Abimelech
his brother. (Judg. 9:6-21)

The criticism of this fable was not only good for that time, but it is yet a fine illustration of the way of the world. Those least competent and worthy are most ready to assume responsibilities and take command.

We also have a fairly well constructed fable in 2 Kings 14:8-10:

Then Amaziah sent messengers to Jehoash, the son of
Jehoahaz, son of Jehu, king of Israel, saying, "Come, let
us look one another in the face." And Jehoash the king
of Israel sent to Amaziah king of Judah, saying, "The
thistle that was in Lebanon sent to the cedar that was in
Lebanon, saying, 'Give your daughter to my son as a
wife.' And a wild beast passed by that was in Lebanon,
and trode down the thistle. You have indeed smitten
Edom, and your heart has lifted you up: glory in that,
and abide at home; for why should you meddle to your
hurt, that you should fall, even you, and Judah with
you?"

The criticism intended by this fable is easily reached. Amaziah had hired an army of Israelites to assist him against Edom, but the Lord refused to let them go with the Jews. So he paid them, and sent them home. But they were angry, and injured the people of the Jews on their return. Amaziah was successful against the Edomites, and then adopted their idolatry. When he returned, he asked that the matter of bad faith be settled between the armies of the Jews and the Israelites. This brought the reply from Jehoash in the form of a fable.

Section 55.
SIMILE.

Webster defines it.

A word or phrase by which anything is likened in one of
its aspects to another; a similitude; a poetical or imagi-

native comparison. 'A good swift simile, but something currish.'—SHAKESPEARE.

A few examples will suffice for this figure of speech:

And it shall be as when a hungry man dreams, and behold, he eats; but he awakes, and his soul is empty: or as when a thirsty man dreams, and, behold, he drinks; but he awakes, and, behold he is faint, and his soul has appetite: likewise shall the multitude of all the nations be, that fight against mount Zion. (Isa. 29:8)

Nothing need be said about this simile respecting its meaning. The prophet explains it. The nations that will come against mount Zion, while they will dream of getting spoil, will be mistaken, This has particular reference to the coming of Sennacherib, of Assyria, who should gather much spoil from the land of the Jews, and then, the night before he expects to have Jerusalem in his power, would have nearly all his men destroyed in the night by the angel of the Lord.

For as the rain comes down, and the snow from heaven, and does not return there, but waters the earth, and makes it bring forth and bud, and gives seed to the sower and bread to the eater; so shall my word be that goes forth out of my mouth: it shall not return to me void, but it shall accomplish that which I please, and it shall prosper in the thing for which I sent it. (Isa. 4:10-11)

It should be noticed that this is said concerning the promises of Jehovah. What He has offered to those who love to do His will, He will give them. To show His faithfulness in this respect, He presents them with His work for the good of the race in the sowing and gathering of grain. God fulfills His part; and yet if man does not fulfill his part, there will be no harvest. To those who will trust the Lord according to His word, there shall be no disappointment.

And the daughter of Zion is left as a tent in a vineyard, as a lodge in a garden of cucumbers, as a besieged city. Except the Lord of Hosts had left to us a very small

> *remnant, we would have been as Sodom, we would have been like Gomorrah. (Isa. 1:8-9)*

This simile is a very strong one, as the comparison is vivid. A tent in a vineyard or a lodge in a garden of cucumbers would not be expected to be very enduring; a besieged city would certainly be in great danger of destruction; indeed, if it had not been that there was a seed of those who did good and followed God, they would have been ruined before that time, and that as utterly as Sodom and Gomorrah.

> *Lest my fury go forth like fire, and burn so that none can quench it, because of the evil of your doings. (Jer. 4:4)*

> *And the aspect of the fourth is like a son of the gods. (Dan. 3:25)*

> *And he saw the Spirit of God descending as a dove, and coming upon him. (Matt. 3:16)*

> *They are like children that sit in the market place, and call one to another; who say, 'We piped to you, and you did not dance; we wailed, and you did not weep.' (Luke 7:32)*

> *Woe to you, scribes and Pharisees, hypocrites! for you are like whitewashed tombs, which outwardly appear beautiful, but inwardly are full of dead men's bones, and of all uncleanness. (Matt. 23:27)*

> *All we like sheep have gone astray; . . . as a lamb that is led to the slaughter, and as a sheep that before her shearers is dumb: yes, he opened not his mouth. (Isa. 53:6-7)*

> *And when you pray, you shall not be as the hypocrites. (Matt. 6:5)*

The simile always furnishes the means of a comparison by a statement, not a story. It also contains the sign of that comparison. It is plainer than the metaphor, on that account; the metaphor makes the comparison by mentioning one when you know the other is meant, because of some feature or features in the thing referred to that are like the thing that is mentioned.

In many popular works these figures are used interchangeably. But they are more easily explained when properly defined.

Section 56.
THE SIMILITUDE.

This is a drawn-out or prolonged simile. It differs from an allegory, in that it is constituted of similes, and not of metaphors. It differs from the parable, in that it is made from statements, but is not woven into a story. The similitude frequently *contains* its own explanation. An allegory is frequently *followed* by an exposition. So are parables. We have a number of parables in the New Testament which, in the form we have them, are properly denominated similitudes. They may have been presented in the parable form, but, if so, they have been reduced to the form of statement, and are not parables as we have them. This should not excite any wonder, as they did not define figures of speech as we do. In Luke 4:23, we have the word *parable,* where, in our custom, it should be proverb. Indeed it is so rendered in the King James Version. Jesus says: "Doubtless you will say to me this parable: Physician, heal thyself." Of course that is not a parable, in the sense in which we use the term. It also occurs in Heb. 9:9; 11:19, and in the Common Version is rendered "figure."

In many other places we have been so long accustomed to calling them parables, that it is like sacrilege to us to have them called anything else. And yet there is no name given to them in the Scriptures.

> *Therefore everyone who hears these words of mine, and does them, shall be likened to a wise man, who built his house upon the rock: and the rain descended, and the floods came, and the winds blew, and beat upon that house; and it did not fall: for it was founded upon the rock. And everyone that hears these words of mine, and does not do them, shall be likened to a foolish man, who built his house upon the sand: and the rains descended, and the floods came, and the winds blew, and beat upon*

*that house; and it fell: and the fall of it was great. (Matt.
7:24-27)*

Here the comparison is clear, by means of this double simile or
similitude. It would have been a parable if the same thought had been
put into the form of a story, and exhibited in that way.

*And he said, "This is the how the kingdom of God is: as
if a man should cast seed upon the earth; and should
sleep and rise night and day, and the seed should spring
up and grow, he knows not how. The earth bears fruit of
herself; first the blade, then the ear, then the full corn in
the ear. But when the fruit is ripe, immediately he puts
forth the sickle, because the harvest is come. (Mark
4:26-29)*

This, again, is called a parable; but if our definitions are correct, it
is a similitude.

What is usually called the parable of the lamp (Mark 4:21-22), is
properly a metaphor. This, however, will be seen under that figure of
speech.

*Suffer hardship with me, as a good soldier of Christ Je-
sus. No soldier on service entangles himself in the affairs of this life; so that he may please him who enrolled
him as a soldier. And if also a man contends in the
games, he is not crowned unless he has contended law-
fully. The husbandman that labors must be the first to
partake of the fruits. Consider what I say; for the Lord
shall give you understanding in all things. (2 Tim. 2:3-
7).*

Part of this has the exact form of the metaphor, but it contains the
likeness or sign of comparison, and therefore must be catalogued as a
similitude.

Many of the Psalms are in the form of similitude. It was a favorite
form of expression with the writer. We are sorely tempted to give a
number of these, but we must desist for lack of space.

Hide not your face from me in the day of my distress
Incline your ear to me;
In the day when I cal,l answer me speedily.
For my days consume away like smoke,
And my bones are burned as a firebrand,
My heart is smitten like grass, and withered;
For I forget to eat my bread.
By reason of the voice of my groaning
My bones cleave to my flesh.
I am like a pelican of the wilderness;
I am become as an owl of the waste places.
I watch, and am become
Like a sparrow that is alone upon the housetop.
My enemies reproach me all the day;
They that are mad against me do curse by me
For I have eaten ashes like bread,
And mingled my drink with weeping,
Because of your indignation and your wrath
For you have taken me up, and cast me away.
My days are like a shadow that declines;
And I am withered like grass. (Psa. 102:2-11)

Here we have a goodly number of similes for the purpose of expressing the condition of the writer. He was weak, short-lived, hated by many, and under the wrath of God. But to put it in that form would not do for an Oriental. He must have something stronger and more vivid.

A beautiful similitude is found in Psa. 90:4-6:

For a thousand years in your sight
Are but as yesterday when it is past,
And as a watch in the night.
You carry them away as with a flood; they are as a
sleep.
In the morning they are like grass which grows up.
In the morning it flourishes, and grows up;
In the evening it is cut down, and withers.

This song is supposed to have been composed by Moses, and gives forth his thought respecting the shortness of human life. God's years shall not fail, but the time allotted to man is but *"as a watch in the night."*

Section 57.
THE METAPHOR.

This is from the two Greek words, *meta,* beyond, over, and *phere-in,* to bring, to carry. Webster says of it:

> *A short similitude; a similitude reduced to a single word; or a word expressing similitude without the signs of comparison. Thus, 'that man is a fox,' is a metaphor; but 'that man is like a fox,' is a simile, similitude, or comparison.*

The metaphor is briefer and more pungent than the simile. On that account it was more frequently used by the ancients. It presents characteristics by the means of a representative of the thought that is intended to be conveyed, by calling one thing by another term which denotes the characteristic which is to be made prominent. The simile gently says that *is like it*; the metaphor says it *is it.* "I will devour them like a lion" (Hos. 13:8), is a simile; "Judah is a lion's whelp" (Gen. 40:9), is a metaphor.

The Bible is full of metaphors, and yet we must not now offer many. But we must have enough, that we may understand the allegory.

> *In that very hour there came certain Pharisees, saying to him, 'Get out, and go from here: for Herod would happily kill you.' And he said to them, 'Go and say to that fox, Behold I cast out devils and perform cures today and tomorrow, and the third day I am perfected.'*
> *(Luke 13:31, 32)*

If He had said, "Go tell that man that is like a fox," it would have been a simile, but it would have lacked its force.

In Jer. 2:13, we have two metaphors, one by which God would be understood in His providential and benevolent character, and the other to indicate the condition into which Israel had come by forsaking His service:

> *For my people have committed two evils; they have forsaken me, the fountain of living waters, and hewed cisterns for themselves, broken cisterns, that can hold no water.*

In the song that Moses taught to the children of Israel, God presents His willingness to destroy the wicked, by the use of the metaphor (Deut. 32:42):

> *I will make my arrows drunk with blood,*
> *And my sword shall devour flesh;*
> *With the blood of the slain and the captives,*
> *From the head of the leaders of the enemy.*

When the Savior gave the institution of the supper, He did it in the most beautiful of metaphorical language (Matt. 26:26-28):

> *And as they were eating, Jesus took bread, and blessed, and broke it; and he gave to the disciples, and said, 'Take, eat; this is my body.' And he took a cup, and gave thanks, and gave to them, saying, 'Drink you all from it; for this is my blood of the covenant, which is shed for many into the remission of sins.'*

Paul presents this thought without the use of the metaphor (1 Cor. 10:16):

> *The cup of blessing which we bless, is it not a communion of the blood of Christ? The bread which we break, is it not a communion of the body of Christ?*

But in 11:23-25 he employs the same figure that the Lord did in instituting it. This shows that they regarded the one form of expression as containing the same as the other. To say this is the communion of the body and blood of Christ, is metonymy of the agent; to say that these are *like* the body and blood, would be a simile, but the beauty and strength would have been removed in that way; hence the Master chose the form of the metaphor as the most expressive.

In John 6:32-65 is the finest collection of metaphors to be found anywhere. Some deal with this chapter as they do with the institution of the supper, in a spirit of legalism, as if the Master had been delivering a lecture on chemistry—and in that way rob themselves of the thought and sweetness of the teaching. There were those present on that occasion that did the same thing, and hence thought He had given them some very hard sayings. They were about as low-minded as the Samaritan woman, reported in John 4: Whosoever would drink of the water he would give, would never thirst, made her wish for that water so that she would not have to come there and draw. And when the Savior told the disciples that He had bread to eat that they did not know about, they said, "Has someone brought him food to eat?"

So they failed, about as signally as did the woman, to catch the meaning of His words. They did this again when they were on their way to Caesarea Philippi (Matt. 16). They had forgotten to take bread, and in His teaching He said to them, "Beware of the leaven of the Pharisees and Sadducees;" and they regarded it as a rebuke for not having provided bread. John seemed to understand this style of speech better than any of the other disciples, and therefore has made more frequent use of the Savior's metaphors. John 2:19, "Destroy this temple, and in three days I will raise it up," had a meaning which the Jews pretended not to understand. Chap. 7:37-38, is so full of beauty and strength that John explains it, lest some would not be able to understand it:

> Now on the last day, the great day of the feast, Jesus stood and cried, saying, 'If anyone thirsts, let him come to me, and drink. He that believes on me, as the Scripture has said, out of his belly shall flow rivers of living water.'

It would be as reasonable to interpret this literally as Matt. 26:26-28, or the many figures of John 6.

> You are the salt of the earth: but if the salt has lost its savor, wherewith shall it be salted? It is from that point

*forward good for nothing, but to be cast out and trod-
den under foot of men. You are the light of the world. A
city set on a hill cannot be hid. Neither do men light a
lamp and put it under a bushel, but on the stand; and it
shines to all that are in the house. Even so, let your light
shine before men, that they may see your good works,
and glorify your Father who is in heaven. (Matt. 5:13-
16)*

They were not said to be *like* salt, nor to have the *qualities* of
light, or be *in view* of the world as a city on a hill, but *they were all
these.*

*Do you not know that a little leaven leavens the whole
lump? Purge out the old leaven, so that you may be a
new lump, even as you are unleavened. For our Passover also has been sacrificed, even Christ: Therefore, let
us keep the feast, not with old, leaven, nor with the leav-
en of malice and wickedness, but with the unleavened
bread of sincerity and truth. (1 Cor. 5:6-8)*

In a church like that at Corinth, a man living with his father's wife
would have a bad influence—so corrupting that ruin would be almost
sure to follow. Start a social disorder of that nature, and the church
will come to nothing unless the evil is removed very soon. It works
like leaven, till it overcomes the entire body.

In Eph. 3:18, the love of Christ is presented by breadth and
length, and height and depth, as if it were something that might be
weighed—measured with a yard-stick. This metaphor is difficult to
explain, and yet it is understood by everyone. All know that Paul
meant to say that it is more profound than man can comprehend.

*Jesus answered and said to him, 'Truly, truly I say to
you, Unless a man is born anew, he cannot see the
kingdom of God.' Nicodemus says to him, 'How can a
man be born when he is old? Can he enter the second
time into his mother's womb, and be born?' Jesus answered, 'Truly, truly I say to you, Unless a man is born*

of water and the Spirit, he cannot enter into the king-dom of God.' (John 3:3-5)

If Jesus had said that a man must pass through a process that is *like* a birth, it would have been a simile; but the form of expression here used is that of the metaphor—a man must be born again.

The metaphor is employed by Paul twice (Rom. 6:3-4, and Col. 2:12):

Buried with him in baptism, in which you were also raised with him through faith in the working of God, who raised him from the dead.

Therefore, we were buried with him through baptism in-to death: that like Christ was raised from the dead through the glory of the Father, so we also might walk in newness of life.

In one respect, the latter of these quotations has the feature of a simile, but on the whole it is better explained by the use of the meta-phor. The burial was not literal—they could not have been entombed with the Savior. It was therefore only in the likeness of that occur-rence. If the sign of that likeness had been used, it would have been a simile; but the burial stated, it has the form of the metaphor.

Metaphors are frequently taken from the characteristics of ani-mals.

Issachar is a strong donkey,
Couching down between the sheepfolds:
And he saw a resting place that it was good,
And the land that it was pleasant;
And he bowed his shoulder to bear,
And became a servant under taskwork. (Gen. 49:14-15)

Here the characteristics of the donkey are ascribed to Issachar. If it had been said that he should be like a donkey, in that he would be satisfied with plenty to eat and be willing to bear the burden placed upon him, then it would have been a simile; but the metaphor presents the thought in a more rugged way—*Issachar is a strong donkey.*

Verses 16-17, are a beautiful metaphor:

Dan shall judge his people,
As one of the tribes of Israel.
Dan shall be a serpent in the way,
An adder in the path,
That bites the horses' heels,
So that his rider falls backward.

A play is first made on the word Dan, which means a judge; and then the character of the man and the tribe is given by the serpent which he is said *to be.*

Gad, a troop shall press upon him:
But he shall press upon their heel. (ver. 19)

Here, again, a play is made upon the word Gad, which means a troop; and then the characteristics of the Gileadites come to view in this metaphor.

Naphtali is a deer let loose. (ver. 21)

This is very expressive. In his history, or that of his descendants, he has more running to do than any other of the tribes. Stationed at the northeast of their territory, and most of the attacks on the land coming from that direction, they always first affected the tribe of Naphtali. He is first to be carried away, on that account.

Benjamin is a wolf that gorges.
In the morning he shall devour the prey,
And at even he shall divide the spoil. (ver. 27)

In this way Christ is called a husband (2 Cor. 11:2). He is the Lamb of God that takes away the sins of the world, and also the Lion of the tribe of Judah.

All animate and inanimate creation has been put under tribute by this figure to represent God and his people, and also the enemies of the race. Christ is a vine, a shepherd, a door, a rock, a fountain, a servant, and the Captain of our salvation. God is spoken of as having ears and eyes, and hands and feet, and hinder parts; as hating, being jealous, divorcing Israel, and permitting his wife to return again, after she had played the harlot. Thus by the use of the metaphor vivid description is given, that all may understand.

Section 58.
THE ALLEGORY.

This word comes from *allos,* other, and *agoreuein,* to speak in the assembly, to harangue. Webster says:

> *A figurative sentence or discourse, in which the principal subject is described by another subject resembling it in its properties and circumstances. The principal subject is thus kept out of view, and we are left to collect the intentions of the writer or speaker by the resemblance of the secondary to the primary subject."*

> *The distinction in Scripture between a parable and an allegory is said to be, that a parable is a **supposed** history, and an allegory a figurative application of **real** facts. An allegory is called a continued metaphor. Bunyan's Pilgrim's Progress, and Spenser's Faery Queen are celebrated examples of the allegory.*

In Hart's Rhetoric, page 167, the figures mentioned are shown in their relation to each other:

> *Difference between Allegory and Metaphor.—Allegory differs from Metaphor in two respects. First, it is carried out into a greater variety of particulars, making usually a complete and connected story. Secondly, it suppresses all mention of the principal subject, leaving us to infer the writer's intention from the resemblance of the narrative, or of the description to the principal subject.*

> *Points in common.—Allegory, Metaphor, and Simile have this in common, that they are all founded in resemblance, there being in each case two subjects, a primary and secondary, having certain points of likeness. In Simile, this resemblance is expressed in form, as when it is said, 'Israel is like a vine brought from Egypt, and planted in Palestine.' In Metaphor the formal comparison is dropped, as when it is said, 'Israel is*

*a vine brought from Egypt,' etc. In Allegory, both the formal comparison and the principal subject are dropped, and the secondary subject is described by itself, leaving the application entirely to the imagination of the reader, as when it is said, 'God brought a vine out of Egypt and planted it in Palestine.' The reader knows that by **vine** is meant God's people, Israel. Yet Israel is not once mentioned, and there is neither metaphor nor simile, though there is likeness.*

This Allegory occurs in Psa. 80, and is as follows:

'Thou broughtest a vine out of Egypt: Thou didst drive out the nations, and plantedst it. Thou preparedst room before it. And it took deep root, and filled the land. The mountains were covered with the shadows of it, And the boughs thereof were like cedars of God. She sent out her branches to the sea, And her shoots to the River. Why hast thou broken down her fences, So that all they which pass by the way do pluck her? The boar out of the wood doth ravage it, And the wild beasts of the field feed on it.

I do not agree with this author in the supposition that an allegory can be constructed and yet no metaphor be employed. In the illustration from the Psalm, there are a number of metaphors. Indeed the allegory stands to the metaphor as the similitude or the parable does to the simile. It is made by arranging metaphors into a story, or statement of fact, or secondary subject, by which the primary is to be understood.

In a work on Composition and Rhetoric, by Quackenbos, page 248, is found a very direct statement:

It will be seen that an allegory is a combination of kindred metaphors so connected in sense as to form a kind of story. The parables of Scripture, as well as fables that point a moral, are varieties of this figure. Some-

*times an allegory is so extended as to fill a volume; as
in the case of Bunyan's Pilgrim's Progress.*

This statement is satisfactory, except that it is not quite correct to say that a parable is constructed of kindred metaphors. The truth is, metaphors are not used in the construction of parables. The remark, however, comes from a lack of clear views as to the difference between a parable and a fable.

Mr. Terry, in his work on Biblical Hermeneutics, says:

*An allegory is usually defined as an extended metaphor.
It bears the same relation to the parable which the metaphor does to the simile. In a parable there is either
some formal comparison introduced, as 'the kingdom of
heaven is like a grain of mustard seed,' or else the imagery is so presented as to be kept distinct from the
thing signified, and to require an explanation outside of
itself, as in the case of the parable of the sower. . . . The
allegory contains its interpretation within itself, and the
thing signified is identified with the image, as, 'I am the
true vine, and my Father is the husbandman' (John
15:1); 'Ye are the salt of the earth' (Matt. 5:13). The allegory is a figurative use and application of some supposable fact of history. The parable uses words in their
sense, and its narrative never transgresses the limits of
what might have been an actual fact. The allegory is
continually using words in a metaphorical sense and its
narrative, however supposable in itself, is manifestly
fictitious.*

Most allegories are simple, that is, they are for a single purpose and have but one line of metaphorical representation regarding the presentation of the thought. But some of them are double, or, they are in the form of antithesis; there are two lines of metaphors, for the purpose of presenting two lines of thought, and these two lines of thought are put in the form of antithesis, one is set over against the other. Paul is more given to this kind of allegorical illustration than any other writer in the Scriptures.

Or ever the sun, and the light, and the moon, and the stars, be darkened, and the clouds return after the rain: in the day when the keepers of the house shall tremble, and the strong men shall bow themselves, and the grinders cease because they are few, and those that look out of the windows be darkened, and the doors shall be shut in the street; when the sound of the grinding is low, and one shall rise up at the voice of a bird, and all the daughters of music shall be brought low; yea, they shall be afraid of that which is high, and terrors shall be in the way; and the almond tree shall blossom, and the grasshopper shall be a burden, and the caper-berry shall fail (Eccl. 12:2-6).

In this way Solomon would exhort young men to seek after the Lord before the time of age comes on, when the weaknesses and fears of old age shall be realized. Here is a splendid list of metaphors, in which the light stands for the hope of youth; and the clouds returning after the rain, the dubiety of age. The keepers of the house are the arms as they are the defenders of a man, and the strong men are the legs, which are not now competent to bear him around as before. The grinders (teeth) are few and the doors (lips) close because there are no teeth now to hold the jaws apart. These grinders make but a feeble impression on their work, and the eyes are looking as if through a glass darkly. Every noise now startles him, and the slightest weight is a burden. He finds no pleasure in the sense of taste as he once did, and even the caper-berry fails to give him appetite. The hair is white, giving the old man the appearance of the almond tree, for soon shall the silver thread of life be snapped, and all the vitality of life poured out as the golden bowl, broken at the cistern.

When Jesus was at the house of Matthew, they came to Him with the question as to why His disciples did not fast, and insinuated that they were somewhat disorderly in that they did not keep the customs of the people. The Master responds by the use of an allegory. See Matt. 9:16,

And no man puts a piece of undressed cloth upon an old garment; for that which should fill it up, takes from the garment, and a worse tear is made. Neither do men, put new wine into old wineskins: else the skins burst, and the wine is spilled, and the skins perish: but they put new wine into fresh wineskins, and both are preserved.

In this, Jesus recognizes the propriety of clothing religious thoughts and convictions with appropriate forms. But fasting was a symbol of grief, and as they could not be sorry while He was with them, it was impossible for them to fast without acting a lie. And as to their paying any attention to the forms and customs which they kept, it would not be appropriate for them to do so. His teaching was new, and the old forms in which their convictions might find protection, would not be sufficient to retain the new wine of truth that He was furnishing to the world. Hence He would have to give to them such forms and rites as would be appropriate to the truth He was then giving them.

Put on the whole armor of God, so that you may be able to stand against the wiles of the devil. For our wrestling is not against flesh and blood, but against the principalities, against the powers, against the world rulers of this darkness, against the spiritual hosts of wickedness in the heavenly places. Therefore take up the whole armor of God, that you may be able to withstand in the evil day, and, having done all, to stand. Therefore stand, having girded your loins with truth, and having put on the breastplate of righteousness, and having shod your feet with the preparation of the gospel of peace; moreover taking up the shield of faith, with which you shall be able to quench all the fiery darts of the evil one. And take the helmet of salvation, and the sword of the Spirit, which is the word of God. (Eph. 6:11-17)

This is Paul's description of the defensive armor, of the Christian's means of defense. It is one of the easiest allegories in the Scriptures to interpret. The foes are clearly announced and their manner of warfare was well understood. Only one set of foes were out of sight; the spiritual hosts. Still, with the needed preparation, they should not fear. Let them be righteous, think, and speak, and live the truth, filling their hearts and their minds with the hope of salvation in Christ, and walking in the commandments of the Lord, and the darts of the enemy and missiles from ambush would do them no harm. The false teaching and the influences of wicked men would not harm them.

I will cite a few double allegories—those in which there are two lines of thought, one put over against the other. These are difficult of interpretation, from the fact that they have twice as much in themselves for the mind of the interpreter to deal with, and also when we have the two lines of thought, we have yet to find the purpose of the comparison. Fortunately for us, in the allegories of the apostle Paul, he has let us in on the secret, and told us what he wished to accomplish by the figures:

> *For if the casting away of them is the reconciling of the world, what shall the receiving of them be, but life from the dead? And if the firstfruit is holy, so is the lump: and if the root is holy, so are the branches. But if some of the branches were broken off, and you, being a wild olive, was grafted in among them, and became a partaker with them of the root and the fatness of the olive tree; do not glory over the branches: but if you glory, [remember] it is not you that bears the root, but the root bears you. You will say then, 'Branches were broken off, that I might be grafted in. True; by their unbelief they were broken off, and you stand by your faith. Do not bet high-minded, but fear: for if God did not spare the natural branches, neither will he spare you. Behold then the goodness and severity of God: toward them that fell, severity; but toward you, God's goodness, if you continue in His goodness: otherwise you also shall be cut off. And they also, if they do not continue in their unbelief, shall be grafted in: for God is able to graft them in again. For if you were cut out of that which is by nature*

a wild olive tree, and were grafted contrary to nature into a good olive tree: how much more shall these, which are the natural branches, be grafted into their own olive tree? (Rom. 11:15-24)

This allegory has given more trouble to exegetes than any other in the Bible, and it should certainly be managed with care. A number of the rules for the interpretation of figurative language will be demanded, that all possibilities for mistake shall be avoided:

1. Paul was the apostle to the Gentiles (11:1).
2. But he was a Jew, of the tribe of Benjamin (ibid).
3. God had not cast off His people whom he foreknew (2).
4. For many of them remained faithful to God (2-5).
5. But for Israel to be saved, the dependence must be upon grace, not the deeds of the law (6-7).
6. Those who had depended upon this scheme of salvation by grace had found it (7).
7. Those who refused that grace, had been blinded and hardened by that refusal (7-10).
8. But the whole nation had not been cast away, nor had they stumbled so as to fall, and not rise again.
9. By the temporary fall of Israel, salvation had been secured for the Gentiles.
10. If their fall had been the enriching of the world, their rising would be much more fruitful of good results (11-12).
11. Paul hoped to stimulate them to thought and action by presenting to his people the glory conferred on the Gentiles through the acceptance of the Messiah (13-14).
12. Those who had failed to retain the favor of God, had failed through unbelief.
13. The Gentiles had succeeded by faith.
14. Hence, if the Gentiles did not continue in faith, they would be cast off.
15. If the Jews should not abide in unbelief, they would be returned to the favor of God.

16. It was much more reasonable, then, to suppose that the great mass of the Jews would, in the future, turn and accept the Savior, their own Messiah, than to have expected that the Gentiles would do.

17. Then (25-32) Paul argues that the Jews can finally accept the Messiah. Hence we now see that his allegory was a part of his argument to show that the Jews can finally turn to the Lord and be saved; and that if they do turn and accept their Messiah, it will be like a resurrection from the dead.

18. The tame olive tree represents the Jews in a state of favor.

19. The wild olive tree certainly stands for the Gentiles, at a time when they did not know God.

20. The only difference, therefore, between the wild and the tame olive trees is a difference in culture and favor.

21. Hence, when the Jews were broken off, they were separated from their former condition of culture and favor.

22. The first fruit, and the root, are figures of the same thought, and were presented to show that God had not cast off Israel as a people. The only thing in their history that would prove that, was not what Abraham had done, or what he had been, but the fact that some of the Jews had accepted of Christ, and were saved. Hence these were the first fruit, or the wave loaf that was offered on the Pentecost, which, being accepted, the whole harvest might be eaten.

23. The Gentiles were then to know that the Jews had not been sundered by an act of the Almighty, but those who had failed had done so for the lack of personally accepting of the Messiah, and that they were all, therefore, on an equality: any Jew might be saved, and any Gentile be lost; on both sides, it would depend upon personal faith and obedience to the will of the Savior.

In the interpretation of this allegory, many more things are put into it than Paul ever thought of. They go to work to find a full grown tree, trunk and bark and root, and then to demand something to answer in the place of every feature of a tree. This is the way that parables and types are interpreted to death. Nothing is said about Abraham, nothing about the trunk of the tree, nothing about the tree being a church. Every bit of it has to be injected into the passage. Indeed, if the tame olive tree meant church, the wild olive tree would mean church, and then we would have *a tame church and a wild church!* But if we keep before the mind the purpose of the figure, and the rules of interpretation, there is no trouble.

Paul's allegory of the two covenants, found in the second letter to the Corinthians (3:6-16) is next to the two olive trees in respect of difficulty in interpretation. It reads:

> *But our sufficiency is from God; who also made us sufficient as ministers of a new covenant; not of the letter, but of the spirit: for the letter kills, but the spirit gives life. But if the ministration of death, written, and engraved on stones, came with glory, so that the children of Israel could not look steadfastly upon the face of Moses for the glory of his face; which glory was passing away: how shall not rather the ministration of the spirit be with glory? For if the ministration of condemnation is glory, much rather does the ministration of righteousness exceed in glory. For truly that which has been made glorious has not been made glorious in this respect, by reason of the glory that surpasses. For if that which passes away was with glory, much more that which remains is in glory. Having therefore such a hope, we use great boldness of speech, and are not as Moses, who put a veil on his face, that the children of Israel should not look steadfastly on the end of that which was passing away: but their minds were hardened: for until this very day at the reading of the old covenant the same veil remains unlifted; this veil is done away in Christ. But to this day, whenever Moses is read, a veil lies upon their heart. But whenever they shall turn to the Lord, the veil is taken away.*

The change in the terms in which Paul presents the metaphors of this allegory, has been a source of darkness. When we come to know the versatility of the man, we will not expect him to continue the same form of expression. He is rich in language, and changes the forms of expression more for the beauty of the composition than for any other apparent reason. That there should ever have been any trouble in the passage, seems strange to one that is familiar with it. It is plain at the first sight, that the two legs of the antithesis are the New Covenant in contrast with the Old Covenant; and that to make that contrast as bold as it ought to be, he selects its very heart—the ten commandments. This fact has frightened many commentators from making any clear and definite statement as to the teaching of this Scripture. Some way it has gotten into theology that the Decalogue is an essential part of the New Institution; hence Paul must not be permitted to say anything to the contrary.

We may get the exact thought of this allegory by placing these legs of the antithesis over against each other. So we arrange two columns—the one headed Old Covenant, or Law, and the other headed New Covenant, or Gospel:

Old Covenant	New Covenant
1. They were not ministers.	They were ministers.
2. The letter kills.	The Spirit gives life.
3. It was the ministration of death, written and engraved on stones, which was glorious, but was passing away.	The ministration of the Spirit had much more glory, and was *not* passing away.
4. The ministration of condemnation was with glory.	The ministration of righteousness exceeded it in glory.
5. It had no glory in this respect, by reason of the greater glory.	It far surpassed in glory.
6. It was passing away.	It remains.
7. Moses put a veil upon his face.	We use great boldness of speech.
8. They could not look steadfastly on the end of that which was passing away.	This remains, and may be clearly seen.
In the reading of this, the veil was unlifted.	This darkness that troubled the world in former times is removed

	in Christ.

There should not remain any trouble in the mind of anyone as to the teaching of this allegory. Suppose that it does say that even the Decalogue was passing away! It was no more than he said elsewhere in clear, didactic speech (Col. 2:14-18). Whatever Christ has given us remains, for it cannot pass away. He has condemned every sin and maintained every virtue. He is the one mediator between God and men, and it belongs to Him to say, in all respects, what shall, and what shall not, be law. Hence His apostles must be heard.

Paul's allegory of the two women (Gal. 4:21-5:1), has the same object in view as the one just noticed. It is clearer, however, in that the apostle himself interprets it for us:

> *Tell me, you that desire to be under the law, do you not hear the law? For it is written, that Abraham had two sons, one by the handmaid, and one by the freewoman. Howbeit the son by the handmaid is born after the flesh; but the son by the freewoman is born through promise. These things contain an allegory: for these women are two covenants; one from Mount Sinai, bearing children to bondage, which is Hagar. Now this Hagar is Mount Sinai in Arabia, and answers to the Jerusalem that now is: for she is in bondage with her children. But the Jerusalem that is above is free, which is our mother. For it is written,*
>
> *Rejoice you barren, that bears not;*
> *Break forth and cry, you that travails not;*
> *For more are the children of the desolate than of her which has the husband.*
>
> *Now we, brethren, as Isaac was, are children of promise. But as then he that was born after the flesh persecuted him that was born after the Spirit, even so it is now. Howbeit what does the scripture say? Cast out the handmaid and her son: for the son of the handmaid shall not inherit with the son of the freewoman. There-*

*fore, brethren, we are not children of a handmaid, but
of the freewoman. With freedom did Christ set us free:
therefore stand fast, and do not be entangled again in a
yoke of bondage.*

One who has read what the apostle has to say in all his epistles,
has no trouble with this passage. Indeed, if we had read nothing from
any other writing of his, this would seem to be very plain. Here are
two sets of metaphors: Hagar (bondage), Sinai (law, or the law that
was given on Sinai); Jerusalem that then was. On the other hand we
have Sarah (freedom), Jerusalem that is above; children of promise;
made free in Christ. So far the antithesis is complete. But now, having
these two institutions, or covenants, what about them? Can they be
blended? "Cast out the bondmaid and her son, for the son of the
bondmaid shall not inherit with the son of the freewoman." Cast out
the Old Covenant, that was given at Mount Sinai, for it shall not have
possession along with the covenant of Christ by which we are made
free.

Section 59.
METONYMY.

The etymology of the word indicates its meaning. It is from the
Greek words *meta,* change, and *onoma,* name, hence a change of
name; the employment of one name or word for another. Webster
says of this figure:

*A trope in which one word is put for another; a change
of names which have some relation for each other, as
when we say a man keeps a good table, instead of good
provisions; we read Virgil—that is, his poems, or writings; they have 'Moses and the prophets'—that is, their
books, or writings; a man has a clear head—that is, an
understanding, or intellect; a warm heart—that is, affections.*

Many times this figure bears a close resemblance to the metaphor
and the allegory. All figures of speech are related to each other, in
that they are employed for the purpose of comparing one thing with

another. The metonymy is one of the most definite of tropes [figures of speech]. It is capable of such divisions and subdivisions as will enable us to apply definite rules in the exegesis of the passage containing it. Hence, for the sake of perspicuity, we will consider it under its several heads.

Section 60.
METONYMY OF THE CAUSE.

By this figure the *cause* is stated while the *effect* is intended.

(1). God and Christ and the Holy Spirit are frequently mentioned, whereas the result of their efforts in the redemption of the race is intended.

But you did not so learn Christ. (Eph. 4:20)

That is, you did not so learn the teaching of Christ respecting the manner of living.

When Christ, who is our life, shall be manifested, then shall you also with him be manifested in glory. (Col. 3:4)

Christ is our life, in that we have life through Him: He is the cause of life; He is named, but the effect of His work is intended.

Which veil is done away in Christ. (2 Cor. 3:14)

Here the word Christ stands for the New Covenant of which He is the author.

And he came by the Spirit into the temple. (Luke 2:27)

Simeon had received a communication before that, assuring him that he should not die till he had seen the Christ. And now that Joseph and Mary were there, be is informed by the Spirit that the promise of the Lord is being fulfilled, and if he will go into the temple he can see the Savior. So in 2 Cor. 3:6, it is said that the "letter kills, but the Spirit gives life." The word 'Spirit' is here employed for the New Institution which had been given by His inspiration. In the same way, Jesus says (John 6:36), "The words that I speak to you, they are Spirit and they are life."

He that does good is of God. (3 John 11)

That is, he is living according to the truth which God has taught.

(2). Parents are put for their children.

> *And Noah awoke from his wine, and knew what his*
> *youngest son had done to him. And he said,*
> *Cursed be Canaan;*
> *A servant of servants shall he be to his brethren.*
> *And he said.*
> *Blessed be the Lord, the God of Shem*
> *And let Canaan be his servant.*
> *God enlarge Japheth,*
> *And let him dwell in the tents of Shem:*
> *And let Canaan be his servant. (Gen. 9:25-27)*

It is clear to everyone, at sight, that the curse has respect to the *posterity* of these men. Enlarging Japheth was not increasing the bulk of the man, but making his descendants numerous.

> *I will divide them in Jacob,*
> *And scatter them in Israel. (Gen. 49:7)*

Of course this refers to the descendants of Jacob—the tribes when they should be located in the land of promise. And so it was Simeon obtained a little corner of the country down toward Egypt, and Levi had no tribal possession. They received forty-eight cities, and were distributed among the other tribes.

In Num. 23:7, Balaam said that Balak had sent for him to come and curse Jacob and defy Israel. Jacob had been dead many years. It was the *people* of Israel or Jacob. So it is in the following chapter of the parables of this prophet. All the way through the Scriptures the word Jacob, or Israel, represents the people that had descended from him. So it is with the tribes—the name of the head of the tribe passes upon the tribe, so that the people of the tribe of Reuben are named from the oldest son of Jacob, and so on to the close. Even Ephraim and Manasseh come to be terms by which we are to understand the people that sprang from them.

"Jacob have I loved, but Esau have I hated" (Rom. 9:13), was not said concerning those twin boys, but their children, some twelve hundred years after their progenitors were dead. See Mal. 1:2-3:

> *'I have loved you,' says the Lord. Yet you say, 'Wherein have you loved us?' 'Was not Esau Jacob's brother?' says the Lord: 'yet I loved Jacob; but Esau I hated, and made his mountains a desolation, and gave his heritage to the jackals of the wilderness.'*

> *'Shall I not in that day,' says the Lord, 'destroy the wise men out of Edom, and understanding out of the mount of Esau? And your mighty men, O Teman, shall be dismayed, to the end that everyone may be cut off from the mount of Esau by slaughter. For the violence done to your brother Jacob shame shall cover you, and you shall be cut off forever. In the day that you stood on the other side, in the day that strangers carried away his substance, and foreigners entered into his gates, and cast lots upon Jerusalem, even you were as one of them.' (Obadiah 8-11)*

These Scriptures show that the language was not concerning Jacob and Esau when they were children, or before they were born, but was used concerning their descendants, many centuries after these patriarchs were dead. And the good and sufficient reasons that are given for loving Jacob and hating Esau are based upon national character.

(3). *Authors are put for the works which they have produced.*— This is one of the most common forms of metonymy at the present time. We inquire of the student if he has read Virgil, Homer, Xenophon, etc., by which we mean to ask if he has read the writings of these men. In Luke 16:29-31, the Savior makes Abraham say to the rich man in hades, that his five brethren back in the world had Moses and the Prophets, and if they would not hear them, they would not give heed to one though he should go to them from the dead. The meaning is easy: they had what Moses had said in the law, and what the prophets had written by way of warning the people against iniquity, and the truth there taught was the same that anyone else would have taught them if it should please the Lord to send them such warning. Hence, if they would not listen to the instruction already furnished, it would be unreasonable to expect them to attend to the same things if re-furnished by some inferior agent.

> *And beginning from Moses and from all the prophets, he interpreted to them in all the scriptures the things concerning himself. (Luke 24:27)*

No one is in doubt, for a single moment, as to the meaning of this language. It can have but one meaning. These disciples had misunderstood the prophecies respecting their Messiah; they held the common view that when He should come, He would remain forever, and reign as an earthly king. And when the Savior was crucified, their hopes were destroyed. Now they had been astonished at what the women said to them that morning, when they reported that they had seen a vision of angels declaring that their Lord was not in the grave, but that he had risen from the dead. But the teaching of the Scriptures on that subject was not known to them. Hence the Master makes them understand that the word of the Lord teaches that He must die and rise again. And again, that evening, as the ten were met together in the city, Jesus came and stood in their midst, and opened their minds to the word of the Lord on that subject, and showed them that they taught that the Christ should die and rise again (verses 44-47). So it was with the apostles when they went to preach the gospel—they had to begin with the Scriptures of Moses and the Prophets, and show to the Jews everywhere that they had foretold that the Messiah should die for men (Acts 17:1-3). This is the meaning of Acts 15:21: "For Moses from generations of old has in every city them that preach him, being read in the synagogues every Sabbath." Not Moses, but the law that was given *through* Moses. The same figure is found in 2 Cor. 3:15: "Wherever Moses is read" that is, the law given by him.

(4). *Instruments are put for their effects.*—These instruments, being supposed to be the immediate cause, are spoken of, whereas the result of their use is intended.

*At the mouth of two witnesses, or three witnesses, shall
he that is to die be put to death. (Deut. 17:6)*

Here the mouth is put for the testimony to be spoken by it. So in Matt.
18:16:

*That at the mouth of two witnesses or three every word
may be established.*

From Acts 15:7-11, we learn that the Gentiles were converted by
Peter's mouth—that is, it was by the mouth of Peter that they first
heard the word of the gospel and believed.

In this way Christ is said to be our peace (Eph. 2:14-16), our wisdom, righteousness, sanctification, and redemption (1 Cor. 1:30). He
is the means, the cause, the instrument in the hands of the Father, by
which we have all these.

*Think not that I came to send peace on the earth: I came
not to send peace, but a sword. (Matt. 10:3-1)*

Christ was not intending to send a sword on the earth in any literal
sense. The sword is the instrument of war, and stands for that disturbance which would follow the introduction of the truth of redemption.

*Notwithstanding, if he continue a day or two, he shall
not be punished: for he is his money (Ex. 21:21).*

This is the case of a man smiting his servant. Had it been another
man, he would have been compelled to make good the time lost, and
to cause the man to be healed. But in case of smiting his servant, he
does not make good the time; but simply loses it. His servant was his
money—that is, he was the means or the instrument of money.

Very many times the sword, the bow, and spear are spoken of, instead of the work which they were expected to accomplish, in which
we have plain cases of the metonymy of the cause (Ex. 5:3; Lev. 26:6;
Isa. 1:20; Jer. 43:11; Rom. 8:35).

Section 61.
METONYMY OF THE EFFECT.

The effect is put for the cause. The cause is meant, but the effect
is named.

Cast your bread upon the waters: for you shall find it
after many days. (Eccles. 11:1)

A man casting bread on the water will not find it again; and Solomon did not intend to say the silly thing that he has been accused of saying. Let the bread stand for the bread seed, or wheat, sown on the water from a skiff, to fall into the alluvial deposit below, and, with the going down of the stream, spring up and grow, and you will get the idea of sowing in hope.

And he answered and said, 'He that sows the good seed
is the Son of man; and the field is the world; and the
good seed, these are the sons of the kingdom; and the
tares are the sons of the evil one; and the enemy that
sowed them is the devil.' (Matt. 13:37-38)

The sons of the kingdom were not sown there by the Son of man; what was done by the Savior was the sowing of the truth, giving to the world the word of the Living God, which has resulted in the Christians referred to. So it is with the children of the evil one—the devil did not sow them, but he presented the world with the falsehood, and gave the influences that have brought them into being, or made them the children of the wicked one. They are the effect, not the cause.

See, I have set before you this day life and good, and
death and evil. (Deut. 30:15)

Everyone sees these as the result of serving God or refusing that service. The life and the good, the death and the evil, were the results of that which he presented to them.

In Luke 11:14, we read that Jesus was casting out a demon, and it was dumb. And then we are informed that when the demon was gone out, the man spoke. Now, as to the condition of the demon, nothing is intended to be affirmed. It was the effect of the demon on the man possessed by it. The man was dumb, and the possession made him dumb. The effect is spoken of, whereas the cause was meant. Christ is the resurrection and the life (John 11:25). He is our wisdom, and righteousness, and sanctification, and redemption; He is our life, and our peace—that is, he is the cause of all these things to us. So is the kingdom of God righteousness and joy and peace in the Holy Spirit—that is, these are blessings derived therefrom. These are the effects. In all these the effect is mentioned, while the cause is understood.

Section 62.
METONYMY OF THE SUBJECT.

In this form of the figure, we have the subject announced, while some property belonging to it, or circumstance, is referred to. These things are meant, but the subject is named.

(1). *The subject put for the adjunct: some mere appendage or circumstance dependent upon it.* "You shall love the Lord your God with all your heart," means with the *affections* (Deut. 6:5). In Acts 4:32, it is said that the disciples were of one heart and one soul—that is, they were one in feeling, wish, faith, desire to glorify the Lord. In 1 Samuel 1:13, we are told that Hannah spoke only in her heart—that is, in her mind. David prayed that the meditation of his heart might be acceptable in the sight of the Lord. In that use of the word, the thinking power of the heart is intended. In Luke 2:19, it is said that "Mary kept all these sayings, pondering them in her heart." The shepherds related what had occurred to them in the field, in the visit of the angels, and she remembered them, and thought over them frequently. In Acts 8:22, Peter said to Simon the sorcerer, "Repent therefore of this your wickedness, and pray the Lord, if perhaps the thought of your heart shall be forgiven you." The power of believing is ascribed to the heart (Rom. 10:9-10); also the power to reason (Mark 2:6-9); and the power to judge (1 John 3:20). Now, no one of these passages fully represents the heart of man. In each of these we have an adjunct, a quality, or power. So it is in all those Scriptures in which we have the different kinds of hearts referred to—the hard heart, the evil heart of unbelief, the upright in heart, the pure heart, the tender heart, the faint heart. These conditions and qualities are mentioned, not to indicate the whole heart. In this way an examination may be conducted. For instance, it would not be agreed as to the meaning of the word 'heart' as found in the Scriptures. The question might be decided by an induction of the whole number of things said of the heart; for a scriptural definition must certainly be equal to the whole number of things said of it. In this, it would be found that the heart is said to imagine, to think, to reason, to meditate, to understand, to believe, to fear, and to love. Having, in this way, learned what the heart is supposed to be, it will be easy to understand the divine plan for the change and control of that heart.

(2). *The container is put for the contained.*—Gen. 6:11: The earth was corrupt, means that the people living in the earth were corrupt. John 1:29: that takes away the sin of the world—that is, of the people of the world. John 3:16-17: "God so loved the world"—that is, He so loved the human race "that he gave his only begotten Son, that whoever believes on him should not perish, but have everlasting life." Psa. 105:38: "Egypt was glad when they departed"—that is, the Egyptians were glad. See Matt. 3:56: "Then Jerusalem, and all Judea, and all the region round about Jordan went out to him; and they were baptized by him in the river Jordan, confessing their sins." No one thinks of these *places* doing all that, but all know that the *people* living in those places are meant.

In Matt. 11:20-24, Jesus is reported as upbraiding the cities wherein most of His mighty works had been done, and he says if the mighty works which had been done in Chorazin and Bethsaida had been wrought in Tyre and Sidon, they would have repented in sackcloth and ashes; and that if the works that had been done in Capernaum had been wrought in Sodom, it would have remained till that time, and that it would be more tolerable for the land of Sodom and Gomorrah in the day of judgment than for that city. Any reader will observe that not the cities nor the country of Sodom was in His mind, but the people who lived there. Luke says of Cornelius, that he was a devout man, and one that feared God with all his house—that is, he feared God, with all the members of his household. Ex. 2:1: "There went a man of the house of Levi." Prov. 11:29: "He that troubles his own house shall inherit the wind." Not the *building* in which he lives, but the members of his *family.* Ezek. 18:31: "For why will you die, O *house* of Israel?" means the *descendants* of Jacob. In 2 Sam. 7:13, the

Lord promises David to build him a *house*. It is then explained to mean that He would set up his son on the throne, and through his family put one on the throne at last who should never fail. The meaning of this language will be still more apparent by reading Isa. 9:6-7. And when, in the course of centuries, this family seems to be giving way, and likely to fail utterly, it was foretold that *David's house* should be reinstated in its former glory.

> '*In that day will I raise up the tabernacle of David that is fallen, and close up the breaches thereof; I will raise up his ruins, and I will build it as in the days of old; that they may possess the remnant of Edom, and all the nations which are called by my name,' says the Lord that does this,"* (Amos 9:11, 12).

Now, from the use of this language, by James (Acts 15:13, 17), it is evident that the tabernacle of David is simply the house of David, and that in the re-establishment of the house, we have the Christ placed upon the throne, to rule it with judgment and with justice from henceforth, even for evermore; now not to rule fleshly Israel only, but spiritual Israel.

(3). *The possessor put for they thing possessed.*—In this use of the figure the possessor is named but the thing possessed is to be understood.

> *Hear, O Israel: you are to pass over Jordan this day, to go in to possess nations greater and mightier than yourself, cities great and fenced up to heaven, a people great and tall, the sons of the Anakim, whom you know, and of whom you have heard say, 'Who can stand before the sons of Anak?' Know therefore this day, that the Lord your God is he who goes over before you as a devouring fire; he shall destroy them, and he shall bring them down before you: so shall you drive them out, and make them to perish quickly, as the Lord has spoken to you. (Deut. 9:1-3)*

These nations were composed of men and women and children, but they were not to be their possession, for they were to drive them out; but their possession was to be in the cities which they had built and the land on which they lived. Hence these cities and lands were their possession. So the cities and lands are not mentioned, but nations are mentioned; though their possessions were intended.

For they have devoured Jacob,
And laid waste his habitation. (Psa. 79:7).

Here is a double metonymy—first, the word Jacob refers to his descendants; and second, his descendants stand for the land they owned and occupied.

Deut. 10:9: Therefore Levi has no portion nor inher-
itance with his brethren; the Lord is his inheritance. See
Josh. 13:33.

The name of the Lord is here put for the sacrifices that should be given to the tribe of Levi. These sacrifices were the Lord's possession and they are given to this one tribe. Hence, to speak literally, Moses would have said that Levi had no possession with the other tribes, but their inheritance should be the sacrifices made to the Lord. But by the figure of metonymy, he says *the Lord is his inheritance.*

In Tit. 2:14, 1 Pet. 2:9, Christians are presented as the inheritance of the Lord. Hence, by this figure (Matt. 25:31-40), the Lord indicates that he can be fed and clothed in the persons of His disciples. "I was hungry, and you fed me"—that is, they fed His disciples, who are His possession. In strict accord with this is the language of the Master to Saul: "Why are you persecuting me?" He regarded the disciples as His own, and hence a part of Himself.

Many times the church is presented under the figure of a body—the body of the Lord Jesus Christ. Hence, by the use of this figure we have the word 'Christ' many times in the New Testament, in the place of the body, or church, which He owned. This is why Paul says, "For as many of you as were baptized into Christ, have put on Christ" (Gal. 3:27). By this we come into covenant with Him, hence into His church; and by this figure Paul says "into Christ."

(4). *The subject is sometimes named, whereas something following that, or connected with it, is intended.*—The burdens of Isaiah respecting the different countries, were evils or calamities that were coming upon them. But what follows the announcement of each one of these burdens is the prediction of the coming affliction (Isa. 13:1; 15:1; 17:1; 21:1; 22:1; 23:1).

Also the promise is put for the faith that receives it:

> *That is, it is not the children of the flesh that are children of God; but the children of the promise are reckoned for the seed. (Rom. 9:8)*

The whole contrast, however, is not respecting the promise so much as the manner of receiving that promise. The Jews had the idea that the promise was to be enjoyed because of fleshly relation to Abraham. Paul assures them that it is not so, but that the blessings of the Lord are appropriated by faith. Hence the word 'promise' is used for the faith that accepts it.

In Gal. 4:28, that thought is presented in the same way: "We, brethren, as Isaac was, are children of promise." By reading 3:25-27, this language is interpreted: "For you are all sons of God through faith, in Christ Jesus."

In like manner sin is presented, instead of the offering that is to be made for its removal.

> *If you do well, shall you not be accepted? And if you do not do well, sin waits at the door: and to you shall be his desire, and you shall rule over him. (Gen. 4:7)*

In this argument the Lord makes Cain to understand that there was no reason for a fallen countenance. The inheritance was his; his place was higher than that which belonged to his brother; and Abel would look to him for guidance and protection. If he did well, he would be accepted; and if he did not do well, for whatever of wrong might be found in him, the sacrifice would be easily made, as if the animal was already crouching at the door, waiting for the services to be rendered. Hence, while the word 'sin' is employed, *the sin-offering is intended.* See Ex. 29:14; Lev. 10:17; Hos. 4:8; Isa. 53:10, where the

Hebrew has *sin,* though our translators have felt it to be their duty to add the word *offering,* lest the language should not be understood. And we can scarcely suppress the wonder that it did not occur to them to do so in some New Testament cases.

> *Him who knew no sin he made to be sin on our behalf;*
> *that we might become the righteousness of God in him.*
> *(2 Cor. 5:21)*

Literally, Christ could not be sin; He was wholly without sin; and the only way for the language to be true is by the use of this form of metonymy. He became a sin-offering for us.

> *So Christ also, having been once offered to bear the sins*
> *of many, shall appear a second time, apart from sin, to*
> *them that wait for him, to salvation. (Heb. 9:28)*

He shall come without a sin-offering the next time. He made the sin-offering the first time; at the next He will come in judgment, not to make a sacrifice for the race.

(5). The thing signified is put for the sign.

> *Seek you the Lord and his strength;*
> *Seek his face evermore. (1 Chron. 16:11)*

This is repeated in Psa. 105:4.

> *Arise, O Lord, into your resting place;*
> *You, and the ark of your strength. (Psa. 132:8)*

It is evident that the ark was the sign of the strength of Jehovah. It was always so regarded when taken into battle. But in those passages, the strength is mentioned rather than the ark which signified it.

> *The king shall mourn, and the prince shall be clothed*
> *with desolation. (Ezek. 7:27)*

Here the word *desolation* refers to the sackcloth, or some other sign of sorrow indicated by the dress of the princes.

Very many times in the Scriptures the word '*mourn*' is employed where some symbol of sorrow is intended. "We have mourned to you, and you have not lamented." These children in the market had made the sound of mourning. There was a great deal of unreal mourning then, as now. There were hired mourners, who went about the streets making hideous noises and telling the good qualities of the dead. This is called "mourning," but of course it is only a symbol that is meant. The land of Israel is said to mourn, and the cities of Judah mourn, and Zion mourns and languishes. This can have no other meaning than that the land was neglected, the crops failed, and altogether there were everywhere the signs of lamentation, as if the land had been dressed in sackcloth and draped in the deepest sorrow. We now say of persons that they are wearing mourning, when they are wearing some badge of grief.

(6). Many times actions are said to be performed when they have only been permitted, or even foretold.

> *That my soul may live because of you. (Gen. 12:13)*

That is, if Sarah would claim to be his sister, they would not put him to death, but *permit him to live.*

> *Then I said, "Ah, Lord God! Surely you have greatly deceived this people and Jerusalem, saying, 'You shall have peace'; whereas the sword reaches to the soul."*
> *(Jer. 4:10)*

God had not told them that they should have peace in their iniquity, but He had permitted their prophets to do so.

Ezek. 13:19-22 speaks of slaying the souls that should not die, and saving the souls that should not live. This was done by the false dreamers, as they told the things that were not true. The mere telling of the things is spoken of as if they were done.

> *Moreover also I gave them statutes that were not good, and judgements in which they should not live; and I polluted them in their own gifts, in that they caused to pass through the fire all that open the womb, that I might make them desolate, to the end that they might know that I am the Lord. (Ezek. 20:25-26)*

This cannot refer to any law that God ever gave to that people; indeed, the idea that the first-born child should be offered in sacrifice was not in existence at the time that God's law was given to them.

The thought is that He gave them this bad law by their own hands—allowed them to do it—because of their wish in the matter, that they might reap the fruits of their own folly, and learn that He was the Lord.

> *I have this day set you over the nations and over the*
> *kingdoms, to pluck up and break down, and to destroy,*
> *and to overthrow; to build, and to plant. (Jer. 1:10)*

And yet the truth is, Jeremiah had been appointed simply to foretell these calamities that were about to come upon the nations for their iniquity.

> *Therefore I have hewed them by the prophets; I have*
> *slain them by the words of my mouth: and your judge-*
> *ments are of the light that goes forth. (Hos. 6:5)*

No more is meant than that the ruin and general disaster had been foretold by the prophets of the Lord.

> *What God has cleansed, do not make common. (Acts.*
> *10:15)*

God had removed the partition from between Jew and Gentile, and hence all the ceremonies of the Jewish institution, and had called the Gentiles clean as well as the Jews. It does not mean that they were already pure in His sight, but that the whole world would be accepted on the same terms in Christ.

> *And whatever you shall bind on earth shall be bound in*
> *heaven. (Matt. 16:19)*

Not that these men could bind anything upon men as a requirement of the Lord, but they could announce the things which had been given to them, and that the Lord declared would be ratified in the upper courts.

> *Whoever's sins you forgive, they are forgiven to them.*
> *(John 20:23)*

This does not mean that it belonged to men to forgive sins which had been committed against God, but they could make known the conditions of such heavenly forgiveness, and that should be approved in heaven.

(7). An action is sometimes said to have been accomplished when all that is meant by it is that an occasion was given.—In nearly all the lives of the kings of Israel, there is a statement that "he followed in the ways of Jeroboam, the son of Nebat, who made Israel to sin." Of course he did not make those men to sin who lived after his time, nor did he compel others to sin who lived at the same time that he did; but he set the example, and that led them into sin.

This is the subject being stated, whereas the agent only is intended. So a man is said to do that which his action occasions, or which he causes to be done. In Acts 1:18, Judas is spoken of as having obtained a field with the reward of iniquity. It was the money that he obtained for the delivery of the Savior from the hands of the priests that bought the field, and the act is attributed to him because he was an actor in the matter, and what he did led to the consummation of that purchase.

> *Do not destroy with your meat him for whom Christ died. (Rom. 14:15)*

It would only be the example that might lead the man into idolatry. One does not use meat as a destructive instrument, as though it were a weapon.

> *For how do you know, O wife, whether you shall save your husband? or how do you know, O husband, whether you shall save your wife? (1 Cor. 7:16)*

> *Take heed to yourself, and to your teaching; continue in these things; for in doing this you shall save both yourself and them that hear you. (1 Tim. 4:16)*

Of course, these cases of one person saving another refer to the effect their actions and teachings have in the way of influence on others, to cause them to accept of the Lord and be saved.

In this way it is said that Jesus made and baptized more disciples than John. Yet Jesus did not baptize in person. He caused it to be done, and therefore the baptizing was credited to Him. The angels that came to Abraham at Mamre were regarded as men, yet one of them is the Lord, or the Lord's agent in the destruction of the doomed cities, and in the blessing of Abraham.

In Gen. 28:13; 31:11, 13, the Lord God of Abraham is referred to as having appeared to Jacob while on his way to Paddan-aram; but in 48:16, he is called the 'angel' that had saved Jacob. In this way the angel is called by the name of Him whom he represents. He was simply the agent of the Lord.

(8). *Sometimes a statement is made as complete when the thought is only comparative.* Those who were acquainted with that figure would not be liable to be misled by it. But it differs so much from our didactic style of speech, that we need to be reminded of the custom in the days of the Scriptures.

> *Thus says the Lord of hosts, the God of Israel: 'Add your burnt offerings to your sacrifices, and eat flesh. For I did not speak to your fathers, nor commanded them in the day that I brought them out of the land of Egypt, concerning burnt offerings and sacrifices: but this thing I commanded them, saying, Hearken to my voice, and I will be your God, and you shall be my people.' (Jer. 7:21-23)*

But we know that God *had* given them commandments concerning burnt offerings and sacrifices. Hence we find here the comparative. Higher than these services was His demand for obedience. Compare 1 Sam. 15:22.

> *If any man comes to me, and hates not his own father, and mother, and wife, and children, and brethren, and sisters, yes, and his own life also, he cannot be my disciple. (Luke 14:26)*

If this had to be understood literally, it would contradict what the Master said on the mount (Matt. 5:43-48). Indeed, it would contradict all we know in both Testaments respecting the duty of man. To honor father and mother, was taught in the Decalogue, and endorsed by the Savior. Indeed, it was regarded as one of the great commandments to love one's neighbor as himself. Besides, to absolutely hate, as here indicated, would make a man a demon. This is not a parallel with Matt. 10:37, "He that loves father or mother more than me is not worthy of me;" for that was given to the twelve in Galilee; but this was spoken in Perea, a good while after that. And yet there is no doubt that the meaning of the two passages is the same. The "hate" of Luke 14:26 is comparative; hence it is, *love less*.

> *For our wrestling is not against flesh and blood. (Eph.*
> *6:12)*

This must be understood in a comparative sense. We do wrestle with flesh and blood; and no man knew it better or presented it in any stronger light than did the apostle Paul. In Gal. 5:19-21, and in the whole of Rom. 7, he treats on the danger of being in the body, and shows the only way of escape. Hence the meaning of the passage is, *We wrestle not against flesh and blood **only***. While that is one of our foes, it is not the *only* one.

> *Be no longer a drinker of water, but use a little wine for*
> *your stomach's sake and your often infirmities. (1 Tim.*
> *5:23)*

Here, again, beyond any question, the thought is comparative. He does not intend to prohibit the use of water, but prescribes a little wine with it, on account of some physical infirmity.

In this way a very large number was spoken of as the whole. There went out to John the Baptist, "Jerusalem, Judea, and the region round about Jordan; and they were baptized of him in the river Jordan." Yet there were many whom he would not baptize, calling them a generation of vipers; there were many who would not be baptized by him, of whom Jesus said, "they rejected the counsel of God against themselves, not being baptized by him." And still it is said that Jesus made and baptized more disciples than John; and that was said, too, of His work in the same country; thus only comparatively a large number were baptized of John.

In Gen. 5:24, it is said that "Enoch walked with God: and he was not; for God took him." When it says that he was not, it only means that he was not on the earth.

Joseph is not, and Simeon is not, and you will take Ben-
jamin away. (Gen. 42:36)

Of course, Jacob may have thought that Joseph was dead; but that was not to be supposed respecting Simeon, whom they had left in Egypt as a hostage. He did not mean that they were not in existence, as some have argued, but that they were not where he could secure them.

Again, on the positive side (Matt. 5:48), we are required to be perfect, even as our Father in heaven is perfect. And even though this refers to having love for all, and doing good to all, still it is furnished as a pattern which we are to copy, and in which we are to do our best as long as we live.

Section 63.
METONYMY OF THE ADJUNCT.

In this form of the metonymy the adjunct [a non-essential] is put for the subject: the subject is intended, but the adjunct is named.

(1). Sometimes an incidental, or that which is in addition to the subject, is mentioned, whereas the subject is meant.

Then shall you bring down my gray hairs with sorrow to
the grave. (Gen. 42:38)

Then shall you bring me to the grave in sorrow. The gray hairs only relate to the age.

I said, 'Days should speak, and multitude of years
should teach wisdom.' (Job 32:7)

The abstract thoughts of days, and multitude of years, stand for the man who had seen them.

Circumcision and uncircumcision stand for Jews and Gentiles, because this mark on the Jew made him to differ from every other people (Rom. 3:30; Gal. 2:9).

In Rom. 11:7, the abstract thought of *election* stands for those who, from among Israel, had accepted the Christ, and thereby had become the elect of God.

For every shepherd is an abomination to the Egyptians.
(Gen. 46:34)

The thought is that a shepherd is an abominable thing or person; the abstract, *abomination,* is employed for the person or thing that was regarded with loathing.

For you were once darkness, but are now light in the
Lord. (Eph. 5:8)

Darkness is the abstract for persons who were unenlightened by the power of saving truth. Being the light in the Lord, has just the opposite thought.

I thank you, O Father, Lord of heaven and earth, that
you did hide these things from the wise and understand-
ing, and revealed them to babes. (Matt. 11:25)

Here are the qualities of men, real or claimed, put for the men themselves. In literal language, these heavenly truths had not been given to the supposed wise men of the country, but rather to the humble and the unpretending.

(2). *The thing contained is put for the container.*—In metonymy of the subject we saw that the container was frequently put for the contained; but this is just the opposite.

This stone, which I have set up for a pillar, shall be
God's house. (Gen. 28:22)

We would say, a rather peculiar kind of house. Instead, the meaning is that the place where he set it up should be God's house.

Opening their treasures, they offered to him gifts, gold
and frankincense and myrrh. (Matt. 2:11)

What they opened was the wallets, or bags, in which these treasures were contained; the treasures are put for the bags that contained them.

The *"outer darkness"* of Matt. 22:13, refers to the place of darkness—the quality of the place having been given for the place itself. And the *marriage* of Matt. 25:10 is the place where the marriage was to be. Demons cried out, and said this or that; whereas it was done by those who were possessed by them. So are the qualities of the person described by assigning those characteristics to the demons themselves. The container is intended, but the contained is mentioned. Acts 16:13: *"A place of prayer"* is a place where people were accustomed to meet for prayer.

(3). Time is put for the things which are done or happen.

> *Men that had understanding of the times, to know what*
> *Israel ought to do. (1 Chron. 12:32)*

They understood the things done, and the condition of affairs (verses 29-30). The history of David had been written by Samuel and Nathan and Gad, giving his reign and his might, "and the times that went over him," that is, the things done in those times. Esth. 1:13: "Then the king said to the wise men, which knew the times"—that is, the things that were occurring. 2 Tim. 3:1: "But know this, that in the last days grievous times shall come." Grievous conditions and conduct. Deut. 4:32: "For ask now of the days that are past"—the events of the past. Mark 14:35: Christ prayed in the garden that the hour might pass from Him—that is, that the suffering and trial might pass—if consistent with the will of the Father. John 12:27: "Now is my soul troubled; and what shall I say? Father, save me from this hour. But for this cause I came to this hour." This is the struggle that is in the mind of the Savior, found in the last quotation.

Days are said to be good or evil, according to the things done in them (Gen. 47:9; Eccles. 7:10; Eph. 5:16).

A day is called in honor of some person, because of something done therein, or something promised to be done on that day. Hos. 1:11: "For great shall be the day of Jezreel." This day was in the future, when the language was written—the greatness was to come.

> *And when he drew near, he saw the city and wept over*
> *it, saying, 'If you had known in this day, even you, the*
> *things which belong to peace! But now they are hid*
> *from your eyes. For the days shall come upon you, when*
> *your enemies shall cast up a bank about you, and com-*
> *pass you round, and keep you in on every side, and shall*
> *dash you to the ground, and your children within you;*

and they shall not leave in you one stone upon another;
because you knew not the time of your visitation.' (Luke
19:41-44)

Even at that late hour, if they could have discerned the signs of the times, and known and acknowledged the Savior, their city and their own welfare would have been secured.

For further investigation of this use of the subject, read Job 18:20; Psa. 137:7; Ezek. 22:4; Obad. 12; Micah 7:4; Psa. 37:13.

The *day of the Lord* is spoken of as the day of judgment; but sometimes the destruction of Jerusalem, because it was a typological prophecy of that coming event (Job 24:1; Isa. 13:6; Joel 1:15; 2:1-2; Amos 5:20; Zeph. 1:14-18; 2:2). While these do not look directly at the day of judgment for the whole race, they have in view a punishment from the Lord. But many times the day refers to the judgment scene (Mal. 3:2, 17; 4:1, 3, 5; Matt. 24:36, 50; 25:13; Acts 2:20; Rom. 2:5, 16; 1. Cor. 1:8; Phil. 1:6; 2 Thess. 1:7-10).

This custom of speaking of the day in honor of someone was of long standing. The days of victories of the ancient generals and kings were known by their names. This is why the resurrection of the Savior on the first day of the week, gave to that day his name, *"the Lord's day"* (Rev. 1:10). It rendered that day sacredly His own, because he had conquered death and the grave for the whole race on that day. This day should not be called the Sabbath; it is *"the Lord's day,"* and should be kept in honor of him (Acts 20:7; 1. Cor. 16:1, 2).

The Passover is frequently used, when the paschal lamb is intended (Ex. 12:21; 2 Chron. 30:17; Mark 14:12-14; Matt. 26:17-19).

(4). *Sometimes things are spoken of according to appearance, opinions formed respecting them, or the claims made for them.* Thus in Jer. 28:1, 5, 10, Hananiah is called a prophet. This was reputation, rather than fact. Ezek. 21:3: "Will cut off from you the righteous and the wicked." These were *apparently righteous,* rather than really so. Matt. 9:13: "I came not to call the righteous, but sinners." The Lord does not mean to say that those men who complained against Him were righteous, but that such was their claim. Compare Luke 18:9. In

Luke 2:41-48, Joseph is spoken of as the father of Jesus, because he was supposed to be. Compare 3:23; John 6:42.

> *For seeing that in the wisdom of God the world through*
> *its wisdom knew not God, it was God's good pleasure*
> *through the foolishness of the preaching to save them*
> *that believe. (1 Cor. 1:21)*

This is not Paul's estimate, but the estimate of the Greek philosophers—it was foolishness to them (verses 22:24). In Gal. 1:6, Paul wondered that they were so soon turned away to another gospel; not because he thought there could be any other gospel, but because they thought the gospel of Christ ought to be conglomerated with the Law of Moses, which would make a false teaching of it. Matt. 12:27: "If I by Beelzebub cast out devils, by whom do your sons cast them out?" He does not mean to say that they cast out demons, but that they thus claimed.

> *Shall I and your mother and your brethren indeed come*
> *to bow down ourselves to you to the earth? (Gen. 37:10)*

Jacob did not refer to Rachel as the mother of Joseph, for she had been dead for a number of years, but to Leah, who was not his mother, but seemed to be.

Psa. 72:9: "His enemies shall lick the dust," must refer to their prostration, and hence seeming to lick the dust. Compare Isa. 49:23; Micah 1:10.

> *The queen of the south shall rise up in the judgement*
> *with the men of this generation, and shall condemn*
> *them, for she came from the ends of the earth to hear*
> *the wisdom of Solomon; and behold, a greater than Sol-*
> *omon is here. (Luke 11:31)*

Of course this coming from the ends of the earth is taken by appearance. There are many such expressions (Deut. 4:32; 30:4; Neh. 1:9; Matt. 24:31). And with all our scientific knowledge, we continue to say that the sun rises and sets.

Angels are spoken of as men (Gen. 18:16; 19:10; Luke 24:4; Acts 1:10), because they were in the form of men—it was the appearance, not the fact.

(5). The action, faith, or feeling, stimulated or caused by anything, may be employed, instead of the thing which caused such action, affection, or feeling.—The senses are put for the things apprehended by them. Rom. 10:17: "So belief comes of hearing, and hearing by the word of Christ." Read this in connection with the preceding verses, and it is apparent that the hearing is put for the gospel heard. In 1 Cor. 1:21, the 'foolishness of preaching' is not preaching, but the thing preached which was decided to be foolishness in the minds of the philosophers. Gal. 3:2-5, the hearing of faith, is the gospel received. Matt. 14:1, Herod heard the report of what Jesus was doing. It was the faith in the statements made that gave him trouble, for which the 'hearing' stands. Many times the word 'faith' denotes the doctrine on which it was founded. Acts 6:7: "And a great company of the priests were obedient to the faith." Gal. 1:23: "He that once persecuted us, now preaches the faith."

> But before faith came, we were kept in ward under the law, shut up to the faith which should afterwards be revealed. So that the law has been our tutor to bring us to Christ, that we might be justified by faith. But now that faith is come, we are no longer under a tutor. (Gal. 3:23-25)

Eph. 4:5: There is one faith. Ver. 13: "Till we all attain to the unity of the faith."

1 Tim. 4:1: "In latter times some shall fall away from *the faith.*" (Tit. 1:13; Jude 3; Rev. 2:13).

Love is put for the object of love. Jer. 2:33: "How you trim your way to seek love!"—to seek some object of affection.

Jer. 12:7: "I have given the dearly beloved of my soul into the hand of her enemies"—the dearly beloved *one.*

Fear is often put for the object of fear. Prov. 1:26: "I will mock when your fear comes"—that is, when some object approaches that shall terrify you. Isa. 8:13: "The Lord of hosts, him shall you sanctify;

and let him be your fear, and let him be your dread." That is, fear the Lord, and be in dread of Him.

> *Except that the God of my father, the God of Abraham, and the Fear of Isaac, had been with me, surely now you would have sent me away empty. (Gen. 31:42)*

Thus Jacob is made to remind Laban that the God of Abraham, who was feared by Isaac, was his defense.

(6). A sign is put for the thing signified.

> *The sceptre shall not depart from Judah,*
> *Nor the ruler's staff from between his feet,*
> *Until Shiloh come;*
> *And to him shall the obedience of the peoples be. (Gen. 49:10)*

Judah was characterized for strength, and should hold a ruling power till the time of the coming of the Messiah. This ruling power is signified, rather than stated.

> *And the key of the house of David will I lay upon his shoulder. (Isa. 22:22)*

This was said of Eliakim, the son of Hilkiah, and it is splendid typology of the coming Son of David, who *shuts, and no man opens; opens, and no man shuts.*

Zech. 10:11: "And the sceptre of Egypt shall depart away"—that is, the power to rule, which is signified by the sceptre.

> *And Abram said to the king of Sodom, 'I have lifted up mine hand to the Lord, God Most High, possessor of heaven and earth, that I will not take a thread...' (Gen. 14:22-23)*

The thought is, that Abram had sworn to that effect, as the hand was lifted up in affirmation.

> *He breaks the bow, and cuts the spear in sunder. (Psa. 46:9)*

As the bow and the spear were the weapons of war, breaking them is to cause war to discontinue.

My sword goes forth out of its sheath against all flesh...
(Ezek. 21:4)

The sign of destruction was the sword, hence general destruction is threatened. So in Matt. 10:34, Christ had come to send a sword—contention, and disturbance, as in war. To beat swords into plowshares and spears into pruning-hooks, is to quit war and cultivate the arts of civilization (Isa. 2:3-4). To bow the knee is the sign of reverence and worship (Isa. 45:23; Phil. 2:10; Eph. 3:14). To wear sackcloth was to mourn, as they did that in the time of very great distress:

When I made sackcloth my clothing, I became a proverb
to them. (Psa. 69:11)

(7). *The names of things are presented for the things themselves.*—In many passages the name of the Lord, or of God, denotes Jehovah.

The name of the God of Jacob set you up on high. (Psa. 20:1)

O give thanks to the Lord, call upon his name. (Psa. 105:1)

The name of the Lord is a strong tower. (Prov. 18:10)

Behold, the name of the Lord comes from far. (Isa. 30:27)

Pour out your fury upon the heathen that know you not, and upon the families that call not on your name. (Jer. 10:25)

Joel 2:32; Acts 2:21; Rom. 10:13: "Call upon the name of the Lord"—that is, they were to call on the Lord.

Names are given in the place of persons. In the Common Version of Acts 1:15, "And the number of names together were about an hundred and twenty," meaning the number of persons.

"But you have a few names [a few persons] in Sardis which did not defile their garments" (Rev. 3:4).

Sometimes names are given to denote character or condition.

*Afterward you shall be called The city of righteousness,
the faithful city. (Isa. 1:26)*

The thought is that, having been cleansed by having all their sin removed, they would be a people that would be faithful in the service of the Lord.

*You shall no more be termed 'Forsaken'; neither shall
your land any more be termed 'Desolate': but you shall
be called 'Hephzibah' [my delight is in her], and your
land 'Beulah' [married]: for the Lord delights in you,
and your land shall be married. (Isa. 62:4)*

The reason that *they* should be called the city in which the Lord delighted, was that they *should be that city*; and the reason that they should be called married, was that they *should be married.*

*So then if, while her husband lives, she be joined to an-
other man, she shall be called an adulteress. (Rom. 7:3)*

That is, she shall be an adulteress in actuality.

Section 64.
SYNECDOCHE.

This word is from the Greek *sunechdeechesthai,* meaning to receive jointly. But the meaning now given to the trope is not easily traced from the origin of the word. It is usually spoken of as a figure of speech by which we speak of the whole by a part, or a part by using a term denoting the whole. But while this is the main feature of this trope, it by no means exhausts it.

(1). *The whole is put for a part.*—"For we have found this man a pestilent fellow, and a mover of insurrections among all the Jews throughout the world" (Acts 24:5). Now, after making all due allowance for the fact that Tertullus was a lawyer and had a case to gain, still the assertion that Paul was moving insurrections throughout the world is too large, except by the figure of synecdoche, that allows the whole to be put for the part.

In Luke 2:1, it is affirmed that from Caesar Augustus there went out a decree that all the world should be enrolled. This could not have embraced more than the Roman provinces.

Rom. 1:8: The faith of the brethren was spoken of throughout the world. In Acts 19:27, it is stated that not only Asia, but the world, worshiped Diana.

By this figure the kingdom of Christ is spoken of many times, when but a single feature of that kingdom is meant. The parables spoken in Matt. 13 are inexplicable on any other hypothesis.

"The kingdom of heaven is likened to a man that sowed good seed in his field." Some have gone to work to show some analogy between the kingdom as a whole and a man sowing in the field. But this is to fail of the purpose of the parable. The kingdom is not represented by a man, nor by the seed, nor by any other feature of the whole parable, but by all of them, and more, too. The truth is, the word 'kingdom' is used in this limited sense—the whole being stated, whereas a part only was intended. The Savior's purpose, in all these parables and similes, was to remove certain errors from their minds respecting the coming of His kingdom. They thought that it would come like all the kingdoms they knew anything about, and therefore with spears and bows and battering-rams. He wished to teach them that it was not that kind of kingdom, and that it could not gain its victories in that way. Its success was to depend upon truth, planted in the hearts of the people; and when it would grow, then would it bear fruit. So you see that the man who was to sow the seed was just one feature in that institution. By the figure of synecdoche the word 'kingdom' is employed, whereas there is only the one element meant.

"The kingdom of heaven is like a grain of mustard seed." It would be the extreme of folly to undertake to find the analogy between the kingdom of Christ as a whole, and a grain of mustard. One feature of the kingdom is illustrated by it—it has a small beginning and a grand result. Again we have the word 'kingdom' employed, only to give one thought with respect to it.

"The kingdom of heaven is like to leaven, which a woman took, and hid in three measures of meal, till it was all leavened." Again there is but one point of analogy—that of a gradual enlarging from a small beginning to a grand final result. Hence the word 'kingdom' is employed for the one idea of a quiet but certain gain, till the influence shall reach the ends of the earth.

"The kingdom of heaven is like to a treasure hidden in the field." In one particular only is it like a treasure—it has great value. So with the pearl of great price: while the similitude of the "*net and the fishes*" gives the feature of the judgment. Take every parable illustration of the kingdom of heaven, and it is the use of the synecdoche—the word 'kingdom' being used, whereas there is but a single feature of that institution intended.

> *Then were there brought to him little children, that he should lay his hands on them, and pray: and the disciples rebuked them. But Jesus said, 'Suffer the little children, and forbid them not, to come to me: for of such is the kingdom of heaven.' And he laid his hands on them, and departed thence. (Matt. 19:13-15).*

They brought these children to Jesus for a blessing, and He gave it to them, for it belonged to them. Here it is evident that the word 'kingdom' is used to indicate the blessings to be conferred by the king. They had not sinned, and in that sinless condition they had a right to these blessings. Indeed, this verse has been rendered by the best authority in the country, "*To such as these belongs the kingdom.*"

"For the kingdom of God is not eating and drinking, but righteousness and peace and joy in the Holy Spirit" (Rom. 14:17). No one thinks that Paul had in his mind the kingdom as an entirety. He is not talking about the king, and the subjects, and the laws, and the officers, and territory, and the throne for the king, nor of the judgment and the punishment that shall follow those who have been disobedient, but of the one great feature of holy living and peace in the service of God. Some of them made this service to consist in forms and ceremonies and nice distinctions about meats, but he wished to have a larger view of the service of God and its blessedness than that; so he employs the word 'kingdom' for the one thought.

Under this figure, Lazarus (Luke 16:23) is put for the spirit of Lazarus. The angels carried him to Abraham's bosom, and yet the body of the poor man was lying at the gate of the rich man, and the dogs were his attendants. In John 19:42; 20:2, we have this figure used for the body. *"There they laid Jesus"*—that is, the body of Jesus. And Mary came and told the apostles that they had taken away her Lord. But in the twelfth verse the distinction is clearly made; she stooped down and saw two angels sitting, one at the head and the other at the foot, where the body of Jesus had lain. So in Luke 24:3: "And they entered in, and found not the body of the Lord Jesus."

(2). *A part put for the whole.*—Sometimes the spirit is spoken of as a possession. Christ gave up the spirit to the Father, and Stephen commended his spirit to the Lord Jesus. The Master said: *"Blessed are the poor in spirit."* In this he might be understood to mean that the man was the being, and the spirit a mere dweller, or some feature of his mentality. In Rom. 1:9, Paul says that "I serve in my spirit, in the gospel." Here Paul is one thing and the spirit another, or a mere possession. When Paul was in Athens, *"his spirit was provoked within him,* as he beheld the city full of idols." But sometimes the other form is found, and the mental man is spoken of to indicate the whole man. In Gen. 46:27, "All the souls of the house of Jacob, which came into Egypt, were seventy." The word 'soul' here, as in many places in the Bible, stands for person. One part of the person is named, but the *whole* person is intended. In other places, however, the outer and inner man are spoken of as the two great features of the man. In the whole of the seventh chapter of the Roman letter, Paul shows the struggle that was going on between the spirit that consented to that which was good, and the flesh that demanded that which was not good. So in Gal. 5:16-24, the same struggle for the mastery is indicated. In 2 Cor. 4:16, Paul says that, "Though our outward man is decaying, yet our inward man is renewed day by day." Here is something mentioned as the real self, having an outward man and an inward man, both of which are the property of this single self.

> *And I think it right, as long as I am in this tabernacle, to stir you up by putting you in remembrance; knowing*

that the putting off of my tabernacle comes swiftly, even as our Lord Jesus Christ signified to me. Yes, I will give diligence, so that at every time you may be able, after my death, to call these things to remembrance. (2 Pet. 1:13-15)

Here the apostle speaks of himself living in a tent, or tabernacle, which is soon to be laid aside. Putting this tabernacle aside is explained to be death; hence, living in this tabernacle was living in the body. The body, then, was the tabernacle, and the inner man, or the spirit, was the real man.

But in 1 Thess. 5:23 and Heb. 4:12, there are indicated three entities in the man—spirit, soul, and body. It is, then, very evident that, in many passages, a part is put for the whole.

This is many times the case with the salvation of sinners. The whole number of conditions are indicated by the use of one. Generally the first one is mentioned—that of faith—because without it nothing else could follow. Men were to call on the name of the Lord, in order to be saved (Rom. 10:17); they must believe on the Lord Jesus Christ (Acts 16:31); they must repent of their sins (Acts 17:30); they must be baptized in the name of the Lord (Acts 22:16). But it is common to have one of these mentioned, without any statement as to the presence of any other.

(3). *Time is put for a part of time.*—All the way through the Scriptures the Oriental form of expression is found, in this respect.

"Of them shall you take your bondmen forever" (Lev. 25:46). Whatever construction may be put upon this passage, they have long ceased to take bondmen from the strangers around them.

"And my covenant shall be in your flesh for an everlasting covenant" (Gen. 17:13). In Gen. 13:15, God promised the land of Canaan to Abram and his seed forever. In Num. 25:13, to Phinehas was promised an everlasting priesthood. It failed a long time ago. Sometimes men have been staggered at the discovery of this fact, and have almost reached the conclusion that these statements were never made by the God of heaven at all. Others have concluded that wherever *eternity* or *everlasting* occurs, only limited duration is intended. But this will not do, for it limits the blessedness of the righteous, and the years of God himself. He is the same, and His years shall not fail; from everlasting to everlasting He is God. It will not do to rush from one extreme to another. The word *'forever'* exhausts the period to which it belongs. If it was said to a king, "live forever," it meant a long life, and yet the life of a man. If it referred to a nation, it was to extend till that nation would be scattered and the nationality be destroyed. If we could know that it related to time, we could be sure that it would exhaust the period. But if it reach beyond the precincts of time, there then being no limit, it must have all the meaning that can attach to the word. Hence, because a word is sometimes used in a figurative sense, it does not follow that it is always to be so understood.

(4). *The plural is put for the singular.*—The ark that carried Noah across the flood rested on the mountains of Ararat (Gen. 8:4). It could not have rested on more than one. To one accustomed to their style of speech there would be nothing strange in the expression. There were three ranges of hills, or mountains, and in one of these ranges the ark rested.

"And it came to pass, when God destroyed the cities of the Plain, that God remembered Abraham, and sent Lot out of the midst of the overthrow, when he overthrew the cities in which Lot dwelt" (Gen. 19:29). But Lot only dwelt in one city—Sodom.

"Who would have said to Abraham, that Sarah should nurse children?" (Gen. 21:7). She never had but one child, and no other was ever promised. In Gen. 46:7, when Jacob was going into Egypt, it is indicated that he took "his sons, and his sons' sons with him; his daughters, and his sons' daughters." But Jacob never had more than one daughter—*Dinah*—the one who was defiled by Shechem.

"Thus says the Lord, 'Stand in the ways, and see, and ask for the old paths, where is the good way, and walk therein, and you shall find rest for your souls'" (Jer. 6:16). Here the *paths* denote that which is right in the sight of the Lord, and therefore could not have been different. This path meant the good way in which they were to walk.

This may account for the singular being used by one apostle and the plural by another, when describing the same thing. Matthew and

Mark usually differ in this respect. Matthew has two men possessed by demons in Gadara; Mark tells of but one. Mark tells of one blind beggar at Jericho that wished to be healed; Matthew has two. Mark describes the ride into Jerusalem to be on a colt whereon man never sat; Matthew has *an ass and a colt.* Mark and Matthew both say that they who were crucified with Jesus reproached him; while Luke declares that one defended his claims by rebuking the other (Luke 23:39-43). To say that they reproached Him when only one did it, would not have been out of harmony with general custom at that time. A number are frequently said to have done a thing, when it is certain that but one of the number did it. This may be all there was in the remark of Paul to the sergeants (Acts 16:35, 37), "They have beaten us publicly, uncondemned, men that are Romans." We know that Paul was a Roman citizen; but that Silas was, could hardly be sustained by this text.

(5). *The singular is put for the plural.*—This is commonly understood when the statement is a general one. When God ordained marriage, it was not for the one man and woman in the garden—it was not for them that it was said, "Therefore shall a man forsake father and mother, and shall cleave to his wife"—for it meant all men; so that marriage was instituted for the race.

"And God said, Let the waters bring forth abundantly the moving creature that has life, and let fowl fly above the earth" (Gen. 1:20). The moving creature and the fowl do not mean one of each, but the whole family of each. In Ex. 8:17; 13:15, we have the plagues of Egypt that came upon *man and beast.* While the words man and beast do not mean all men and all beasts, they do mean all those that were exposed in Egypt, belonging to the dominion of Pharaoh. The term is singular, but the meaning is plural.

> *I will sing to the Lord, for he has triumphed gloriously:*
> *The horse and his rider has he thrown into the sea. (Ex. 15:1)*

> *Yes, the stork in the heaven knows her appointed times;*
> *and the turtle and the swallow and the crane observe*

*the time of their coming; but my people do not know the
ordinance of the Lord. (Jer. 8:7)*

Here a number of things are spoken of in the singular, while the whole number is intended: the stork, the turtle, the crane, stand for all such.

"The ox knows his owner, and the ass his master's crib" (Isa. 1:3). All oxen, and all asses, is the meaning. Lev. 11:29 tells of some unclean animals, such as the weasel, the lizard, and the mouse. In Deut. 7:20, God promised to send the hornet, and drive out the inhabitants; and in Josh. 24:12, they are reminded that God had sent the hornet, and had driven out the people in that way. Of course it was not any one hornet that did that work. He is to be regarded as a numerous hornet! This is, perhaps, the proper interpretation of Gen. 6:16, respecting the light in the ark, which God appointed.

(6). A definite is put for an indefinite number.

"That she has received of the Lord's hand double for all her sins" (Isa. 40:2). The word *double* stands for plenty.

"Render to her even as she rendered, and double the double according to her works" (Rev. 18:6). That is, she must be punished sufficiently.

*God has spoken once,
Twice have I heard this. (Psa. 62:11)*

*Howbeit in the church I would rather speak five words
with my understanding, that I might instruct others also,
than ten thousand words in a tongue. (1 Cor. 14:19)*

In this he is understood to mean that he would prefer to use a very few words that would instruct the people than a great number that would not do any good. Elkanah said to Hannah (1 Sam. 1:8), "Am I not better to you than ten sons?"—that is, than a whole family of sons?

*A rebuke enters deeper into one that has understanding
Than an hundred stripes into a fool. (Prov. 17:10)*

That is, than any number of stripes.

"If a man beget an hundred children" (Eccles. 6:3). A great number.

"For the child shall die an hundred years old, and the sinner being an hundred years old shall be accursed" (Isa. 65:20). This is a strong figure for the blessings that would be for them when they should return from their captivity in Babylon.

One thousand stands for a higher number, and yet indefinite, many times.

> *And showing mercy to thousands, of them that love me*
> *and keep my commandments. (Ex. 20:6)*

Here the thousands include the whole number of those that love the Lord, and keep His word.

> *The Lord, the God of your fathers, make you a thousand*
> *times so many more as you are. (Deut. 1:11)*

That is, increase your number very greatly.

> *He cannot answer him one of a thousand. (Job. 9:3)*

> *For every beast of the forest is mine,*
> *And the cattle upon a thousand hills. (Psa. 50:10)*

Ten thousand stands for a very great number, but sometimes as indefinite as the others.

> *And when it rested, he said, Return, O Lord, to the ten*
> *thousands of the thousands of Israel. (Num. 10:36)*

> *A fiery stream issued and came forth from before him:*
> *thousand thousands ministered to him, and ten thousand*
> *times ten thousand stood before him. (Dan. 7:10)*

> *And the number of them was ten thousand times ten*
> *thousand, and thousands of thousands. (Rev. 5:10)*

Everyone understands by these expressions a very great number, but no one thinks of the number being accurately made out.

The words hour, day, year, are employed with the same latitude. Jesus said to the disciples the night before the crucifixion, "Could you not watch with me one hour?"—that is, just a little while.

Numbers, among the ancients, were very loosely kept. All the antediluvian patriarchs seem to have died on their birthdays, for they were so many years old. The same is true of the men who lived on this side of the flood. And yet we do not think but what they lived months and days, more or less, just as the people do now.

If we take the ordinals among the Greeks, first, second, third, etc., they are always to be relied upon; but if we have the indication in the use of the cardinals, one, two, three, etc, we may feel sure that it is not as we would say it. Jesus says that He was to be in the heart of the earth *three days and three nights;* and again, that He would *rise again on the third day.* As we speak, this could not be true. See John 2:19; Mark 8:31; Matt. 16:21. And by reading 1 Kings 12:5-12, both styles of record will be found.

(7). *A general name is put for a particular name.*—"All flesh" stands for all human beings. Psa. 145:21. "And let all flesh bless his holy name, for ever and ever."

> *And the glory of the Lord shall be revealed, and all flesh shall see it together: for the mouth of the Lord has spoken it. The voice of one saying, 'Cry.' And one said, 'What shall I cry? All flesh is grass.' (Isa. 40:5-6)*

> *Because by the works of the law shall no flesh be justified. (Rom. 3:20)*

> *And preach the gospel to the whole creation. (Mark 16:15)*

It is not meant to preach the gospel to the animal creation, but to the human family. The word 'creature' stands here for the human race only.

In the time of Abraham it was said that "the Canaanite was then in the land" (Gen. 12:6). But this is the general for a large number of tribes into which the descendants of the fourth son of Ham had been divided. It is not certain that the races of giants—the Anakim, the Avim, the Emmim, the Horim, the Rephaim, the Zuzim, or the Zamzummim—were descendants from this line or not; but the probabilities are that they were. At any rate, the Canaanite includes the Amorites (between Hebron and the salt sea, that afterwards spread to the east side of the Jordan, and occupied the country from the river Arnon on the south, to the north line of Bashan); the Arkites (at Arka, opposite the northern part of Lebanon); the Arvadites (around Arad); the Girgashites (around the sea of Tiberius); the Hamathites (around Hamath, in the extreme north of the land); the Hittites (around Hebron); the Hivites (about the foot of Hermon); the Jebusites (about Jerusalem); the Perizzites (in Samaria); the Sinites (south of Arka); the Zerarites (south of Arad); and probably the Zidonians (at Zidon).

It is quite common, in all ages of the world, to speak of the smaller tribes by mentioning the larger, which contained the smaller.

(8). Sometimes a special name or word is put for a general.

He makes wars to cease to the end of the earth;
He breaks the bow, and cuts the spear asunder;
He burns the chariots in the fire. (Psa. 46:9)

That is to say, God is the great peace-maker, and he accomplishes the work by the destruction of the means of warfare.

By this rule, bread is used in the place of food in general.

Command that these stones become bread. (Matt. 4:3)

Give us this day our daily bread. (Matt. 6:11)

That is, our daily food. Many times the word *meat* is used in the same sense. These special names are employed because they are leading, and therefore indicate the whole line of food in general.

In Dan. 12:2, *many* is put for *all mankind,* for, though the thought to be conveyed is the restoration of Israel from Babylon, yet the scene is laid on the general resurrection of the dead. Hence the "Many that sleep in the dust of the earth" meant all that sleep in the dust of the earth (see 2 Cor. 2:6).

In Mark 16:16, "He that believes" stands for *all* who believe, etc. In Psa. 1:1: "Blessed is the man," means blessed are *all* men who walk as indicated in that place. In like manner we have father, mother, brother, sister, daughter, son, etc., used for relatives that are more distant. They are the particular things used for the general. Consult Gen. 1:21; 17:4; 24:38-40; 29:12; 28:9; 3:20; Judg. 5:7; Rom. 16:13; Deut.

15:7; 23:19; Ruth 4:3; Mark 3:35; Josh. 7:19; Matt. 1:6. It will be found in the genealogy of Matthew, that there are skips where even the form of begat is used. We are ready to excuse Luke, in adopting the Septuagint in giving the line of Salmon, Boaz, Obed, Jesse, David; and yet from the birth of Boaz to the birth of David, there is scarcely less than four hundred and fifty years of time, which would demand that each father mentioned should have been about one hundred and fifty years old when his son was born. And yet men were not as long lived then as now. David was an old and worn out man at seventy, and Solomon reaches the end of life under sixty. It is better to concede that there are vacancies in the account, and that they did not choose to fill them, and have thus used the terms in a larger sense, giving the specific for the general, as in Rom. 1:16. In many other places the word 'Gentile' occurs for all heathen.

Section 65.
PROVERB.

This seems to come from the Latin *proverbium*, from *pro*, before, or for, and *verbum*, a word. A sentence condensed into a word, or its smallest form. Webster says of it:

> *1. An old and common saying; a phrase which is often repeated; especially a sentence which briefly and forcibly expresses some practical truth, or the result of experience and observation; a maxim; a saw. 'The proverb is true, that light gains make heavy purses; for light gains come often, great gains now and then.'—BACON.*

> *2. Hence a striking or paradoxical assertion; an enigma. 'His disciples said to him, Lo! now speakest you plainly, and you usest no proverb.'—WYCLIFFE'S BIBLE, 1551.*

> *3. A byword; an expression of contempt. Thou shall become an astonishment, a proverb, and a byword, among all nations (Deut. 28:37).*

A proverb, then, may be regarded as a short, pithy sentence, containing a complete and valuable thought. Its value may be judged (1) by its prominence and value of truth; (2) its brevity; (3) its elegance and beauty.

It is constructed of several different figures of speech, and when they are employed the rules that relate to their interpretation should be used.

As they were in the habit of calling nearly all figures parables, several times in the New Testament the word 'parable' is used where, according to our forms of speech, we would say 'proverb.' Once before we mentioned Luke 4:23 (See Parable), and also the parable of the fig tree (Matt. 24:32) are proverbs: When the fig tree puts forth leaves, the summer is nigh.

Here are a few model parables.

> *Out of the wicked comes forth wickedness. (1 Sam. 24:13)*
>
> *It is more blessed to give than to receive. (Acts 20:35)*
>
> *The days are prolonged, and every vision fails. (Ezek. 3:22)*

The form of that last one was good enough, but God found fault with its substance on the ground that it was not true (ver. 23). They used another that looked well enough, but was faulty on the same account: "The fathers have eaten sour grapes, and the children's teeth are set on edge" (Ezek. 18:2).

Sometimes they spoke of proverbs as dark sayings (John 16:25, 29).

These sayings, or "words of mine" (Matt. 7:24), might be called proverbs. Indeed, the Sermon on the Mount is almost made up of terse, forceful sentences, each one containing a great volume of truth. From 1 Kings 4:32; Eccles. 12:9, Solomon seems to have spoken many proverbs which have not been reported to us. The whole book of Proverbs should be studied, in order to be familiar with this form of speech.

It was used by the ancients, as by us, for the purpose of making the truth appear with greater force, and to be remembered longer. "The legs of the lame are not equal." "Consistency thou art a jewel." "He laughs best who laughs last." Ahab, king of Israel, is the author of a very fine proverb. It was in answer to Benhadad, king of Syria: "Let not him that girds on *his armor* boast himself as he that puts it off" (1 Kings 20:11).

> *It has happened to them according to the true proverb,*
> *The dog turning to his own vomit again, and the sow*
> *that had washed to her wallowing in the mire. (2 Pet.*
> *2:22)*

That illustrates those who are low in their disposition and practices, who then turned to be Christians, and then permitted their old desires and customs to control them.

A proverb may be enlarged into a parable, simply by the use of a story which will contain the thought that would otherwise be put into a brief sentence. The parable of the Good Samaritan (Luke 10:25-37), might be made into a proverb: "To be neighbor, is to show kindness." And while that truth might be as potent to one who wished it, yet it would not enforce itself on the mind as well as in the parable form in which the Savior put it.

Section 66.
IRONY.

From the Greek *eironeia,* dissimulation; as a figure, it means to dissemble in speech—to say one thing, while another is meant. In modern language, this would usually be known as "sarcasm" (but see next section for more on that). Webster says of this word:

> *A kind of ridicule which exposes the errors or faults of others by seeming to adopt, approve, or defend them; apparent assent to a proposition given, with such a tone, or under such circumstances, that opposite opinions or feelings are implied.*

Irony can be detected (1) by a statement made by the author: he sometimes says that certain things were said in mockery. (2) It is sometimes apparent from the tone or accent, or the manner of the speaker. (3) Sometimes it will be recognized by the character of the address: if the speaker has been dealing in that kind of dissimulation for the purpose of ridicule, it will be the easier detected. (4) The extravagance of praise, when we know both the subject and the author, will enable us to note the intent. (5) When the language was used orally, and has been printed, there may be nothing in the form of words to denote that it was an ironical speech; but if we can get the opinion of those who were present, it will assist us; for they would be able to discover in the tone or the accent what has been lost to us by distance and time.

The Scriptures contain many examples of irony, but, with the rules we have given already for its detection, we will cite but a few, for the real meaning in any case is not difficult.

> *And it came to pass at noon, that Elijah mocked them, and said, 'Cry aloud: for he is a god; either he is musing, or he is gone aside, or he is in a journey, or peradventure he sleeps, and must be awakened.' (1 Kings 18:27)*

> *And when he had come to the king, the king said to him, 'Micaiah, shall we go to Ramoth-gilead to battle, or shall we forbear?' And he answered him, 'Go up, and prosper; and the Lord shall deliver it into the hand of the king.' And the king said to him, 'How many times shall I adjure you that you speak to me nothing but the truth in the name of the Lord?' And he said, 'I saw all Israel scattered upon the mountains, as sheep that have no shepherd: and the Lord said, These have no master; let them return every man to his house in peace.' And the king of Israel said to Jehoshaphat, 'Did I not tell you that he would not prophesy good concerning me, but evil?' (1 Kings. 22:15-18)*

There is nothing in the form of this address that would enable us to discern the irony in it. But Ahab knew the man, and perhaps detected in the tone and accent of the speech the ironical under-current.

> *No doubt but you are the people,*
> *And wisdom shall die with you. (Job 12:2)*

The wisdom these men supposed they possessed, but did not actually possess, made it necessary that the patriarch should deal in a very rugged language to bring them to their senses.

> *Go and cry to the gods which you have chosen; let them save you in the time of your distress. (Judg. 10:14)*

> *Already you are filled, already you have become rich, you have reigned without us: yes and I desire that you did reign, that we also might reign with you. For, I think, God has set forth us the apostles last of all, as men doomed to death: for we are made a spectacle to the world, and to angels, and to men. We are fools for Christ's sake, but you are wise in Christ; we are weak, but you are strong; you have glory, but we have dishonor. Even to this present hour we both hunger, and thirst, and are naked, and are beaten, and have no certain dwelling-place; and we toil, working with our own hands: being reviled, we bless; being persecuted, we endure; being defamed, we entreat: we are made as the filth of the world, the offscouring of all things, even until now. (1 Cor. 4:8-13)*

The wisdom that this church supposed they possessed, but did not actually possess, made it necessary that the apostle should deal in very rugged language to bring them to their senses.

"But others mocking said, They are filled with new wine" (Acts 2:13). Of course they meant to be understood as saying that they were drunk; but being full of sweet wine would not make them drunk. They meant what we now mean when we say of a man that *"he is happy,"* or that he *"he is full of milk."* They say one thing, but mean another.

Section 67.
SARCASM.

This is from the Greek *sarkasmos,* from *sarkadzein,* to tear flesh like dogs; to bite the lips in rage; to speak bitterly; to sneer. Webster says of it:

> *A keen, reproachful expression; a satirical remark uttered with some degree of scorn or contempt; a taunt; a gibe; a cutting jest.*

It is so related to irony that it is quite common for them to be regarded as the same. It differs, however, from the usual form of irony in its severity and evident spitefulness. It is only used for the purpose of reproof and condemnation, and when the soul is too angry to secrete its bitterness. It is used to condemn some action by seeming to order it, or decide the claims of those who are condemned.

> *And they plaited a crown of thorns and put it upon his head, and a reed in his right hand; and they kneeled down before him, and mocked him, saying, 'Hail, King of the Jews!' (Matt. 27:29)*

> *In like manner also the chief priests mocking him among themselves with the scribes said, 'He saved others; he cannot save himself. Let the Christ, the King of Israel, now come down from the cross, that we may see and believe.' (Mark 15:31-32)*

The Savior uses sarcasm in His fierce condemnation of the self-righteousness of the Jews. They were punctilious in the payment of tithing on mint and dill and garden spices; they were strict in keeping the traditions of the fathers, but had little respect for the authority of God Himself.

> *And he said to them, Full well do you reject the commandment of God, that you may keep your tradition. (Mark 7:9)*

In Paul's anger at the high priest at Jerusalem (Acts 23:3-5), he gives vent to his feelings by the use of sarcasm.

And when God told the Jews to get drunk and spew, He used the severest form of sarcasm.

Section 68.
HYPERBOLE.

Greek *huper,* above, over, beyond; and *bolee,* from *bolein,* to throw. Webster says:

> *A figure of speech in which the expression is an exaggeration of a meaning intended to be conveyed, or by which things are represented as much greater or less, better or worse, than they really are; a statement which exaggerates through passion or intense excitement.*

"And there we saw the Nephilim, the sons of Anak, which come of the Nephilim: and we were in our own sight as grasshoppers, and so we were in their sight" (Num. 13:33). This was the report of the ten spies whose faith failed them. And, according to Deut. 1:28, they also said: "The cities are great and fenced up to heaven." In 9:1, Moses repeats this to the Israelites just before they passed over the Jordan.

In Gen. 41:49, it is said that Joseph "laid up corn as the sand of the sea, very much." God said to Abraham (Gen. 13:16), "And I will make your seed as the dust of the earth; so that if a man can number the dust of the earth, then shall your seed also be numbered."

When the Midianites had overrun the land of Israel, for several years, the Lord raised up Gideon for their deliverance. But the insignificance of the army of the Lord, when compared to the Midianites and the help they had provided, is strongly expressed by Judg. 7:12: "And the Midianites and the Amalekites and all the children of the east lay along in the valley like locusts for multitude; and their camels were without number, as the sand which is upon the sea shore for multitude."

> *And the Philistines assembled themselves together to fight with Israel, thirty thousand chariots, and six thousand horsemen, and people as the sand which is on the sea shore in multitude. (1 Sam. 13:5)*

And God gave Solomon wisdom and understanding exceeding much, and largeness of heart, even as the sand that is on the sea shore. (1 Kings 4:29)

But I am a worm, and no man;
A reproach of men, and despised of the people. (Psa. 22:6)

Again, in verses 14-15:

I am poured out like water,
And all my bones are out of joint:
My heart is like wax;
It is melted in the midst of my bowels.
My strength is dried up like a potsherd;
And my tongue cleaves to my jaws;
And you have brought me into the dust of death.

David expresses his sorrow in a very strong light in Psa. 6:6-7:

I am weary with my groaning;
Every night I make my bed to swim;
I water my couch with my tears.
My eye wastes away because of grief;
It waxes old because of all my adversaries.

And there are also many other things which Jesus did, which if every one should be written, I suppose that even the world itself would not contain the books that should be written. (John 21:25)

All the nations are as nothing before him; they are counted to him less than nothing, and vanity. (Psa. 40:17)

To me, who am less than the least of all saints, was this grace given. (Eph. 3:8)

There need be no rule for the interpretation of the hyperbole, except to keep the purpose of the author before one's mind, and the language will interpret itself. It is simply an intensification, and not used with any intent to misrepresent the facts in the case. Of course, to make these statements literal will find the Bible guilty of many false-hoods; but when we treat such figures in the Scriptures as we treat them elsewhere, there is no danger of failing to comprehend them.

Section 69.
THE APOSTROPHE.

Greek *apo,* from, and *strephein,* to turn, a turning from, or away from. In rhetoric it is a turning away from the real auditory, and addressing an imaginary one.

(1). When this audience is from the inanimate world, it is common to call it Personification. Yet there is a clear distinction between ascribing to them powers and volition and knowledge which do not belong to them, and addressing a speech to them. Personification is present, but it is not all; the turning aside from the regular discourse, and speaking to another than the real audience, makes it Apostrophe.

> *O you sword of the Lord, how long will it be before you are quiet? Put up yourself into your scabbard; rest, and be still. How can you be quiet, seeing the Lord has given you a charge? (Jer. 47:6-7)*

> *O death, where is your victory? O death, where is your sting? (1 Cor. 15:55)*

> *O Jerusalem, Jerusalem, which kills the prophets, and stones them that are sent to her! how often would I have gathered your children together, even as a hen gathers her own brood under her wings, and you would not! Behold, your house is left to you desolate: and I say to you, 'You shall not see me, until you shall say, Blessed is he that comes in the name of the Lord.' (Luke 13:34-35)*

(2). When the address is to an absent person, it is pure apostrophe.

> *And the king was much moved, and went up to the chamber over the gate, and wept: and as he went, he said, 'O my son Absalom, my son, my son Absalom!*

Would to God I had died for you, O Absalom, my son,
my son!' (2 Sam. 18:33)

This is an address to the absent son as though he were present, and is the unmixed apostrophe.

The finest and boldest apostrophe found in any book is to be read in Isa. 14:9-20. It is properly regarded as the prophet's address to the king of Babylon. The man of God had seen his work of disaster until he was sick at heart, and now that the Lord permits him to see what is reserved for that power that had trampled every other to the ground, he delivers the matter with zest:

Hell from beneath is moved for you, to meet you at your
coming: it stirs up the dead for you, even all the chief
ones of the earth; it has raised up from their thrones all
the kings of the nations. All they shall answer and say to
you, 'Are you also become weak as we? Have you be-
come like us? Your pomp is brought down to hell, and
the noise of your viols: the worm is spread under you,
and worms cover you. How you are fallen from heaven,
O day star, son of the morning! How you are cut down
to the ground, you who laid low the nations! And you
said in your heart, I will ascend into heaven, I will exalt
my throne above the stars of God; and I will sit upon the
mount of congregation, in the uttermost parts of the
north: I will ascend above the heights of the clouds; I
will be like the Most High. Yet you shall be brought
down to hell, to the uttermost parts of the pit.' They that
see you shall narrowly look upon you, they shall consid-
er you, saying, 'Is this the man that made the earth to
tremble, that shook kingdoms; that made the world as a
wilderness, and overthrew the cities thereof, that did not
loose his prisoners to their home?' All the kings of the
nations, all of them, sleep in glory, every one in his own
house. But you are cast forth away from your tomb like
an abominable branch, clothed with the slain, that are
thrust through with the sword, that go down to the

stones of the pit as a carcass trodden under foot. You shall not be joined with them in burial, because you have destroyed your land, you have slain your people; the seed of evil-doers shall not be named forever. (Isa. 14:9-20)

This is a most wonderful address, especially when we realize that the prophet was talking to a man who was not yet born, and whose end was two hundred years away. He might have presented this in the usual form of prophecy, but he could not have given to it the strength and force that was desired. Hence he calls up the king of Babylon, and delivers to him the sentence of death, and even permits the slain kings to rise up from the grave and taunt him for not having a place in which to be buried; and the unseen is set into a roar of laughter at the pretensions of this mighty man.

Section 70.
PERSONIFICATION.

This is a figure of speech by which human characteristics are put on non-human objects or creatures. A singing mountain, clapping trees, angry waters, etc. This is frequently employed in the Hebrew Scriptures. Indeed, it is now a staple in the market of communication, and we use it so commonly ourselves that we have almost ceased to think of it as a figure of speech.

And it came to pass, as he made an end of speaking all these words, that the ground clave asunder that was under them: and the earth opened her mouth, and swallowed them up, and their households, and all the men that pertained to Korah, and all their goods. (Num. 16:31-32)

The earth opening her mouth indicates volition, and intent to remove those rebels against the Lord and His servant.

Therefore do not be anxious for tomorrow: for tomorrow will be anxious for itself. Sufficient to the day is the evil thereof. (Matt. 6:34)

Here is a day or some period of time spoken of as having the reason and interest of men.

> *The sea saw it, and fled*
> *Jordan was driven back.*
> *The mountains skipped like rams,*
> *The little hills like young sheep. (Psa. 114:3-4)*

> *The mountains saw you, and were afraid;*
> *The tempest of waters passed by*
> *The deep uttered his voice,*
> *And lifted up his hands on high.*
> *The sun and moon stood still in their habitation;*
> *At the light of your arrows as they went. (Hab. 3:10-11)*

Here the mountains, the sea, and the sun and the moon are endowed with powers which belong to the human race, and are not in the choice of inanimate things.

"If any man thinks himself to be religious, while he does not bridle his tongue, but deceives his heart, this man's religion is vain" (Jas. 1:26). In this text the apostle ascribes to the tongue of man an independent power, as if it were some ferocious animal. In 3:9-10, he has another use of it, very much the same.

Job, in his valuation of wisdom and search for understanding, says some beautiful things respecting its home being in the mind of God.

> *The deep says, 'It is not in me':*
> *And the sea says, 'It is not with me.' (Job. 28:14)*

> *Destruction and Death say,*
> *'We have heard a rumor of it with our ears.' (ver. 22)*

In these texts the sea and death and destruction are regarded as considering questions which are worthy of the best minds of mortals.

> *The whole earth is at rest, and is quiet: they break forth*
> *into singing. Yes, the fir trees rejoice at you, and the ce-*
> *dars of Lebanon, saying, 'Since you are laid down, no*
> *feller is come up against us.' (Isa. 14:7-8)*

This was the rejoicing of nature at the thought of the destruction of the king of Babylon. Isaiah sees everything as conforming to the feelings of the people of the Lord respecting the breaking down of that power that had retained them in bondage away from their own land. So again, when he is permitted to see the Jews returning home, it seems to him as if the very land itself will be frantic with joy at the sight, once more, of the children of that country.

> *For you shall go out with joy, and be led forth with peace; the mountains and the hills shall break forth before you into singing, and all the trees of the field shall clap their hands. (Isa. 55:12)*

Thus he gives to them all the volition and thought and feeling that belonged even to men.

> *Go up, you horses; and rage, you chariots; and let the mighty men go forth: Cush and Put, that handle the shield; and the Ludim, that handle and bend the bow. For that day is a day of the Lord, the Lord of hosts, a day of vengeance, that he may avenge him of his adversaries: and the sword shall devour and be satiated, and shall drink its fill of their blood. (Jer. 46:9-10)*

Here the horses and chariots and the sword are filled with animation, and have desires that are to be satisfied with the destruction of those who oppose their country.

Fables can only be constructed by the use of this figure of speech. From first to last, human ability must be ascribed to the lower animals, or to inanimate creatures.

Section 71.
INTERROGATION

This is a figure of speech when it is employed for the purpose of affirming or denying with great force. It is not an inquiry into any proposition, but asking rhetorical questions as a way of finishing the point, and is to be understood as the conclusion of all investigation. The question is only asked because it serves as a basis for some conclusion which the speaker desires to reach.

Nicodemus says to them (he that came to him before, being one of them), 'Does our law judge a man, except it first hear from himself and know what he did?' (John 7:50-51)

He meant to say that the law did not permit any man to he condemned without first having been heard, and he meant to say it with force.

Am I not free? Am I not an apostle? Have I not seen Jesus our Lord? Are you not my work in the Lord? (1 Cor. 9:1)

Surely Paul does not ask these questions for the sake of any light he might gain respecting them. He meant to say, 'These things are so, and you know them to be so; these are facts about which there is no doubt.'

Are all apostles? Are all prophets? Are all teachers? Are all workers of miracles? Do all have gifts of healings? Do all speak with tongues? Do all interpret? (1 Cor. 12:29-30)

Here are seven questions to which a negative answer was expected. Indeed, they are presented as if they were the conclusion on the subject—as if he had said: 'You know that all are not apostles, etc.'

Are they not all ministering spirits, sent forth to do service for the sake of them that shall inherit salvation? (Heb. 1:14)

It was not because Paul, or anyone else, doubted that the angels were ministering spirits, that he puts the question, but because on that point there was no dispute, as if he had said, 'You know that they fill that mission.'

Job indulges this style; and the Lord, when He speaks to Job, presents the thought with great force in this way.

Can you, by searching, find out God? Can you find out the Almighty to perfection? (Job 11:7)

Zophar the Naamathite, tries this form of emphasis (see Job 20:4, 5):

> *Do you not know this of old time,*
> *Since man was placed upon earth,*
> *That the triumphing of the wicked is short,*
> *And the joy of the godless but for a moment?*

He is not inquiring after anything that Job might know on that subject, but using this figure as the best way of enforcing his thought.

When the Lord answered Job out of the whirlwind (38-41), everything, almost, was put in this terse way:

> *Who is this that darkens counsel*
> *By words without knowledge?*
> *Where were you when I laid the foundations of the*
> *earth?*
> *Have you commanded the morning since your days be-*
> *gan?*
> *Have you entered into the springs of the sea?*
> *Have the gates of death been revealed to you?*
> *Have you entered the treasuries of the snow?*
> *Has the rain a father?*
> *Out of whose womb came the ice?*
> *Canst you bind the cluster of the Pleiades,*
> *Or loose the bands of Orion?*

These are but a few for the whole; for God's reproof of this man was by the use of the Interrogative, making him to understand that he had undertaken to speak on subjects with which he was not acquainted. The reproof had its desired effect, for he was made to feel that his knowledge was not sufficient to the topics on which he had spoken.

But one of the finest figures of this kind is to be read in Rom. 8:31-35:

> *What shall we say then to these things? If God is for us,*
> *who is against us? He that spared not his own Son, but*
> *delivered him up for us all, how shall he not also with*
> *him freely give us all things? Who shall lay anything to*

the charge of God's elect? It is God that justifies; who is he that shall condemn? It is Christ Jesus that died, yes rather, that was raised from the dead, who is at the right hand of God, who also makes intercession for us. Who shall separate us from the love of Christ? Shall tribulation, or anguish, or persecution, or famine, or nakedness, or peril, or sword? (Rom. 8:31-35)

Section 72.
PROLEPSIS.

This is from the Greek *pro,* before, and *lambanein,* to take; hence to take beforehand. Of this figure Webster says:

1. (Rhet). 'A figure by which objections are anticipated or prevented'—BISHOP BRAMHALL.

2. 'An error in chronology, when an event is dated before the actual time: a species of anachronism'— THEOBOLD.

3. A necessary truth or assumption; a first or assumed principle.

The works on Rhetoric seem to know nothing of this figure, and yet it is one of the most common in all languages. In the Scriptures we have Bethel spoken of at the time that Abraham came into the land of Canaan (Gen. 2:8), and yet at the time of Jacob's flight from the face of his brother, he slept there; and because of the visitation of the angels it received its name (Gen. 28:10-19). When the writer gave the account, it had long been known by that name, and he therefore speaks of it by the name commonly spoken by the people. So with Hebron; it was called Mamre, and Hebron is a later name; but because it was known by that name when the account is written, it is so denominated in the earlier record (Gen. 13:18; 23:2; 35:27; 14:14). In this way Moses is said to have seen as far north as to Dan (Deut. 34:1-5). In Josh. 19:47, the country is described, indicating that place in the far north where a portion of the tribe dispossessed the people of Laish, or Leshem, and built up a city, and called it Dan. But there was no place by that name when Moses looked from the top of Nebo; and certainly not when Abraham pursued the kings of the east. The account is completed, then, after the tribe had built up that city; and the name is carried back on the same principle by which we speak of "*President Garfield, when, he was a boy.*" We do not mean to say that he was then President, but because he afterwards came to that position, we feel that we can carry back these honors, in mentioning his earlier life. So we hear of what General Grant did when he was a boy. He was not General then, but as the people have become accustomed to calling him General, we do so when referring to his early life.

"And the man called his wife's name Eve; because she was the mother of all living" (Gen. 3:20). At that time she was not a mother of any one. But when Moses wrote, she stood at the maternal head of the race. So he borrows from the then present knowledge and lends to Adam.

> *And the man said, 'This is now bone of my bones, and*
> *flesh of my flesh: she shall be called Woman, because*
> *she was taken out of man.' Therefore shall a man leave*
> *his father and mother, and shall cleave to his wife: and*
> *they shall be one flesh. (Gen. 2:23-24)*

The ordination of marriage would seem to be from Adam. In Matt. 19:5, the Savior indicates that it was from God. But it is quite certain that God did not proceed at that time to instruct Adam on that subject. But long before Moses wrote the account of the beginning, marriage had been ordained, and the remark is thrown in here when the man and his wife were created, because at the time of the writing the institution had long been known. The Savior is right in attributing it to the Father, for He was its author.

In the tenth and eleventh chapters of Genesis, where the three sons of Noah are written up, with their posterity, the form of writing is frequently proleptic. The account runs many centuries in advance of the time. The history had been made when Moses wrote the account, and therefore he borrows from that future record.

> *And the Lord said to her,*
> *Two nations are in your womb,*

And two peoples shall be separated even from your bowels;
And the one people shall be stronger than the other people.
And the elder shall serve the younger. (Gen. 25:23)

This would be strange, if literally true. There were the potencies; and from those two sons should spring two nations, and by the figure of prolepsis they are said to be present.

Now a certain man was sick, Lazarus of Bethany, of the village of Mary and her sister Martha. And it was that Mary, which anointed the Lord with ointment and wiped his feet with her hair, whose brother Lazarus was sick. (John 11:1-2)

This anointing did not occur yet for about three months, but John speaks of it as having already taken place, because when he wrote the account it was generally known that she did this (John 12:5).

So in Matt. 10:4, Judas is mentioned as the one who betrayed Christ, and yet it was more than a year before the betrayal took place. He dates the event ahead, because at the time of writing it was known to almost everyone who it was that betrayed Him. On the same principle the Savior says (Matt. 22:30), "For in the resurrection they neither marry, nor are given in marriage, but are as angels in heaven." Here they are spoken of as having passed into the resurrection state already, and they were a long ways from it; but in the contemplation of that condition He correctly speaks of it as present, and puts "they are," for *they will be.* When the object is high, the intervening distance becomes trivial. Hence the Messianic prophecies are generally spoken of as if the event was just at hand, or even in the past. "For to us a child is born, to us a son is given" (Isa. 9:6). In view of the ascension and coronation that were soon to follow, Jesus came to His disciples and said, "All authority has been given to me in heaven and on earth" (Matt. 28:18).

Care must be taken that we do not avoid any facts respecting the time of any event. It will be easy to say that any reference to time, present or past, is a proleptic statement. We must be sure that we are not making a contradiction in the word of God by the introduction of this figure. However, there is but little danger in the hands of any conscientious man, for the presence of the figure is so guarded that there is no mistaking it. And when there is no such necessity laid upon us, we will do better not to regard the language as proleptic.

Section 73.
PARALLELISM.

Greek *parallelismos,* from *para,* beside, and *allelo,* each. As a figure of speech, it is placing beside each other several lines having the same or similar meaning. Bishop Lowth maintains that it is the sole characteristic of Hebrew poetry; that it is a certain equality, resemblance, or relationship, between the members of each period; so that in two lines, or members of the same period, things shall answer to things, and words to words, as if fitted to each other by a kind of measure or rule. Such is the general strain of Hebrew poetry. The origin of this form of poetical composition among the Hebrews is supposed to be the chanting of songs, when one company or choir answers another. It is understood that Moses and Miriam (Ex. 15), conducted their joyful singing in that way. In 1 Sam. 18:7, it is quite certain that the women in their praises of David and Saul gave a song in this way. So it was when Deborah and Barak rejoiced against Sisera and his men, that they sang back and forth at each other in this responsive way. But to call this the origin of parallelism is certainly to miss the facts.

The mind is most likely to give off poetry when highly wrought by love, triumph, or anger. There are few poets among farmers on level land, who pass their time in an even way. The imagination necessary to that kind of composition is not aroused. But those who live in mountainous countries, and are frequently thrown into a highly excited condition, will dream and talk in poetry. In the song of Deborah and Barak it is clear that the construction was the result of an exultant state of mind. They are not now angry, but they rejoice that their enemies have been destroyed. But in the response of Mary to Elizabeth, it can be seen that her heart is overflowing with love and gratitude to God for his wonderful works.

> *And Mary said, My soul doth magnify the Lord,*
> *And my spirit has rejoiced in God my Savior.*
> *For he has looked upon the low estate of his handmaid-*
> *en.*
> *For, behold, from henceforth*
> *All generations shall call me blessed.*
> *For he that is mighty has done to me great things;*
> *And holy is his name.*
> *And his mercy is to generations and generations*
> *On them that fear him.*
> *He has showed strength with his arm;*
> *He has scattered the proud in the imagination of their*
> *heart.*
> *He has put down princes from their thrones,*
> *And has exalted them of low degree.*
> *The hungry he has filled with good things;*
> *And the rich he has sent away empty.*
> *He has helped Israel his servant,*
> *That he might remember mercy;*
> *(As he spoke to our fathers)*
> *Toward Abraham and his seed forever. (Luke 1:46-55)*

A careful reading of this address will cause any one to see the parallel lines and rhythm in the heart wrought to the highest tension with love for and praise to God. But when Laban followed the fleeing Jacob out of Paddan-aram, and overtook him in the mountains of Gilead, his mind was highly wrought, but in a very different way.

> *What have you done, that you have stolen away una-*
> *ware to me,*
> *And carried away my daughters, as captives of the*
> *sword?*
> *Why did you flee secretly,*
> *And steal away from me;*
> *And did not tell me, that I might have sent you away*

with mirth,
And with songs, with tabret, and with harp? (Gen.
31:26-28)

Laban then makes a search for his *teraphim,* and finds nothing that was his, and Jacob is angry, and chides in the same way:

What is my trespass?
What is my sin,
That you have hotly pursued after me?
Whereas you have felt about all my stuff,
What have you found of all your household stuff?
Set it here before my brethren and your brethren,
That they may judge between the two of us. (verses 36-37)

I think it certain that this figure of speech had its origin in the passions of the people, for it is well-suited as a method of giving vent to their feelings. A short, crisp, terse sentence or statement, and another following just like it in sentiment, gives the emphasis that is in a heart full of love or anger.

There are so many forms of parallelism that it will be better to treat it under the several heads into which it is naturally divided.

Section 74.
SYNONYMOUS PARALLELISM.

This is when the lines contain the same thought, or nearly the same thought.

Adah and Zillah, hear my voice;
You wives of Lamech, hearken to my speech
For I have slain a man for wounding me,
And a young man for bruising me.
If Cain shall be avenged sevenfold,
Truly Lamech seventy and sevenfold. (Gen. 4:23-24)

This may be denominated *identical,* for some of these lines contain exactly the same thought. Adah and Zillah were the same as the wives of Lamech, and the man that wounded him was the same as the young man that bruised him. In such cases we have the same thing repeated for the sake of beauty and force.

(1). *The first form of this kind of parallelism is identical,* for the comparison is made by employing a part of the same words, intended to convey the same thought.

> *You are snared with the words of your mouth,*
> *You are taken with the words of your mouth. (Prov. 6:2)*

> *The floods have lifted up, O Lord,*
> *The floods have lifted up their voice;*
> *The floods lift up their waves.*
> *Above the voices of many waters,*
> *The mighty breakers of the sea,*
> *The Lord on high is mighty. (Psa. 93:3-4)*

In Isa. 55:6-7, we have a parallelism that is more nearly of this order than any other, and therefore we quote it:

> *Seek the Lord while he may be found,*
> *Call upon him while he is near:*
> *Let the wicked forsake his way,*
> *And the unrighteous man his thoughts:*
> *And let him return to the Lord,*
> *And he will have mercy upon him;*
> *And to our God, for he will abundantly pardon.*

(2). A similar synonymous parallelism is one in which the lines have the same meaning, or nearly the same, but not couched in the same words.

> *Does the wild ass bray when he has grass?*
> *Or the ox low over his fodder?*
> *Can that which has no savor be eaten without salt?*
> *Or is there any taste in the white of an egg?*
> *My soul refuses to touch them;*
> *They are as loathsome food to me.*
> *Oh that I might have my request;*
> *And that God would grant me the thing that I long for!*
> *Even that it would please God to crush me;*

That he would let loose his hand, and cut me off. (Job 6:5-10).

A good example of this is found in Hosea 11:8, 9.

How shall I give you up, Ephraim?
How shall I deliver you, Israel?
How shall I make you as Admah?
How shall I set you as Zeboim?
Mine heart is turned within me,
My compassions are kindled together.
I will not execute the fierceness of my anger,
I will not return to destroy Ephraim
For I am God, and not man;
The Holy One in the midst of you. (Hos. 11:8-9)

At their presence the peoples are in anguish;
All faces are waxed pale.
They shall run like mighty men;
They climb the wall like men of war;
And they march every one on his ways,
And they do not break their ranks.
Neither does one thrust another;
They march every one in his path
And they burst through the weapons,
And do not break off their course.
They leap upon the city;
They run upon the wall;
They climb up into the houses;
They enter in at the windows like a thief. (Joel 2:6-9)

You shall tread upon the lion and adder:
The young lion and the serpent you shall trample under feet. (Psa. 91:13)

Section 75.
ANTITHETIC PARALLELISM

This is *that in which lines and sentences are made to oppose each other*. Truth is often made to appear by the use of antithesis; and this may be done in poetry, as well as elsewhere.

(1). Simple antithetic parallelism is that in which the sentences opposed are simple.

> *In the multitude of people is the king's glory:*
> *But in the want of people is the destruction of the*
> *prince.*
> *He that is slow to anger is of great understanding:*
> *But he that is hasty of spirit exalts folly.*
> *A sound heart is the life of the flesh:*
> *But envy is the rottenness of the bones.*
> *He that oppresses the poor reproaches his Maker:*
> *But he that has mercy on the needy honors him.*
> *The wicked is thrust down in his evil-doing:*
> *But the righteous has hope in his death.*
> *Wisdom rests in the heart of him that has understand-*
> *ing:*
> *But that which is in the inward part of fools is made*
> *known.*
> *Righteousness exalts a nation:*
> *But sin is a reproach to any people.*
> *The king's favor is toward a servant that deals wisely:*
> *But his wrath shall be against him that causes shame.*
> *A soft answer turns away wrath:*
> *But a grievous word stirs up anger.*
> *The tongue of the wise utters knowledge aright:*
> *But the mouth of fools pours out folly. (Prov. 14:28-*
> *15:2)*

(2). A compound antithetic parallelism is one in which the sentences opposed are compound, or have less of the directness and simplicity of the former.

The ox knows his owner, and the ass his master's crib:
But Israel doth not know, my people do not consider.
(Isa. 1:3)

Come now, and let us reason together, says the Lord:
Though your sins be as scarlet, they shall be as white as
snow;
Though they be red like crimson,
They shall be as wool.
If you be willing and obedient, you shall eat the good of
the land
But if you refuse and rebel, you shall be devoured with
the sword. (verses 18-20)

In chapter 54:7-8, we have this form of parallelism, though it seems a kind of mixture.

For a small moment I have forsaken you;
But with great mercies I will gather you.
In overflowing wrath I hid my face from you for a mo-
ment;
But with everlasting kindness I will have mercy on you."

Section 76.
SYNTHETIC PARALLELISM.

This is where the words and sentences do not answer to each other. There may, however, be several lines running parallel bearing certain relations to each other, as our blank verse, with a view of bringing out a certain thought.

(1). *The corresponding synthetic parallelism* is where the correspondence is between relative sentences. Sometimes the responding thought is found in one sentence, and sometimes in two or more.

The Lord is my light and my salvation; whom shall I
fear?
The Lord is the strength of my life; of whom shall I be
afraid? (Psa. 27:1)

Anyone will see that these sentences contain the same thought, and that the author repeated the thought of the first in the second, for the sake of strength. In Psa. 35:25-26, we have a more difficult form of this figure:

> *Let them not say in their heart, 'Aha, so would we have*
> *It':*
> *Let them not say, 'We have swallowed him up.'*
> *Let them be ashamed and confounded together, that re-*
> *joice at mine hurt:*
> *Let them be clothed with shame and dishonor, that*
> *magnify themselves against me.*

It will be seen that these sentences respond to each other; that they present the same view, but that they do so in different ways. In this way thought is intensified by being set forth in this compound or double manner.

(2). *Cumulative synthetic parallelism.*—This is ordinarily climactic: each line or sentence is supposed to be a gain on the preceding one in some particular, until the purpose of the author finds satisfaction in a completed statement. The full truth might have been stated at the beginning, but the bearing, force, and beauty would have suffered by that directness. It should be remembered that this is just as competent to present the descendent as the ascendant scale. From not noticing that thoughts are increased in a downward course as well as in an upward, many beautiful Scriptures have been misinterpreted.

Some examples of the ascendant scale (Psa. 19). In verses one to six, the author gives us a view of the greatness of God, seen in the work of creation.

> *The heavens declare the glory of God;*
> *And the firmament shows his handiwork.*
> *Day to day it utters speech,*
> *And night to night it shows knowledge.*
> *There is no speech nor language;*
> *Their voice cannot be heard.*
> *Their line is gone out through all the earth,*
> *And their words to the end of the world.*

In them he has set a tabernacle for the sun,
Which is as a bridegroom coming out of his chamber,
And rejoices as a strong man to run his course.
His going forth is from the end of the heaven,
And his circuit to the ends of it
And there is nothing hid from the heat of it.

In this way the Psalmist accumulates, and adds to the statements already made, till his mind is satisfied. And having sufficiently praised God for the wonderful work of His hands, for the wisdom and goodness everywhere displayed, he gives us his still higher appreciation of the law of the Lord in the same way. See verses 7-11:

The law of the Lord is perfect, restoring the soul
The testimony of the Lord is sure, making wise the simple.
The precepts of the Lord are right, rejoicing the heart:
The commandment of the Lord is pure, enlightening the eyes.
The fear of the Lord is clean, enduring for ever:
The judgments of the Lord are true and righteous altogether.
More to be desired are they than gold, yes, than much fine gold
Sweeter also than honey and the honeycomb.
Moreover by them is your servant warned:
In keeping of them there is great reward.

To indicate the revealed will of God, the author uses the terms 'law,' 'testimony,' 'precepts,' 'commandment,' 'fear,' 'judgments'; and to show his appreciation of it, has employed the terms 'perfect,' 'sure,' 'right,' 'pure,' 'clean,' 'true'; and says of it, in a general way, that it restores the soul, makes wise the simple, rejoices the heart, enlightens the eyes, endures forever; and, not yet satisfied, he goes on to say that it is more valuable than gold, and more delightful than honey. While it cannot be said that each line is a stronger statement than the preceding one, still, as a cumulative synthetic parallelism, it is very valuable.

Psa. 29:1-9 contains an ode to the voice of the Lord, in which this manner of accumulating thought is followed. It may be studied with profit.

(3). *The descendent scale is seen also in many passages of Scripture.*—Prov. 9:13-17 contains Solomon's view of the woman of folly. She talks a lot, but knows nothing of any value; she shows herself at her own door, and in the prominent places in the city. She calls the attention of those who would otherwise go on and attend to their business, and suggests that secret vices are very pleasant; but her guests are killed. This passage begins with the ways that are not so palpably wrong, but by the cumulative method the whole road to evil is pointed out, and the terrible and awful results are exposed.

The first Psalm, which has been a favorite with preachers as being easy to interpret, has been generally *mis*interpreted because of a lack of acquaintance with this form of parallelism. David's aim is to show the difference between the righteous man and the unrighteous. He changes terms in presenting the man who is not blessed, but the degrees are made known in the other words describing conduct.

If he will have the blessing of the Lord, he must not walk in the counsel of the wicked—no, he must not stand in the path of sinners—no, nor even sit among those who make light of divine things. Nor is that all—not only must he not be on the wrong side, but he must be on the right side: he must delight in the law of the Lord; yes, and must meditate upon it day and night. If he shall thus refuse the wrong and do the right, then he shall be like the tree beside the waters, that shall not be injured by any temporal calamity.

(4). *Irregular synthetic parallelism is one in which the thoughts are brought together in an irregular way.*—We choose to call it 'irregular,' because there are no exact rules or forms by which the thoughts are gathered. Sometimes there are three lines of comparative expression; sometimes there are four; but the first and the third are matched, and the second and fourth; sometimes the first and the last, and the two middle; while at other times there are several lines of comparative thought to be put in antithesis with a line before and one or more afterwards. To illustrate all these irregularities would demand more space than we can give to it.

My son, if your heart be wise,
My heart shall be glad, even mine:
Yes, my reins shall rejoice,
When your lips speak right things. (Prov. 23:15-16)

It is common to call this 'the inverted form,' but it is better called 'the introverted form,' as it reads from the inside out, thus:

My heart shall be glad, even mine,
Yes, my reins shall rejoice,
If the heart of my son is wise,
And his lips speak right things.

One of the loftiest Psalms containing a Messianic prophecy has been composed on the plan of introverted parallelism. So you can understand, we will quote it as we think it should be read, in order to get its meaning (Psa. 35:15-21). In this we will find that ver. 15 matches ver. 21; ver. 16 matches ver. 20; ver. 17 matches ver. 19; and ver. 18 is last, and is the relief that comes in the just judgment of God.

Ver. 15: But when I halted they rejoiced, and gathered themselves together;
The slayers gathered themselves together against me, and I knew it not;
They tore me, and did not cease.

Ver. 21: Yes, they opened their mouth wide against Me:
They said, 'Aha, aha, our eye has seen it.'

Ver. 16: Like the profane mockers in feasts,
They gnashed upon me with their teeth.

Ver. 20: For they speak not peace,
But they devise deceitful words against them that are quiet in the land.

Ver. 17: Lord, how long wilt you look on?
Rescue my soul from their destructions,
My darling from the lions.

Ver. 19: Do not let them that are my enemies wrongfully rejoice over me,
Neither let them wink with the eye that hates me without a cause."

Ver. 18: I will give you thanks in the great congregation;
I will praise you among much people.

I was never able to see why the Psalmist should have stopped in the midst of the crucifixion of the Savior to give praise to the Father, and then repeat the same things, with respect to the mocking of the high priests. But with this reading all is plain.

In Isa. 65:21-22, there is a parallelism in which the alternate lines are in antithesis, answering to each other in that way:

And they shall build houses, and inhabit them
And they shall plant vineyards, and eat the fruit of them.
They shall not build, and another inhabit;
They shall not plant, and another eat.

Sometimes the parallelism is in triplets—there will be three lines expressing the same thing, or one answering to two; at other times there are four expressing the same thing, but this is unusual. The Savior and the apostles many times quote a beautiful parallelism from the Psalms, but it is written in the gospels and epistles in a way that often isn't noticed.

Many times linking is employed for the purpose of intensifying, where the thought is to be repeated either in the same, or nearly the same, words. The meaning of these passages is, many times, mistaken, because people don't recognize the figure of speech that has been employed.

And many peoples shall go and say, 'Come you,
And let us go up to the mountain of the Lord,
To the house of the God of Jacob;
And he will teach us of his ways,
And we will walk in his paths:

> *For out of Zion shall go forth the law,*
> *And the word of the Lord from Jerusalem.' (Isa. 2:3)*

Here the thoughts are repeated in couplets, and joined together, not by way of adding new thought, but to intensify the one already stated.

> *My son, hear the instruction of your father,*
> *And forsake not the law of your mother:*
> *For they shall be a wreath of grace on your head,*
> *And chains about your neck. (Prov. 1:8-9)*

See also Jer. 31:31; Hos. 2:2.

> *Therefore as the tongue of fire devours the stubble,*
> *And as the dry grass sinks down in the flame,*
> *So their root shall be as rottenness,*
> *And their blossom shall go up as dust:*
> *Because they have rejected the law of the Lord of hosts,*
> *And despised the word of the Holy One of Israel. (Isa. 5:24)*

Very many times the use of dividing is necessary, so that negative truth shall have the proper emphasis. Two very striking passages will be enough to cite—Neh. 1:7; 2 Kings 17:34.

There is *need of caution,* however, in the use of this fact. While this figure of speech exists in Scripture, we shall need to exercise care lest many truths be thrown away, by supposing the presence of the figure when it is not present.

CHAPTER X:
FIGURES OF THOUGHT.

There are many things in the Bible which are conveyed to our minds, not in didactic language, nor yet in figurative language, properly speaking. They are figures of thought, rather than figures of speech. Indeed, some of the figures of speech might have been presented as figures of thought. This is true of most of the proverbs, and a large part of the poetry of the Scriptures.

But several features of interpretation still need to be brought out which we cannot consistently call figures of speech. Hence we have introduced the term that heads this chapter, not knowing what else to say.

Section 77.
ANTITHESIS.

This is from the Greek *anti,* against, and *thesis,* a setting. Of this word Webster says:

> *An opposition of words or sentiments occurring in the same sentence; contrast; as, 'When our vices leave us, we flatter ourselves that we left them.' 'The prodigal robs his heir, the miser robs himself.' 'Excess of ceremony shows lack of breeding.' 'Liberty with laws, and government without oppression.'*

If we had two pillars of equal dimensions and height, one set opposite the other, with a compass on top, with one leg resting on each pillar, we would have a mechanical antithesis. There would then be no difference between these, except one would be on the north and the other on the south, the right hand or the left, black or white, etc. But the two legs are supposed to be exactly equal, except in that respect in which the author has seen proper to make them to differ. A rhetorical antithesis has the same basis—thought and purpose. Hence, if at any time there shall be one member of the antithesis which we can understand, we can know what is intended by the other, by knowing that it is the opposite of the one we have described. If we know that one is on the right hand, we know just as certainly that the other is on the left hand; if one is North, the other is South—for such opposites are inherent in the figure. If, at any time, we should be in doubt about what faith is, we may get its opposite (or its *opposites*), and understand it by the things which it is supposed to antagonize.

The question of how faith comes may be settled in the same way. If we can know all the causes of unbelief, and put them into one pillar, knowing that faith is the opposite, we will know that the opposite causes will be the power (or the *powers*) that produce faith.

In the fifth chapter of Matthew we have several uses of antithesis. Jesus says, "You have heard that it was said by them in old time," etc.; "but I say to you" (verses 21, 27, 33, 34, 38, 39, 43, 44). In all this, Christ shows that the righteousness which He should require of His followers was higher than that which was demanded by the Pharisees, or even that of the law.

The duration of the punishment of the wicked can be settled by this law of antithesis (Matt. 25:46): "And these shall go away into eternal punishment: but the righteous into eternal life."

The duration which is the measure of the one of these, must of necessity be the measure of the other, unless the author of the antithesis has seen proper to make a difference in that respect. In this case, so far from making any difference, He has used the same word on both sides; if the eternal life of the righteous is life without end, so is the punishment of the wicked. This is absolutely demanded by the law of antithesis.

In Romans 2:7-10, there is even more need of close attention to this law; hence I quote the whole passage:

> *To them that by patience in well-doing seek for glory and honor and incorruption, eternal life: but to them that are factious, and do not obey the truth, but obey unrighteousness, shall be wrath and indignation, tribulation and anguish, upon every soul of man that practices evil, of the Jew first, and also of the Greek.*

In this antithetical statement there is glory and honor and peace, put over against wrath and indignation, tribulation and anguish. It is easy to see that these are the opposites; but there is one other phrase used that is liable to be missed—'to those that do well, eternal life' shall be the reward. This is, in that place, put as the antithetical thought, but the opposite things mentioned, *in and of themselves,* might not be eternal. So what is the reader to understand? Using the law of antithesis, we understand that since 'eternal life' means eternal glory, honor, and peace, so we are compelled to regard the opposite— wrath, indignation, tribulation and anguish—as eternal. We have no right to suppose that one leg of the antithesis passes through eternity, and that the other is limited to time.

> *So also is the resurrection of the dead. It is sown in cor-*
> *ruption; it is raised in incorruption: it is sown in dis-*
> *honor; it is raised in glory: it is sown in weakness; it is*
> *raised in power; it is sown a natural body; it is raised a*
> *spiritual body. (1 Cor. 15:42-44)*

In the interpretation of this passage, it should be remembered that the only point in the antithesis is between the body as it lived and moved in the world, and what it would be in the resurrection. With that fact clearly in the mind, it will be easy to see the point of comparison. Corruption, dishonor, weakness, animal, are on one side, and incorruption, glory, power, spiritual, are on the other side. The former denotes the body as the man lived in this world, the latter as he may live in the world to come. These expressions mutually explain each other.

The most perfect antithesis to be found in the whole Bible is to be read in 2 Cor. 3:5-13. As this has been cited already for the teaching contained in the passage, we will not quote it again, but would ask the reader's attention to it as a most instructive lesson on this subject.

Section 78.
SYMBOLS.

This is from the Greek *sumbolon,* a sign by which one knows a thing or infers it, from *sun,* with, and *ballein,* to throw, *to throw with, or throw together.* Webster's first definition fairly exhausts its meaning:

> *1. The sign or representation of something moral or intellectual, by the images or properties of natural things; an emblem, a representation; as, the lion is the symbol of courage; the lamb is the symbol of meekness or patience.*

It may be said that types were representatives of thought, but they always represented a something yet to be, or a fact in the scheme of redemption. A symbol may tell the conditions existing at the time, or it may relate to something to occur in the future; in that case they sometimes become typological prophecy—they symbolize the events beforehand and in that way foretell them.

We can better examine the subject under three headings or classes: The *miraculous,* the *material,* and the *visional* (those seen in visions, or in dreams). Several other subdivisions would be allowable, but for our brief space it is not well to introduce them.

Section 79.
THE MIRACULOUS SYMBOLS.

The first we come to is in Gen. 3:24, and the cherubim with a flaming sword at the East of the garden in Eden. Though literally existing, it serves as well to symbolize the fixedness of the word of Jehovah—when Adam and Eve saw this, they would be reminded of what the Lord had said to them. Whether man had been separated from the tree of life to prevent him from living forever in sin and misery, into which he had then fallen, or for some other reason, the point is that the heavens and the earth are all put under tribute to keep the commandments of God.

When Moses saw the burning bush (Ex. 3:2), God's glory was made to appear; it was not so much intended to tell of any future fact, but showed the present majesty and dignity of the God of Abraham, Isaac, and Jacob.

Likewise the pillar of cloud and the pillar of fire that went with the Israelites (beginning Ex. 13:21), was to them a constant symbol of God's presence and watchfulness.

In Ex. 16:10, we are informed of an appearance similar, in the glory of the Lord seen as the people looked towards the wilderness. Just what they saw, may not be known, but we are certain that God made them to understand His glory by what they saw. This was seen in the display made at the Mount of Commandments, when the Lord appeared on the summit in the smoke and the fire, and all the divine manifestation that accompanied the giving of the law (Ex. 20). Often during the wandering of Israel, the Lord manifested His presence in this symbol of His glory.

The acknowledgment of the Son at the time of His baptism, and at the transfiguration (Matt. 3 and 17) may be regarded in the list of miraculous symbols. So also was the coming of the Spirit from the heavens on the day of Pentecost (Acts 2). The apostles had known of its coming, and they were waiting for it. As it had been previously interpreted for them, its meaning was clear. So, when the same symbol was present at the house of Cornelius, Peter was at no loss in understanding it. These divine or miraculous symbols were not prophetic; they did not tell of some future event, but of present truth.

Section 80.
MATERIAL SYMBOLS.

In selecting representatives of this kind of divine instruction, it is very difficult to make any clear and satisfactory distinction between symbols and types, for they frequently overlap each other. It should be remembered that the symbol is supposed to relate to the present, and only concerns the future if the same things will continue to be true; or that the symbol is employed to represent a thought that shall be true in time that is to come. But this is just where the type begins. It gathers its power of expression from the condition of things at the time, and pictures beforehand the things that are to come. Many things are clearly symbols, and others are clearly types; while others seem to have the two thoughts and purposes combined. Many of the most beautiful and instructive of types had, at the time they were given, a symbolic truth of very great importance to present. In all the sacrifices by which sin was to be removed, there was the then-present truth that man, by his sin, had lost his right to live. There was also the thought of divine mercy in the acceptance of the sacrifice, in the place of man who deserved to die. But these become the most powerful and instructive of types as they tell of the coming of that Savior that should suffer death for all men. In the same way we might go through the tabernacle and the temple, and find the beauty and force of symbolic truth in everything that the Lord had given them, for they were object lessons, containing present and valuable truth; but they have a grander reality pointed to in the coming of Christ and His grand accomplishments in behalf of the children of men.

But there are things that are purely symbols. The "testimony," as applied to the tables of the law (Ex. 25:16-21; 31:18), and also called the tables of the covenant (Deut. 9:9) (because on the basis of these God made a covenant with Israel, Ex. 34:27, 28; Deut. 4:13), served as a symbol of God's judgment against sin. The offering of incense from the golden altar symbolized the thought of worship, or the prayers of God's children. And while the worship of the heart is more prominent now than then, it was true then that God required them to draw near to Him in the loftiest devotion of which they were capable. And while the cherubim, stretching their wings on high, overshadowed the mercy seat, and gazed intently at the same place on the mercy seat below, there was ever presented to the Jewish mind the thought that God and the angels are attentive to their worship. And as the tables of the covenant were in the ark, it was necessary that the mercy seat should overlay the ark, for people judged exclusively by that law would all be lost; but mercy rejoices against judgment.

In Isa. 7:4, the prophet calls Rezin, king of Syria, and Pekah, king of Israel, two tails of smoking firebrands. Of course, in the form in which this comes to us, it is a metaphor; but it should be remembered that *what a metaphor is in speech, a symbol is in action, or being.*

This is true of the bread and fruit of the vine of the Lord's Supper (Matt. 26:26-28). "This is my body," "This is my blood," etc., these are both in metaphorical language; but the bread and the fruit of the vine are visible, material symbols of the body and blood of the Savior.

The rainbow that was set in the cloud (Gen. 9:13) was a token or a symbol of the covenant. When Abraham spoke with Abimelech, he told the king of the well the king's men had taken from them, and then symbolized his innocence in the matter by seven lambs (Gen. 21:28-30).

Circumcision was a symbol of the lopping off of sin.

Section 81.
BUT THE GREAT NUMBER OF SYMBOLS ARE VI-SIONAL.

They were seen in vision, in dream or in the wakeful hours, but by the power of God. They are employed as object lessons by which the man of God understands some present truth, or some event to come. Jeremiah foretold many things by the use of these forms. He has sometimes been denominated the acting prophet, on that account.

> Moreover the word of the Lord came to me, saying, 'Jeremiah, what do you see?' And I said, 'I see a rod of an almond tree.' Then the Lord said to me, 'You have well seen: for I watch over my word to perform it.' (Jer. 1:11-12).

The almond tree was the first to blossom—in fact, it seemed never to sleep—and consequently it was regarded as a symbol of wakefulness, or watchfulness.

Then, in the two following verses, there is a symbol of a prophetic character:

> And the word of the Lord came to me the second time, saying, 'What do you see?' And I said, 'I see a seething caldron; and its face is from the north.' Then the Lord said to me, 'Out of the north, evil shall break forth on all the inhabitants of the land.'

A seething caldron, tilted so much as to enable a man to look into the mouth, would be a symbol of a thorough scalding. And the Lord uses it to show what was about to come upon them. The families of the kingdoms of the North would come and sit on the thrones at Jerusalem, and make war with the cities of Judah.

In Gen. 40:1-20, we have the two dreams of the men in prison with Joseph, in Egypt. Each had a dream: one saw what, in symbol, meant that he should be restored—the three branches of grapes were an omen of good; but the other dreamed of the three baskets of white bread, and of the birds picking the meats from the upper, which meant that within three days his head should be lifted up from off him.

Two symbols were presented to Pharaoh in a dream, by which he was to know what was in store for them in the days to come (See chap. 41). The seven fat cows, and the seven lean, that ate them up, and the seven full ears of corn, and seven thin ones, that devoured them, told of seven years of plenty, and then seven other years in which they should not be able to gather food. In a dream quite similar to this, Nebuchadnezzar was made to know of the four universal monarchies, himself being at the head (Dan. 2:1-45). In the first chapter of the book of Revelation we have several beautiful symbols. There are seven golden lamp-stands; someone, like to the Son of man, walking in the midst of them, who holds seven stars in His right hand. We learn that the lamp-stands were the seven churches, and that the seven stars were the seven messengers of the seven churches.

In the tenth chapter of the Acts of the Apostles we are introduced to a symbol furnished for the education of the apostle Peter. He had gone upon the top of the house to pray, and fell into a trance, and saw a vessel, like a great sheet, knit at the four corners, and full of all kinds of animals. And as he gazed upon the object lesson, he was told to arise, and kill, and eat. But he said, 'Not so.' He had kept the law of Moses as it related to food, and did not know that it was removed. This was the first lesson in the series by which he was to know that the Gentiles were to be fellow-heirs and of the same household with the Jews. At first it seems strange that an apostle has to be taught in this way; and yet, when we come to study the matter, we find that they had to learn just as much as the rest of us. While the Lord used their mouths for the purpose of presenting truth to the world, they did not always understand it themselves. Jesus had told Peter (and the rest of the apostles), just days before Pentecost, that they would preach the gospel to *all nations* (Matt. 28:18-20), but it was several years later before its meaning was clear to him.

Section 82.
SPECIAL RULES FOR THE INTERPRETATION OF SYMBOLS.

These rules are few in number, yet we feel that they are needed. So many different things have been twisted to fit some of the symbols, that it is obvious there are many interpreters who follow no rule at all. Each man feels that he must find something in the symbol that will fit the his favorite theology. If he is skillful in cutting and fitting history, he will doubtless succeed.

Rule 1. Many of the symbols have been interpreted, in whole or in part, by their authors. In such cases, we have nothing to do but to accept the interpretation as given.

Rule 2. Some symbols have been interpreted by other inspired authors. This, again, must stand as the interpretation.

Rule 3. Sometimes the symbol has been given in a manner that is difficult, but another writer or speaker has used the same illustration in such a way that there is no doubt as to its meaning. In that case, that which is obvious must interpret the meaning of that which is difficult.

Rule 4. The names of symbols are to be understood literally. When they tell us what they saw and heard, we are to understand them as being exactly what they said. Many times, too, there is peculiar significance to be found in the etymology of the names or words employed. Hence the words used should be subjected to the same rules as if they were found in other composition.

Rule 5. There must be found a resemblance, more or less clear, between the symbol and the thing signified. If this resemblance was not close, it is probable that the author would have selected some other.

Rule 6. The condition of those to whom the symbol was given must be known, if possible, because the meaning which they would get out of it, is the meaning that the author intended to put into it.

The valley of dry bones (Ezek. 37:1-14) was to teach the restoration of the Jews from their captivity. The lesson given to Jeremiah (18:1-10), by the potter's vessel that became marred, represented the house of Israel. And ignoring the fact that these have been explained by divine authority, they have been as lavishly interpreted as any other symbols; so that almost everything has been made out of them.

In Jer. 24, we have a symbol of two baskets of figs. After the description of the figs—that one basket was very good, and the other very bad—it is explained to mean that those captives in Babylon who were true to the Lord were good figs, and should be brought back again; but the bad people, including Zedekiah, their king, should be too bad for any use, and therefore should be tossed to and fro from Egypt to Babylon, until they should be utterly destroyed. God has interpreted it, but that does not always protect the symbol from abuse at the hands of those who have a particular theory to advance.

In Isa. 22:22, there is a prophecy concerning Christ, in which it is said that on Him should be laid the key of the house of David. The word 'key,' of course, means that he should not only be in the line of kings, but that he should sit upon the throne of David, and that he should have the power that would rightly belong to Him as David's descendant. The same word, when the Savior said to Peter, "I will give to you the keys of the kingdom," contained the authority to open it, with all its advantages, to the world. Keys are for the purpose of opening, and it was left for men to tell the world what they were to do to be saved.

When Jacob said, "The sceptre shall not depart from Judah" (Gen. 49:10), everyone would understand it at once to refer to the symbol of power to rule or control. It is its natural and easy interpretation, and there has never been any difficulty in understanding it. But the point is to instruct and encourage men to use the other symbols in the same way.

In Zech. 4-6, there are several symbols that have had about as many interpretations as there have been interpreters. And yet the interpretations that are given in the text are never followed. In doing so, these supposed scholars propose that when the Lord tells us what He means, His statements are not reliable. That splendid lampstand, and the two olive trees that supply with oil, were symbols of the watchfulness and helpfulness of the Lord, which assured Zerubbabel that he should succeed in rebuilding the temple. And so the flying scroll was God's condemnation of thieves and false swearers. Now, when the Lord gives the meaning of the symbol, and the purpose of its exhibition, it is a sin to refuse to accept it. Speculations are only excusable when the meaning has not been announced.

In Daniel 2, we have a symbol which is partly interpreted. So there are some things which we know about the dream of the king, and some things that we must interpret by rules. We know that the four sections in that image were four universal empires. We know that the head was the Babylonian government. We know that the three others followed in the order of the silver, the brass, and the iron. We know that during the time of these kings, the God of heaven should set up a kingdom which should never be destroyed. And when we use the divine interpretation as far as it goes, the meaning of the rest is easy to be found.

The whole of the book of Revelation, or nearly the whole of it, is presented by the use of symbols. Self-styled prophets have gone to that book to prophesy, and then compel the apostle John to sanction their imaginations. Not wishing to enter this field, I have only to say that we must take every statement of meaning and purpose found in the book for just what it says. After that, we must remember *where* and *when* the symbols have been used before this; for if they may be found in any clearer light, that usage may help in the interpretation. We must remember *to whom* these symbols were shown, and therefore what he would likely get out of them. We must be careful not to demand too many points of analogy, lest we have *eisegesis,* and not *exegesis.*

Section 83.
TYPOLOGY.

Of course, we mean by this a discourse about types. But then comes the question, *What is a type?* It is from the Greek *tupos,* from *tuptein,* to strike. Hence Webster's first definition. His first, second, and fourth definitions relate to religious truth, and we quote them:

1. The mark or impression of something; stamp; impressed sign; emblem.

2. Impressed form; stamp; kind; sort.

4. A figure or representation of something to come; a token; a sign; a symbol; correlative to antitype. 'A type is no longer a type, when the thing typified comes to be actually exhibited.'—SOUTH.

It is necessary to remark, concerning types—

(1). *That the original meaning of the word is not that which is generally found in the Scriptures.*—It does not generally mean to strike, nor yet the result of striking. We say that we have seen a horse's foot in the clay, when we have only seen the impression of his foot, which would be the type. But when we take the impression of the foot, we really have just the opposite of the foot. So if a man should push his fist onto a ball of putty, he would leave there, not his fist, but the type, or impression, of it. Though this is not the meaning it generally has in the Bible, remembering this original meaning will be of service in the interpretation of types.

(2). *We must never expect the type and the antitype to be the same,* for that would not be type and antitype, but identity. We shall find, therefore, that it is utterly impossible to find something in the antitype that is analogous to every feature of the type, or that the type has perfectly prefigured the antitype. There are many "types" of Jesus Christ in the Old Testament, but none of them were Christ Himself.

(3). *Let us remember that the type has been selected generally for one purpose*, and, finding that purpose, the application will be easy.

(4). *It must foretell something.*—When it is a representation of a present truth or duty, it is a symbol, and not a type.

(5). It must not simply happen to represent something in the future and therefore do as an illustration—*it must have been intended to represent that thought or fact when it was given.* We cannot retroactively create types.

(6). *The Scriptures should be made to interpret them,* as far as possible; and with such definition we must be content.

(7). *While we are always safe in calling anything a type that is described that way in the word of God,* it is *not* necessary to suppose that we are *limited to these statements.* It would not be reasonable that God should have gone through the whole Bible, and explicitly identified every type with the words, "Here is a type."

(8). As in the interpretation of symbols, the *similarity* between *type* and the *antitype* will lead, in most cases to the true meaning.

(9). *Anything, to be a type, must have been a real person, thing, event, or office.*—Not so with the symbols. All the visional symbols were unreal—they were seen by assisted or superhuman sight—they were not actually present, though they appeared to be. But the type is real. Adam was a type of Christ; so were the sacrifices from the foundation of the world; the kings, priests, and prophets, in that they were actually *anointed;* the serpent in the wilderness, Solomon, and Joshua, etc. These were as real as the Savior.

(10). *The antitype is always superior to the type.*—If this were not the case, there would be no reason in the type. The type is always visible at the time it is given, because it is material; but the antitype contains divine or spiritual thought. However, many times there are two or more of them in one line, and one seems to look to another as its fulfillment; yet they are all looking to the final object for their meaning.

(11). *Sometimes figurative language is employed in giving a typical event.*—The figure should be treated as it would be if given under any other circumstances.

(12). *The rules for the interpretation of symbols apply to types as well.*—They have several features in common. In so far as the type becomes a prophecy, history should be carefully examined, that we may have all the facts on both sides.

Section 84.
THE MANY KINDS OF TYPES.

We do not mean, by this heading, that there are differences in the construction of types, or in the rules by which they shall be interpreted, but that there are different sources from which instruction is drawn.

(1). *Typical persons.*—No person, as such, can be regarded as a type in every aspect of his life, actions, and existence. It must be because of some relation, office, or characteristic, that typology is possible. Adam is a type of Christ, in that he is the first of the human race (Rom. 5:12-19; 1 Cor. 15:22, 45). But the features of typology, as they are mentioned by the apostle, are opposites. He represents the Christ by presenting the antithesis of what Christ was and did. He was at the beginning, and Christ at the ending of sin; he was disobedient, Christ was obedient; he brought death, Christ brought life from the dead; he made many sinners, Christ makes many righteous; he was natural, Christ was spiritual; he was from the earth earthy, Christ was the Lord from heaven. All this, however, is according to the original intent of the word of God.

Moses was a type of Christ, in that he was a leader and mediator between God and the people (Deut. 18:15-18). But this language looks to Joshua for its first and partial fulfillment. Joshua was like Moses, in that he led the people. But its meaning is not satisfied till the Savior has come (Acts 3:22-24). It is safe to say, then, that both Moses and Joshua were types of the Messiah. Moses prefigured Him, in that he was a leader, a lawgiver, a prophet, a mediator, and had to die before his followers could cross into the Promised Land. Joshua was a type, in that he led the people—in that he took them across the Jordan into Canaan, which in itself was a type of entering into heaven. And the name "Joshua" is the Hebrew form of "Jesus."

Melchizedek was a type of Christ. (Gen. 14:18-20; Ps. 110:4; Heb. 5:5-10, 6:20, 7:1-17). He prefigured Christ in his priesthood, in his excellent character, and in that he was king and priest at the same time.

David was a type of Christ (Acts 13:33-35; Isa. 9:6). He was not only a king, but was a model for his people, and, in that respect, about as complete a type as could be found.

Solomon was a type of the Messiah, though a more feeble one (2 Sam. 7:13-15; 1 Kings 8:18-20; Rom. 1:1-4). When God promised to establish the house of David, it looked directly to Solomon, but eventually to Christ, as the greater Son of David.

Zerubbabel was a type of Christ (Hag. 1:1-12; Zech. 4:1-10; 6:12, 14). He was not only a deliverer of the people, but he built the temple of the Lord, and returned the people to the pure worship of the Father.

Cyrus, king of Persia, was a type of Christ (Isa. 44:27, 28; 45:1-4). He was the anointed of the Lord. He was not intended as a representative of the Savior's character, and yet in that respect he would do as well as many others; but he was a deliverer. He gave the people liberty, and even helped them to return to Jerusalem.

CHAPTER XI:
PROPHECY.

In the chapter on Figurative Language we have given a number of rules for the interpretation of prophecy, not because it is a figure of speech or a figure of thought, but because so large a part of prophecy is in figurative language, and so much of it has been given by the use of symbol and type.

Section 85.
THE DUTY OF THE PROPHET.

Our word prophet is from the Greek *prophetees* and is compounded of *pro*, before, and *phanai* to speak. Hence it is one who speaks before another or for another. Webster says of this word:

> *1. One who prophesies, or foretells events; a predicter; a foreteller.*
>
> *2. (Scripture) A person illuminated, inspired, or instructed by God to speak in His name, or announce future events, as Moses, Elijah, Isaiah, etc.*
>
> *3. One who explains or communicates sentiments; an interpreter.*
>
> *'School of the prophets (Ancient Jewish History), a school or collection in which young men were educated and qualified for public teachers. These students were called sons of the prophets.'*

His definition of prophecy throws no additional light on the subject.

(1). We are *limited to the Hebrews and Christians for examples* of that spiritual ecstasy that enables one to communicate the mind of God respecting the things that are to come. Among the nations of antiquity we have the augurs, the diviners, and the oracles; but these were nothing more than the guesses of the men who gave the information. Sometimes the guesses were reasonably founded in the appearance of things; at other times, the prophecy was because of a personal wish in the matter, or to get the praise of the king and the people. But because of the uncertainty of the future, they usually clothed their prophetic utterances, if we should call them such, in language that could be interpreted as easily one way as the other. If the king is told to go to battle, and succeeds, then the praise is given to the oracle; but if he falls before the enemy, they return, and the claim is made that the utterance was entirely misinterpreted. The king lost, but the oracle stood firm.

But the Hebrew prophets foretold the things that they did not wish—that were disagreeable to the king and the people, and that were very little likely to occur. Their warnings were not the soothing symphonies of sycophants, but the condemnations of the invisible Jehovah issuing from the secret chambers of the thunder. The true prophet does not necessarily foretell future events, but gives God's message to the world, whether it relates to the future or the present. Abraham was a prophet, in that he spoke for God (Gen. 20:7). Aaron was to be prophet to Moses, by speaking the things that Moses would tell him (Ex. 7:1; 4:16).

The Hebrew word *nabi,* generally used for prophet, means one who boiled forth, or who ran over. The cause of this strange proclamation, however, was regarded as of divine origin; they supposed that God caused the man to speak in that way. It has been supposed that when Saul was numbered with the prophets (1 Sam. 10:11), and afterwards, when his three companies and himself were all made to prophesy at Naioth, that the language means no more than that they were caused to act like the prophet (1 Sam. 19:20-24); not that they foretold any future event, or that they delivered any message from God to men.

(2). The prophetic office of Elijah was to convey the word of God to the court of Ahab, and to condemn the wickedness of his people. This was largely true of Jeremiah and Isaiah as well.

Rightfully enough they were called men of God (1 Kings 13:1-2; 2 Kings 4:7-8; Hos. 9:7). They were called this because they came with God's message and to attend to God's business.

Since the fall of man, when the communion between God and man was clipped because of sin, it has been necessary that someone divinely appointed should be the teacher of the race. Hence, God has raised up seers, revelators, prophets, and has sent them with messages, as the world had need.

Philips (Commentary of Rom. 12:6) urges:

> [T]he New Testament idea of the prophetic office is identical with that of the Old Testament. Prophets are men who, inspired by the Spirit of God, and impelled to theopneustic [God-breathed] discourse, partly removed the veil from the future (Rev. 1:3; 22:7-10; John 7:52; Acts 11:27, 28; 21:10, 11; Comp. 1 Pet. 1:10), partly make known concealed facts of the present, either in discovering the secret counsel and will of God (Luke 1:67; Acts 13:1; Eph. 3:5), or in disclosing the hidden thoughts of man (1 Cor. 14:24, 25), and dragging into light his unknown deeds (Matt. 26:68; Mark 14:65; Luke 22:64; John 4:19); partly dispense to these hearers instruction, comfort, exhortation, in animated, powerfully impassioned language, going far beyond the wonted limits of the capacity for teaching, which, although spiritual, still confines itself within the forms of reason (Matt. 7:28, 29; Luke 24:19; John 7:40; Acts 15:32; 1 Cor. 14:3, 4, 31).

(3). It should be noticed that the prophet is of great value as a historian, and that the prophecies of the Old Testament should be read in connection with the history of the people.—In the history we have ordinarily the hull—nothing more. We have the condemnation of God upon the people, but we do not see the justice. A great reformation has taken place, and we wonder why the condemnations of Jehovah must continue. But if we turn and read the prophets of those times, they show us that the reformation was only on the surface. While they came with their offerings to Jerusalem, and spread their hands before the Lord in prayer, God would not hear them (Isa. 1:16-18). Their hands were red with innocent blood, and their hearts were hard toward the poor in the land, whom they continued to oppress. They give us the inside of history, and make us to know the causes of calamity as we never could know it in any other way.

(4). *Persons are called prophets who interpreted the Scriptures and exhorted the people to faithfulness in the service of God.*—There has not always been a necessity for a revelation. We would think that to be the condition of the church in Antioch. Paul and Barnabas had been there, and had wrought a great work in that city. No doubt that they had made known to the church the whole counsel of God. And yet (Acts 13:1) Barnabas, Simeon, Manaen, and Lucius are mentioned in that roll. In 15:32, Judas and Silas are mentioned as prophets, and in the fulfillment of their duties as such they exhorted the people. In 1 Cor. 14, the prophet was supposed to edify the church, and in verse 24, prophesying was regarded as that gift by which sinners would be converted. This was not a foretelling of future events, for that would not at the time convert any one. It would have to be fulfilled before it would be evident to them that God was directing the affair. It was, therefore, most probably an interpretation of Scripture truth. That gift was, therefore, more desirable than the gift of tongues.

Section 86.
DIFFERENT WAYS IN WHICH PROPHECY WAS DELIVERED.

(1). *Sometimes it was like history written beforehand.*—Samuel (1 Sam. 10:3-6) tells Saul what would occur as he would return home; whom he would meet; what they would have; what they would propose; where he would meet the prophets, and what would come of it all. If he had waited till it was all over, he would have found it necessary only to change the tense in order to give a correct history of the matter. In one of the efforts of Balaam to curse Israel (Num. 24:14-24), he tells what Israel would do to Moab, and to Amalek. Though the language is figurative in a high degree, yet the history of those events is fairly related. Beginning with the thirteenth chapter of Isaiah, and reading to the close of the twenty-third chapter, we have the burdens of Babylon, Moab, Damascus, Egypt, the Wilderness of the

Sea, and of the Valley of Vision. These denunciations are intensified with figures of speech more than is generally found in history, but the evils were told in about as plain language as could be selected. Ezek. 25-32 gives God's condemnation against several nations. Amon, Moab, Edom, Philistia, Tyre: who would slaughter them, the effect, the weeping, the bitter lamentation, the injury to commerce. Zidon: how they should treat Israel after they should return. Egypt: the sword to visit that people, and all the calamities that were to come upon them. In narrating these things, there are many highly-wrought figures employed, but the style is that of the historian of the Oriental type. It seems to the reader that the prophet saw the events beforehand as they really occurred, and spoke of them in the language of the people. The place where the Savior should be born (Micah 5:2), was foretold with all the certainty of a historical record. The time of His birth is clearly announced (Dan. 9:24-27). Also the maltreatment that He received while on trial at Jerusalem (Isa. 50:6). His resurrection, too, is stated in language susceptible of but one interpretation (Psa. 16:8-10). The part that Cyrus took in behalf of the children of Israel is very clearly stated (Isa. 44:28; 45:1).

(2). *Many times the thoughts respecting the future are presented in figurative language, so that it is difficult to get the meaning.—* When the prophet was sent to condemn the sins of the people, he used very burning words; and the interpretation of such passages is attended with some difficulty. But by the rules already agreed to, we can proceed in safety. The symbols that have been employed for the purpose of foretelling the future, are subject to the rules that govern symbolic language. When Jeremiah (27:8; 28:14) made a yoke to show the rule of the king of Babylon, the meaning is so easily gathered that no one has ever been in doubt of it. When Agabus (Acts 21:11) took Paul's girdle, and bound his hands and feet with it, everyone expected to hear of someone being bound; and when he said that it was to be the owner of that girdle, and that the Jews at Jerusalem should bind him, the brethren at once began to try to dissuade Paul from going there. The symbolism in the dreams of Nebuchadnezzar and Pharaoh would seem to be easily interpreted, also the hand-writing on the wall at Babylon. And still the meaning was hidden from the wise men of the times. Dream-books were of no value whatsoever. Nothing less than inspiration from the Lord would do.

(3). *The peculiarities of the prophets are maintained in their writings.*—It is clear, to every attentive reader, that they differ as much in their manner of stating things as other men. We conclude, therefore, that in most instances the Lord has furnished the needed intelligence by inspiration, and trusted them with the presentation of it to the people.

Occasionally, of course, there were thoughts that a Hebrew prophet could not get into his mind. In such a case, God had to give him words (1 Pet. 1:11; 2 Pet. 1:21; Acts 2:4). While they did not know the time of the fulfillment of their own predictions, or when the Messiah should come to bless the world, they could understand enough of the history of their own people to present it with clearness and force. But a common error among all Jews, that their Messiah would establish a temporal kingdom, and reign forever without seeing death, would not enable any one of their prophets to know that Christ was to die. It would be as difficult for them to get that thought as it was for the apostles to learn the same lesson—and they could not understand it till it had occurred; and even then it had to be explained to them before they could comprehend it (Luke 24:44-49; John 20:9; 12:34). And yet the prophets did certainly teach that the Christ should die. Hence, as this thought could not have been understood by them, the language must have been given by the Lord directly. Another thought would be about as difficult as that for any Hebrew prophet to understand—that was, that the Gentiles were to have a part in the great salvation of the Lord. This was many times foretold by them, especially by the prophet Isaiah; and I must believe that at such a time he was directed by the Lord in a way above the ordinary manner of inspiration.

(4). *Much of the language of the prophets is very literal.*—This is especially true of those portions which were delivered to the people concerning the sins of the hour. When Jeremiah stood in the gate of Jerusalem, and delivered them a discourse containing a message from the Lord (7:10), he gave them the fact in a plain manner. The same with John the Baptist, a man sent by God with a divine message, who came preaching in the wilderness of Judea. I suppose that there never was a plainer preacher than he. This was true with Elijah. Indeed, it was true with all the prophets of the Lord—when they came to men with a message for that people and that age, it was plainly stated. Some way it has gotten into the minds of many persons that the language of any prophet must necessarily be in symbolic form. When they told their own, or the dreams of others, and gave the meaning, it was in language very easily understood.

Section 87.
THE CHARACTER OF THE PROPHETS.

(1). *God has used the best material for any given purpose that could be found.*—The supernatural is never employed till the natural is exhausted. When Jesus fed the five thousand, or the four thousand, He used the loaves and fishes on hand, as far as they would go. And when they were done eating, the fragments were taken up, "that nothing be lost." When He healed the daughter of Jairus, He told them to give her something to eat. Of course He could have furnished the strength that she needed, but that was not His way. She was then able to take food, and that was the natural way of obtaining strength. So in all that He did, and all that the apostles did, natural resources were employed as far as they would be of service. The same law is found in nature. There is no redundancy. Everything has its place and power; it has its own work to accomplish, and has been assigned to that task. So it is with the history of the dealings of God with men. When He has had work to perform, He has selected the best men that could be found for that work. If they have lacked the qualification necessary to the task, He has sent them to school till they were prepared for the work. He had Moses in school for nearly eighty years, that he should be able to do forty years of good work. The schools of the prophets had the divine approval. They were to prepare young men, as far as they could, for the work to which the Lord might select them. The apostles were not entrusted with any work by themselves, till they had been in the school of the Master for nearly three years. And they were not then prepared for the work of the ministry under the great Commission. After the resurrection of the Savior from the tomb, He continued with them for forty days, speaking to them concerning the kingdom of God; and even then they were in need of a new teacher to *"guide" them "into all truth."* With all these facts before us, and many more that might be presented, we feel certain that when God made choice of a man as a prophet, He selected the best man that could be found.

(2). *The prophets were good men.*—This does not say that they were faultless. They were men, and not only so, but they lived under circumstances in which the development of character was not an easy task. It was an age of ignorance, coarseness, and lust. And yet it is fair to say that they were the best men that could be found. David, with all his imperfections, was one of the grandest characters of that age. He was not perfect, but far above the average for purity, integrity, and piety. When God inspired his songs, that he might tell of the coming of the Lord's anointed, He employed the heart and the pen of the man whom we would select as the best man of the time. It will be said that Balaam, who prophesied, was not a good man, and yet the probabilities are that he had done well in most of his life before his temptation and fall; and then God simply used the man's mouth to say the things that were to stand for a rebuke for those who opposed the children of Israel. Balaam's ass reproved him, and was in no need of character. If Caiaphas said what he did not intend to say respecting the need of one dying instead of all the people, it was not to his praise, nor did God select him as a representative to the race. From all we can learn from the Old Testament and the New Testament prophets, they were among the best men that could be found on the earth at the time. They were not only the best men in point of goodness and firmness, but their qualifications were of the very best. There is no evidence that God has chosen unworthy men for His work. Hence, when we find men making claims to inspiration and divine communications, it is fair to examine the characters of the men. If they are not among the best men of the age in which they live, we may know at once that they are not prophets.

(3). *Women prophesied.*—The woman is not as well fitted to this work as the man, but it has sometimes been the case that good men were scarce, and then the Lord has called good women to do the work that men ought to have done. Even when there were good men, very excellent and godly women have assumed this work. Miriam (Ex. 15:20-21) was a prophetess in leading the women in their holy joy at the time of deliverance from their bondage in Egypt. From Judges 4:4, we learn of Deborah, a prophetess, the wife of Lapidoth, who judged Israel for forty years. When that people were being overrun by Jabin, king of Hazor, for a period of twenty years, purity and piety seemed to be wanting; real men became scarce, and a woman was selected to judge the people and to make known to them the word of the Lord. In 2 Kings 22:14-20, we have an account of Huldah, the prophetess, the wife of Shallum, who lived in the second quarter of the city, to whom Josiah sent his chief of staff to know what would become of that nation for having so long neglected the right ways of the Lord. This, too, it should be remembered, was in the time of the prophet Jeremiah; and for a woman to outrank him, in the estimation of the king, shows a wonderful confidence in her communion with God. In Isa. 8:3, we have the prophetess spoken of, but the language means no more in that case than that she was the wife of the prophet Isaiah. The trouble in the time of Nehemiah (ch. 6), with Sanballat and Tobiah, needed the wisdom that comes down from the Father of Lights. A number of the prophets seemed to have been hired by these men to fill Nehemiah with fear, and among them was the prophetess Noadiah. From this it will appear that a woman may be a prophetess, and not only so, but she may be false, just as a man.

The prophet Joel looked forward to the coming of the kingdom of the Christ, when the Holy Spirit should be given to the saints, and their young men should see visions, and their old men should dream dreams, and on the servants and the handmaids of the Lord the Spirit should be poured, and they should prophesy (Acts 2:17-21). Philip, the evangelist (Acts 21:9), had four daughters that prophesied; and in

1 Cor. 11:5-16, Paul gives directions for the attire of women when they should prophesy.

From this, it is certain that God selects prophets generally from among men; but because of unusual fitness, He has sometimes selected godly women for this responsible work. Of course, in the exercise of these gifts, their speaking had to be public; for the time, they were God's teachers of the multitude. And this would be true whether the prophecy should relate to the foretelling of future events, the condemnation of some present sin, or the explanation of some Scripture, or an exhortation founded upon anything which God had revealed.

(4). *Guilt of pretending to prophetic knowledge not possessed.*— The man who would change a landmark, or in any way deceive the unsuspecting, was held a very guilty man. When the blind lead the blind, all fall into the ditch. But when one pretends to have a communication from the heavens, which he has not received, he purposes to mislead the world to a far greater extent. It is partly on this account that God has been so particular respecting the character of those whom He would send to the world as its teachers. There would be necessarily some rules by which to know the true from the false prophets. If any truth that has been clearly attested shall be contradicted by a pretended prophet, then it should be known that he was a false prophet. If one should say, 'Let us go and serve other gods,' and ask a following on account of some vision or pretended revelation, it should be disregarded, and the man put to death (Deut. 13:1-6). Likewise, if any should preach any other gospel than that which the apostles had preached, he should be accursed; not even an angel from heaven would be at liberty to do such a thing (Gal. 1:6-10).

When one should presume to speak in the name of the Lord that which the Lord had not commanded, he should not be followed nor feared, but put to death; and they were to know whether the Lord had directed him or not by the fulfillment of his prediction (Deut. 18:20-22). Compare Jer. 14:14-15; 23:9-35)—for misleading the people in that way, they should be punished, and their houses with them (Ezek. 13:1-16). We have a case of the punishment of one Hananiah, who prophesied falsehood in the days of Jeremiah. See Jer. 28:1-17. God has been thus protective of His word, lest men should follow false lights to their injury. It was understood by the ancients, that if a man had that communion with God which would enable him to reveal new truth to the world, he would be enabled to do wonders. They got that thought from their history, for the men who brought divine intelligence not known before did possess that power. Though John did not work any miracle, yet it was in the mind of even Herod Antipas that he had risen from the dead; and Nicodemus regarded the Savior as having come from God, because of the signs which He performed (John 3:1-2). In this way pretended revelators in the time of the apostles might be detected (1 John 4:1-6; Rev. 2:2; Amos 2:11).

Section 88.
SCRIPTURAL ACCOUNT OF THE FULFILLMENT OF PROPHECIES.

(1). *The seed of Abraham should be in bondage for four hundred years* (Gen. 15:1-14).—And after the affliction, they should be delivered with great substance. The fulfillment of this will be found by reading Ex. 2:23-12:40.

(2). *The flood of Noah was threatened* (Gen. 6:9-22).—And it came (7:6-8:14).

(3). The land of Canaan was promised to the seed of Abraham (Gen. 12:7).—And it came true, as it may be read in the book of Joshua.

(4). *Isaac promised and given* (Gen. 18:10; 21:1).

(5). *Esau should serve Jacob, and afterwards break the yoke from off his neck* (Gen. 27:39-40).—So we find that David entirely subdued Edom in his reign (2 Sam. 8:14); but in the time of Joram, the son of Jehoshaphat, they broke away from Israel (2 Kings 8:20-22).

(6). Jacob's vision at Bethel (Gen. 28:10-12) was made good in his preservation and return to that land in peace (Gen. 32:9-12; 33:1-20).

(7). Joseph dreamed that he should have the rule over his brethren (Gen. 37:5-8); which came to be true (Gen. 42:6).

(8). In Gen. 49, *Jacob foretells the things that were to occur in the latter times.*—He gives a good outline history of each of the tribes; and we need only to study their after history to see that the patriarch said these things by the word of the Lord.

(9). *Moses foretold the utter corruption and ruin of the children of Israel* (Deut. 31:28-29).—No one who knows their history can deny that the statement he made came true to the letter. The Scriptures are replete with the fulfillment of this prediction.

(10). In Josh. 6:26, after the taking of Jericho, Joshua told them that *anyone who would attempt to rebuild the city, should do so by the loss of his first-born, and that he should set up the gates in his youngest son.* This was fulfilled in one Hiel, more than four hundred years after that (1 Kings 16:34).

(11). *The death of the two sons of Eli in one day* (1 Sam. 2:34).—This was literally kept (1 Sam. 4:11).

(12). In 1 Sam. 10:1-13, we have the account of the prophecy of Samuel *concerning Saul,* and the fulfillment of the prediction.

(13). *Saul's defeat and death* made known (1 Sam. 28:19); and was fulfilled (1 Sam. 31:2-7).

(14). *David invited evil upon him and his house,* in causing the death of Uriah, and in taking his wife; and for it the sword should not depart from his house, and one of his house should rebel against him and take his wives, in the presence of all the people in the daytime (2 Sam. 12:7-12). This is fulfilled in the defiling of Tamar by her half-brother Amnon (13:6-22); in the killing of Amnon by the command of Absalom, two years later (23-30); and in the rebellion and death of Absalom (chaps. 16-18).

(15). The prophecy of Ahijah concerning the division of the ten tribes from Judah and Benjamin, by parting his new garment into twelve pieces, and giving Jeroboam ten of them (1 Kings 11:26-34).—All this came true (12:16-18), when the ten tribes revolted with their chosen leader.

(16). *Ahijah prophesies of the destruction of the house of Jeroboam* (1 Kings 14:10-13).—See its fulfillment in verses 17-18.

(17). The destruction of the house of Baasha (1 Kings 16: 1-12).

(18). *The three years of drought* (1 Kings 17:1-18:41).—Elijah had said that it would not rain except at his word for that time, and the statement was made true by the facts.

(19). Elijah foretold rain, and it came (1 Kings 18:44-46).

(20). The king of Syria, after having been defeated by Ahab, and Israel made to feel safe, the prophet came and told the king to prepare for the return which would occur at the end of the year; and it was so (1 Kings 20:22-26).

(21). *Death of Ahab* (1 Kings 21:19; 22:38; 2 Kings 9:34; 10:11).—For his murder of Naboth, he was told by Elijah that he should perish, and his house. And so he came to his death in a strange way, and came to the place where he had done the wrong to the innocent man in robbing him of his vineyard. And when Jehu came to the throne, all the house of Ahab was destroyed.

(22). *The victory of Jehoshaphat over Moab, Ammon, and Edom* (2 Chron. 20:14-25). —When it was told to the king that these forces were at Engedi, or between Tekoah and the Dead Sea, he was afraid; and the people came together, and, while they worshiped, the Spirit of the Lord came upon Jahaziel, who told them that the Lord would fight for them. So they went out with the singers, and while they praised the Lord, the battle was fought for them, as the Edomites and the Moabites fought each other, and both armies were destroyed.

(23). The Moabites delivered again to Jehoshaphat and Jehoram, by a miraculous sudden flood of waters, according to the word of the Lord by Elisha (2 Kings 3:17-24).

(24). *Plenty supplied in Samaria,* according to the word spoken by Elisha (2 Kings 7:1-18).

(25). *The sons of Jehu were to sit on the throne to the fourth generation,* because he had destroyed Baal-worship out of the land (2 Kings 10:30); and it was fulfilled (15:12). This was certainly a prophecy. Jehu was not the man to receive direct communications from the Lord.

(26). The ruin of Damascus seen by Amos (1:5) in the days of Uzziah, and fulfilled in the fourth year of the reign of his grandson,

Ahaz (2 Kings 16:9).—This also was foretold by Isaiah, three years before its occurrence (Isa. 8:4).

(27). *The destruction of the army of Sennacherib, and his murder at the hand of his own sons* (2 Kings 19:7-37).—This occurred in the time of Hezekiah, and was foretold by Isaiah. He had this vision in whole or in part a good many times. But in this chapter it can be read in prophecy and history. This Assyrian king had spoiled the land, and now loses 185,000 men by the destroying angel, and escapes with 15,000 to his home, to be killed in the temple of Nisroch.

(28). *Josiah destroys the altar of idolatry,* according to the statement of the man of God that went down from Judah to Bethel, in the time of Jeroboam (1 Kings 13:1-4; 2 Kings 23:15-17).

(29). *The captivity in Babylon* (2 Kings 20:17-19; 24:8-16; 25:8-13).

(30). *The time of that captivity* (Jer. 25:1-11; 29:10).—This began in the fourth year of Jehoiakim, and seventy years reaches the first year of Cyrus (2 Chron. 36:22; Ezra 1:1), when the edict went forth that the Jews should return.

(31). *The destruction of Tyre by Nebuchadnezzar.*—It should be remembered that there were two cities by that name: the one was on the shore, and the other was built out into the sea, and away from the continent. Sometimes the prophecies relate to the one of these, and sometimes to the other. With this fact in the mind and the knowledge of the place the city held in the commercial world; that, while it was the daughter of Sidon, it was the great maritime city of the world, trading with Egypt—valley of the Nile, Sihor—and supplying the isle of Kittim, or Cyprus, and trading even as far west as Tartessus, in Spain. It will be seen in the prophecies we refer to, that the city should not only be thrown down, but rebuilt, and sing again like a harlot, and even traffic in holy things, and that the time of her prostration should be seventy years, according to the years of a king or kingdom (Joel 3:5; Amos 1:9; Isa. 23:1-18; Ezek. 26:7-11; 27:3; 29:18). The whole of chaps. 26-29, can be studied with profit on this subject. It would be an easy task to show the fulfillment from history. Nebuchadnezzar was thirteen years in leveling down the walls of this mighty city; and even then he found that the spoils had been removed, when the people had flowed like a river away from the doomed place. It is certain, too, from history, that it was in desolation for a period of seventy years. The same thought can be had from reading Zech. 9:1-3. It will be seen by this text that the city had been rebuilt, and by referring to 1:1; 7:1, we find that it was written in the fourth year of Darius Hystaspes.

(32). *The destruction of Babylon* (Jer. 50:17-18; Jer. 51; Isa. 13:19-22; 44:28, 45:1; Dan. 5:16-31).

It would be easy to continue to notice these prophecies and the fulfillment, as they relate to Egypt, Damascus, Arabia, Philistia, Moab, Ammon, Edom, Assyria, Ethiopia, etc., etc. But we have aimed rather at a sample of these predictions, that we might discover the clearness and force with which they are presented. These men were not telling the things which they wished to have come to pass—not the things which, judged according to human wisdom, were likely to occur. These countries and cities were never in better condition than when their destruction was foretold. These fulfillments can be verified by history, as well as by the statements of the Scriptures.

Section 89.
NEW TESTAMENT PROPHECIES, AND THEIR FUL-FILLMENT.

We have seen already that there were New Testament prophets; that the Spirit of the Lord would not only enable men to dream dreams and see visions, and to prophesy, but that women should have the same endowment. In the giving of the new law, some time would necessarily pass before it would be possible for the whole will of God to be put to record. During the time there was a partial revelation within the reach of the churches, but they would need something to take the place of a revelation; hence the promise that the Spirit of the Lord would give this wisdom, to the extent of their need.

So then you are no more strangers and sojourners, but you are fellow-citizens with the saints, and of the household of God, being built upon the foundation of the apostles and prophets, Christ Jesus himself being the chief cornerstone; in whom each individual building, fitly framed together, grows into a holy temple in the Lord; in whom you also are builded together for a habitation of God in the Spirit. (Eph. 2:19-22)

Also the following chapter, verses 5-6:

Which in other generations was not made known to the sons of men, as it has now been revealed to his holy apostles and prophets in the Spirit; that is, that the Gentiles are fellow-heirs, and fellow-members of the body, and fellow-partakers of the promise in Christ Jesus through the gospel.

The gospel could not all be given at once in all its bearings nor could it be written fast enough to supply the demand of the newly-organized churches. But these prophetic gifts supplied the need for the time. We want to notice a few of these prophetic teachings and warnings, to see in what manner the Lord directed His people.

(1). *The well-known Agabus* (Acts 11:27-28) went down from Jerusalem to Antioch, and warned them of the great dearth that was to come upon the whole land, which came in the time of Claudius Caesar.

(2). *The imprisonment of Paul* (Acts 21:10-11).—This was foretold by the same Agabus, who met the apostle at Caesarea, at the house of Philip. He first fastened his own feet and hands with Paul's girdle, and in that way illustrated what was about to befall its owner.

(3). *The persecution that should come upon the disciples* (Mark 13:9-11; Luke. 21:12-15; Acts 4:3; 16:23; 12:1-4; 6:10-8:3).

(4). *Many shall stumble* (Matt. 24:10).—See the fulfillment 1 Tim. 1:6; 6:10; 2 Cor. 11:13; 2 Tim. 2:17-18.

(5). Mark 9:11: "And he said to them, 'Truly I say to you, There are some of them that stand by here, who shall in no way taste of death, till they see the kingdom of God come with power.'" This kingdom had been expected by the apostles for some time, and now they are glad to know that it is soon to come. They did not know the nature of it, nor the sorrows that would sweep over them before it should be established. Just before the Master ascended into the heavens, He came and told the disciples that all authority in heaven and in earth had been given into His hands (Matt. 28:18). Still the kingdom had not come. But on the Pentecost, the prophecy was fulfilled (Acts 2). Then they were at liberty to announce that He had risen, to occupy the throne of His father David, and that the world must now submit to Him, in order to be saved.

(6). The Holy Spirit would be given to the disciples in a manner not yet enjoyed (John 7:37-38; Luke 24:46-49; Acts 1:4; 2:1-5).

(7). *Jesus foretold His death* (John 2:19; Matt. 16:21). See chaps. 27: and 28: Nothing could have been taught more plainly than the death, burial and resurrection of the Savior.

(8). Acts 2:16-21

> *But this is that which has been spoken by the prophet Joel:*
> *'And it shall be in the last days,' says God,*
> *'I will pour forth from my Spirit upon all flesh*
> *And your sons and your daughters shall prophesy,*
> *And your young men shall see visions,*
> *And your old men shall dream dreams*
> *Yes, and on my servants and on my handmaidens in those days*
> *I will pour forth from my Spirit; and they shall prophesy.*
> *And I will show wonders in the heaven above,*
> *And signs on the earth beneath;*
> *Blood, and fire, and vapor of smoke*
> *The sun shall be turned into darkness,*
> *And the moon into blood,*
> *Before that day of the Lord come,*
> *That great and notable day*
> *And it shall be, that whoever shall call on the name of the Lord shall be saved.'*

This is not a prophecy made in the New Testament, but a prophecy applied in the New Testament. It is found in Joel 2. We quote it here that we may have an application of it, and from it get a rule for the interpretation of prophecies that are confessedly difficult. So far as we have gone, in both Testaments, the interpretation has been easy. Indeed, they have been but little else than history written beforehand. They have been susceptible of but one meaning. But in the one just quoted we have room for much speculation. And the manner of exegesis adopted by many is not likely to give any assurance of the meaning of the passage.

Peter says: *"This is that which has been spoken."* Hence there is a question of truthfulness involved, to begin with. If we take the language, and apply it to something in the future, or remove it from that day and the things then occurring, we call Peter a liar.

Somehow it is in the mind of most commentators that this prophecy demands such a wonder for its fulfillment as the world has never seen. But this is a great mistake. This language is highly figurative, and therefore the rules which governs such language must be applied, just as if they found in other compositions. Now let us turn back to the first verse of the chapter, and see now much of this language had its certain fulfillment on that day:

1. I will pour forth from my Spirit.—That had occurred.

2. *Your sons and your daughters shall prophesy.*—And that also was being fulfilled. While we do not know if the daughters were then engaged in that work, we do know that they were afterwards, and that, too, because of the coming of this gift.

3. The Spirit given to the servants and the handmaidens.—That is answered.

4. *I will show wonders in heaven.*—The Spirit had come from heaven that morning, and the rushing sound of the mighty wind did not move horizontally, but came down; and that sound pointed out the place of meeting to the multitude. No greater sign had been exhibited since the world began.

5. *And signs on the earth.*—And there was the sign of all the signs that had ever been seen—a few unpretending and unlearned men speaking in nine or ten different languages and dialects.

6. *Blood, and fire, and vapor of smoke.*—These were all present that day. That was Pentecost; it was nine o'clock in the morning, and therefore the time at which the great sacrifices were to be offered. They were largely free-will, and the number of people present assures us that it was unusually well attended, and therefore that the sacrifices were many. The blood is running, the fire is burning, the smoke is rising; nay, more—the vapor of smoke, for it comes from the burning of flesh.

7. *The sun darkened, and the moon given the appearance of blood.*—This was certainly the appearance of things that morning. Hence there is no need of going into some far-fetched and imaginary interpretation of the prophecy. It was then being fulfilled, or Peter over-talked the facts in the case.

If we are not at liberty to differ from the conclusions of an inspired man, the question is settled, and the passage is interpreted. This is by far the safer plan—indeed, it is the only one in which there is any safety. The conclusion: "Whoever shall call on the name of the Lord, shall be saved," gave hope to the crowd that, though they had crucified the Lord's Anointed, still they could be saved; therefore they ask, "*What shall we do?*"

In the predictions of the Savior, and in the symbolic prophecy of the Apocalypse, there is work for a large book. But these should be interpreted in the light of history—those that have been fulfilled, and the rest without such advantage. It is not possible for us now to enter so large a field. We will notice one more prediction, or promise, of the Savior.

8. Matt. 16:13-20:

> *Now when Jesus came into the parts of Caesarea Philippi, he asked his disciples, saying, 'Who do men say that the Son of man is?' And they said, 'Some say John the Baptist; some, Elijah; and others, Jeremiah, or one of the prophets.' He says to them, 'But who do you say that I am?' And Simon Peter answered and said, 'You are the Christ, the Son of the living God.' And Jesus answered and said to him, 'You are blessed, Simon, son of*

Jonah: for flesh and blood has not revealed it to you,
but my Father which is in heaven. And I also say to you,
that you are Peter, and upon this rock I will build my
church; and the gates of Hades shall not prevail against
it. I will give to you the keys of the kingdom of heaven:
and whatever you shall bind on earth shall be bound in
heaven: and whatsoever you shall loose on earth shall
be loosed in heaven.' Then he charged the disciples that
they should tell no man that he was the Christ.

From this language, a few things are evident to every careful reader:

(1). Christ was going to establish a kingdom.

(2). The words *kingdom* and *church* are used in this passage as synonyms.

(3). Peter was to have the keys, or serve as gate-keeper.

(4). He could not be the rock on which this kingdom should be built, and be the gate-keeper at the same time.

(5). From many other Scriptures, we know that Christ was that rock (Psa. 118:22; Isa. 28:16; Matt. 21:42; Acts 4:11; Eph. 2:19-21).

(6). The authority of Peter in that kingdom was just that which belonged to the other apostles (Luke 24:46-49; John 20:21-23).

(7). After the kingdom had been established, Peter never claimed any superiority over the other apostles, and they never hinted that he had this type of position either.

Hence the meaning of the promise, or prophecy, of the Savior is clear: that in the near future, He would build His church, or organize His kingdom; that in the establishment of that institution Peter would serve as spokesman, and hence it would be Peter's place to announce the terms of admission. This was fulfilled on the first Pentecost after the ascension of the Savior.

The value of these predictions of the Savior to the apostles was very great. They are of supreme importance to us; as they are fulfilled in history, recorded in the Scriptures, we have a continued line of evidence of the clearest and strongest character (John 13:19; 14:29; 16:4).

Section 90.

PROPHECIES CONCERNING CHRIST.

These prophecies, as we would expect, are the most complete of all the subjects treated by the prophets of the Lord. And yet the men that gave them never fully understood their meaning. Hence it is very evident that many times they told more than they knew. They have seen the character of the Christ in the distance, with all wicked men did to Him, and have told what they saw and felt and heard. Sometimes it would seem that they must have been directed to say the things which God put into their mouths. They tell of the cross, and yet not one of them ever saw any such an instrument of torture and death.

(1). He was to be the seed of the woman (Gen. 3:15; 4:2; Matt. 1:18).

(2). He would be the Son of God (Psa. 2:7; Luke 1:32-35).

(3). He would overcome the serpent (Gen. 3:15; Heb. 2:14).

(4). The seed of Abraham (Gen. 12:1-3; 17:7; 22:18; Gal. 3:16).

(5). The seed of Isaac (Gen. 21:12; Heb. 11:18).

(6). The seed of Judah (Gen. 49:10; Heb. 7:14).

(7). The seed of David (Psa. 132:11; Jer. 23:5; Acts 13:23; Rom. 1:3).

(8). The time of His coming and death (Dan. 9:24-27; Luke 2:1).

(9). Born of a virgin (Isa. 7:14; Matt. 1:18; Luke 2:7).

(10). He was called Immanuel (Isa. 7:14; Matt. 1:22-23).

(11). Born in Bethlehem of Judea (Mic. 5:2; Matt. 2:1; Luke 2:4-6).

(12). Great men shall come and bow down to Him (Psa. 72:10-15; Matt. 2:1-11).

(13). Children slaughtered, in an effort to kill Him (Jer. 31:15; Matt. 2:16-18).

(14). Introduced by John the Baptist (Isa. 40:3; Mal. 3:1; Matt. 3:1-3; Luke 1:17).

(15). Was anointed by the Holy Spirit (Psa. 45:7; Isa. 11:2; 61:1; Matt. 3:16, 17; John 3:34; Acts 10:38).

(16). He was a prophet like to Moses (Deut. 18:15-18; Acts 3:20-22).

(17). Was sent as a deliverer to the people (Isa. 61:1-3; Luke 4:16-21, 43).

(18). He is the light to Zebulun and Naphtali (Isa. 9:1-3; Matt. 4:12-16).

(19). He comes to the temple and cleanses it (Hag. 2:7-9; Mal. 3:1; Luke 19:45; John 2:13-16).

(20). His poverty (Isa. 53:2; Mark 6:3; Luke 9:58).

(21). He was meek, and without ostentation (Isa. 42:1-2; Phil. 2:7-9).

(22). His compassion (Isa. 40:11; 42:3; Matt. 12:15-20; Heb. 4:15).

(23). Was without guile (Isa. 53:9; 1 Pet. 2:22).

(24). Great zeal for the house of God (Psa. 69:9; John 2:17).

(25). He taught by the use of parables (Psa. 78:2; Matt. 13:34-35).

(26). He wrought miracles (Isa. 35:5-6; Luke 7:18-23).

(27). Rejected by His brethren (Psa. 69:8; Isa. 53:3; John 1:11; 7:5).

(28). Hated by the Jews (Psa. 69:4; Isa. 49:7; John 15:24-25).

(29). Rejected by their rulers (Psa. 118:22; John 7:48; Matt. 21:42).

(30). A stone of stumbling and rock of offense (Isa. 8:14; Rom. 9:32; 1 Pet. 2:8).

(31). Betrayed by a friend (Psa. 41:9; 55:12-14; John 13:18-21).

(32). Forsaken by His disciples (Zech. 13:7; Matt. 26:31-56).

(33). Was sold for thirty pieces of silver (Zech. 11:12; Matt. 26:15).

(34). This money was given to buy the potter's field (Zech. 11:13; Matt. 27:7).

(35). He was patient and silent in all His sufferings (Isa. 53:7; Matt. 26:63; 27:12-14).

(36). Smitten on the cheek (Mic. 5:1; Matt. 27:30).

(37). His sufferings were intense (Psa. 22:14-15; Luke 22:42-44).

(38). Was scourged and spit upon (Psa. 35:15; Isa. 50:6; Mark 14:65; John 19:1).

340

(39). His visage was greatly marred (Isa. 52:14; 53:3; John 19:1-5).

(40). He suffered, that he might bear away our sins (Isa. 53:4-6; Dan. 9:26; Matt. 20:28; 26:28).

(41). The rulers, Jews and Gentiles, combine against Him to put Him to death (Psa. 2:1-4; Luke 23:12; Acts 4:27-28).

(42). He was extended upon the cross, and His hands and His feet were nailed to the wood (Isa. 25:10-11; Psa. 22:16; John 19:18; 20:25).

(43). This agony was increased by being numbered among thieves (Isa. 53:12; Mark 15:28).

(44). They gave him gall and vinegar (Psa. 69:21; Matt. 27:34).

(45). He was cruelly mocked (Psa. 22:7-8; 35:15-21; Matt. 27:39-44).

(46). He suffered alone; even the Father's presence was withdrawn (Isa. 63:1-3; Psa. 22:1; Matt. 27:46).

(47). They parted his garments among them, and cast lots for his vesture (Psa. 22:18; Matt. 27:35).

(48). He thus became a curse for us, and bore our reproach (Psa. 22:6; 79:7; 9:20; Rom. 15:3; Heb. 13:13; Gal. 3:13).

(49). He made intercession for the murderers (Isa. 53:12; Luke 23:34).

(50). After his death they pierced him (Zech. 12:10; John 19:34-37).

(51). But did not break a bone of his body (Ex. 12:46; Psa. 34:20; John 19:33-36).

(52). He was buried with the rich (Isa. 53:9; Matt. 27:57-60).

(53). His flesh did not see corruption (Psa. 16:8-10; Acts 2:31).

(54). He rose from death the third day, according to the Scriptures (Psa. 16:8-10; 30:3; Luke 24:6, 31, 34).

(55). He ascended into the heavens (Psa. 68:18; 24:7-9; Luke 24:51; Acts 1:9).

(56). He became a priest after the order of Melchizedek, who was king and priest at the same time (Psa. 110:4; Heb. 5:5-6; Zech. 6:12-13).

(57). He received for Himself a kingdom that embraces the whole world (Psa. 2:6; Luke 1:32; Dan. 2:44; 7:13-14; John 18:33-37; Matt. 28:18-19; Phil. 2:9-10).

(58). His law went forth from Zion and his word from Jerusalem (Isa. 2:1-3; Mic. 4:1-2; Luke 24:46-49; Acts 2:1-40).

(59). The Gentiles should be admitted into his service, (Isa. 11:10; 42:1; Psa. 2:8; John 10:16; Acts 10:44-48; Rom. 15:9-12).

(60). The righteousness of His reign (Isa. 9:6-7; Psa. 45:6-7; John 5:30; Rev. 19:11).

We have sketched through these prophecies, not thinking of furnishing all that might be said of them, or of giving all of them. What we have given is to show what a large portion of the prophecies refer to the coming Savior. When salvation is proposed for the Gentiles, we may be sure that the statements were from the Lord.

Jewish prophets were incompetent to understand any promise made to any other people than those who were of the seed of Abraham. Because they had been the peculiarly favored of the Lord, they looked for all excellence in Judah, and all blessings and favors to be extended only to that people. But God had a different view of the matter, and when he gave promises to the human race, they were upon the basis of *character*. We greatly misunderstand the Bible if we suppose that the Hebrews were the only people that received the revelations of God. Because they were more cultured than those about them, they were put in charge of holy things, and used as a vessel for the preservation of the divine records. God must necessarily bring the Savior into the world through some line, and it would be as well to select that line as any other, and better, for they were the best prepared to furnish the world with the evidences of God's faithfulness in keeping His promises.

We have now seen that all truth centers in the Christ; that He is our prophet, priest, and king; that all the types and ceremonies and symbols that were before the crucifixion looked forward to that event; and that since that time, all ordinances and teachings and promises, look to Him for meaning and fulfillment.

www.ingramcontent.com/pod-product-compliance
Lightning Source LLC
LaVergne TN
LVHW051726080426
835511LV00018B/2910